USING
AUTHORING
IN
EDUCATION

Customizing
Computer-Based Lessons
for Students

Kristie Younghans Davis
Milton Budoff

BROOKLINE
BOOKS
Cambridge, MA

Library of Congress Cataloging-in-Publication Data

Davis, Kristie Younghans, 1949–
   Using authoring in education.

   Bibliography; p.
   Includes index.
   1. Computer-assisted-instruction—Authoring programs.
I. Budoff, Milton, 1929–   . II. Title.
LB1028.66.D38 1986   371.3´9445   85–25492
ISBN 0–914797–10–7
ISBN 0–914797–20–4 (pbk)

Published by
Brookline Books, Inc.
PO Box 1046
Cambridge, MA 02238–1046

Printed in the United States of America.

Table of Contents

1

Introduction

Another presentation about computers in the classroom...

Almost all the teachers were in attendance. Glancing around the room, the chairperson of the in-service committee could almost hear their thoughts. There was Kevin, the new fifth grade teacher, his excitement almost visible. All he needed was something new or different and he was off and running. He had been the first staff member to ask for a computer in his classroom and had done some interesting projects with the students. He would be receptive to the presentation today.

Not far away sat Mary Ellen. Even the way she sat said "show me." A veteran teacher of sixteen years, she had seen a lot of fads. After previewing some of the early software when computers first became available in the district, she had commented that workbooks did as much as those "page turning" programs. Nonetheless, she had found a program she liked, and she had used computers effectively with her students. "I don't want a lot of hype," she'd commented when she heard about this presentation. "If this idea is a good one, I'll give it a try. But I'm going to have to be convinced."

Then there was Bob. He was almost adamant in his refusal to consider using computers with his classes. His arguments were many. Computers were toys, time consuming, too difficult to use. Besides, he

had yet to see a piece of software that was right for his students. As
far as he was concerned, this meeting was just another waste of time.

Anyone associated with the movement of computers into public schools
is familiar with the attitudes and approaches just described. Many educators recognize the potential of this technology and are eagerly exploring a
variety of classroom adaptations. At the other extreme are individuals who
want nothing to do with computers. Perhaps they have seen inappropriate
applications or are disenchanted with unfulfilled commercial promises. Still
other teachers are simply uncomfortable with or even fearful of machines.
These educators are understandably disturbed by administrative directives
that require they use computers with their students. It will take time and
training to help make these teachers comfortable with the new technology.

The vast majority of teachers are neither overly enthusiastic about nor
completely disinterested in computers. Most educators have adopted a
wait-and-see attitude. Leery of miracle cures, these teachers are asking for
concrete examples of sound classroom applications.

Three years ago, when microcomputers became the latest craze, school
administrators and parents uncritically accepted claims that computers
would revolutionize learning in schools. In spite of their inadequate understanding of the roles the computer should play in the learning process,
administrators, parents and policy makers pressed to have computers
quickly introduced into the curriculum.

In the intervening three years, we have learned that the successful utilization of microcomputers in education requires thoughtful and careful
planning. Fortunately, as the intense pressure on schools to adopt microcomputers eases, school administrators now have the time to plan how best
to introduce computers to teachers, students, and staff members.

There are two major reasons why computer users and potential computer users have become more cautious about computers, often adopting a
"show me" attitude toward having computers in the classroom. First, the
computer did not live up to the excessive expectations put forward by the
media. Initially, computer games were a major source of excitement in the
home market. However, children tired of video games, and it became clear
that the magic appeal of the computer fades quickly when the activities are
too repetitive.

This failure to live up to expectations was not limited to the home and
education market. When sales of high tech products slumped in 1985,
investment analysts were quick to report that computer companies had
promised more to the business community than they had delivered. Custo-
mers who spent money hoping for gains in productivity were disappointed,

and that disappointment too often contributed to a disillusionment with the technology.

The second reason for the changed attitude was a general recognition that much of the available software was of poor quality, and presented activities and content in a manner which did not enhance instruction. The software did not meet student needs, and did not capitalize on the innate excitement the computer holds for children.

In addition, advocates of computing in schools have come to realize that computers can only be effectively used in education if teachers are comfortable using them. The computer should not be viewed as a threat or a replacement for the teacher. The computer is one more in the teacher's arsenal of instructional tools—joining the workbook, videotape, flashcard, etc. Understanding how computers work, what kinds of educational tasks are best suited to them, and how to use them to perform those tasks will assist teachers in evaluating the worth of this new technology.

Today, more teachers are aware of the educational goals computers can help accomplish. These goals include:

- stimulating more and higher quality writing output through word processing programs;
- teaching classification and organization of materials by using database software; and
- accessing specialized information; for example, from an electronic encyclopedia.

In the past, schools have attempted to meet the need for teachers to learn about computers by running workshops. Unfortunately, and understandably, the majority of these workshops have been addressed to immediate needs and have rarely focused on training and support needs over the long term. On the other hand, the longer-term courses at colleges do not usually address the nitty gritty of classroom applications.

The demands placed on a teacher's time and energy are significant. Successfully introducing computers to faculty requires clear goals and continuing support from administrators and colleagues. To accomplish these aims, school administrators and school board members must

- clarify the instructional goals for this technology;
- develop training programs for teachers interested in working with computers; and
- develop the organizational mechanisms to support and enhance teacher efforts.

Using Authoring in Education is concerned with successfully integrating computers into the classroom, whether for regular or special education students. The emphasis of this volume is on introducing and describing authoring products. Authoring is a type of computer software which allows computer-based lessons to be customized to meet specific student needs.

We begin with three basic premises:

1. Computers can enhance the learning of slow or inefficient students.
2. Computers should be located in classrooms as well as laboratories.
3. Computers should be viewed as adding to the instructional power of the classroom.

Computers Can Enhance the Learning of Slow or Inefficient Students

Computer-based instructional applications are particularly important for students who learn slowly or inefficiently and have difficulty generalizing what they have learned to new situations. This book does not distinguish between students who simply learn the material slowly and those who qualify for Chapter 1 or special needs programs. We refer to both groups of students as slow or inefficient learners since they share learning problems. Their prior failures discourage them from further learning, but they find interacting with the computer very positive. Thus, these students benefit most from using the computer and find the computer's ability to develop individual learning experiences highly motivating. If the teacher can structure the computer work of these students to make it responsive to their learning needs and style, the students' work output, time spent in productive work, and general motivation to learn should increase.

The computer motivates these students to more systematic, involved, and purposeful learning and permits them to work independently. The computer's immediate feedback provides the student with a strong impetus to continue working. These students seem more willing to accept repetitious material in computer lessons than in traditional learning situations, and so are more likely to work until they master that material. These features of the computer are especially important since these students experience success infrequently. The result is that many of these slow or ineffective learners work on the computer for much longer periods than usual. Chapter 2 discusses the many specific advantages of computers for these students.

Given the stimulating experience of the computer, however, the temptation may be to use computer-based lessons as much as possible with the slow learner. This is probably a mistake since these students need opportunities to apply their learning in a variety of settings using as many instructional materials as the teacher can utilize. Although the computer may be a primary motivator and initial source of learning for these students, it should not become the only medium through which learning takes place.

Computers Should Be Located in Classrooms as Well as Laboratories

A major debate centers on whether computers should be concentrated in a laboratory or placed in classrooms in ones, twos, and threes. Initially, the group teaching orientation of regular education prevailed. Five to twenty computers were clustered in one room for class-size activities. This practice forced a policy of scheduled access and required that a specialist, not the classroom teacher, conduct the classes. Usually students using computers in the setting of a laboratory do so as part of a scheduled activity such as a course on computer literacy, LOGO, or programming. Sequestering computers in laboratories means that students cannot move to the computer when their progress in an activity suggests a useful computer application, such as a drill-and-practice program to review long-division problems or word processing for a report. The result of placing computers exclusively in laboratories is that it is unlikely that computers will become an intrinsic part of the instructional system of the class because they are not physically convenient and readily accessible.

Computers Should Be Viewed as
Adding to the Instructional Power of the Classroom

The computer must be viewed as an instructional tool, powerful but limited. Computers do not replace teachers—computers are teaching tools to be used by teachers. Current educational software and the availability of hardware preclude making the computer the sole or major source of learning. Thus, the computer should be viewed as adding distinctive instructional alternatives as part of a learning sequence, not as replacing elements of instruction.

We refer to this learning sequence as an *instructional scenario.* The concept of an *instructional scenario* is intended to help the teacher identify the unique roles the computer can play in teaching students. The concept both legitimizes current teaching approaches, which remain relevant after the computer has been introduced, and allows teachers to see how computers might increase the educational power of the classroom.

Teachers typically use many different instructional materials and sequence them for the student as he or she masters the elements of a task. An instructional scenario describes this instructional program—the lessons and tools which enable the student to attain an objective. The scenario describes the variety and sequence of instructional procedures planned for the student and reflects the task's prerequisite skills, the conditions under which the student learns best, and those instructional procedures that will help him or her attain the objective.

Scenarios are not necessarily written. They are, however, deliberately formulated in a step-by-step fashion, depending on the student's response to a lesson plan. The choice of activities and their sequence reflects the teacher's philosophy of teaching and knowledge of the student and the student's learning style, strengths, and weaknesses. The teacher selects the activities, identifies the milestones in the process as the student's learning proceeds, and outlines the probable sequence of activities.

Conceptualizing the learning sequence the teacher implicitly uses with a student as an instructional scenario emphasizes two aspects: the constructive process by which the teacher builds or designs a "script" for each student's orderly learning, and the need to think about the usefulness of the various instructional materials or tools available.

Thinking in terms of scenarios helps teachers view when and for what tasks computer-based learning is appropriate, and ensures that the computer is not the only learning medium the student uses.

The logic and use of scenarios is discussed more fully in the prior book in this series, *Microcomputers in Special Education: An Introduction to Instructional Applications* (Budoff, Thormann, & Gras, 1985), and more briefly in Chapter 10 here.

Computers in the Schools

In schools across the country, numerous brands of microcomputers are appearing in classrooms, media centers, and labs. Computers are being used in all disciplines with many types of students. For a variety of reasons, the results have been mixed. As mentioned above, many teachers are skeptical of the benefits of the computer, but this skepticism is useful. Teachers and administrators should be critical evaluators of new materials and methods, and thoughtful users of technology. But it is equally important that this skepticism be accompanied by a willingness to explore new materials.

The problems faced by educators wishing to use computers in the classroom are real and numerous. These difficulties include limited time, lack of training and insufficient assistance, and, most often, insufficient access to the computer itself. By carefully testing new methods and evaluating new information, educators will be better prepared to make decisions regarding which materials, approaches, and programs are most appropriate for their particular situations.

Special education teachers tend to view computer use in the classroom positively because their mandate is to organize instruction according to the student's educational plan. The computer permits them to individualize instruction if the software can be specialized to meet their students' needs. Special education teachers have also recognized that a computer can be a prosthetic device—an instrument that enables a disabled or handicapped student to perform certain tasks despite a disabling condition. As a prosthetic device, the computer may help persons with spinal cord injuries to walk, allow a voiceless child to speak, and enable a blind person to read using optical scanning devices.

Regular class teachers tend to set less well-defined goals for the computer because class size often dictates large-group activities. In addition, many schools still cluster computers in computer labs, thereby limiting student access to them. These teachers recognize that some students could benefit substantially from working with computers individually or in small groups designed to meet the students' learning needs and styles. To accomplish this goal, teachers need access to computers in their classrooms, appropriate software, and training and support which enables scheduling students on the computer at appropriate times during the student's sequence of learning activities.

Authoring Products as a Solution

A major challenge for educators today is to harness computers to meet instructional needs. Often regular and special education teachers see the utility of the computer but are unable to identify software which meets their specific needs. The teacher may actually know the best task structure and what materials are most likely to evoke a response but be unable to locate appropriate software. A program that sounds useful may not be available in the school or district. Most likely, the appropriate software does not exist.

Using Authoring in Education addresses this concern by focusing on a type of software that allows the computer's instructional offerings to be tailored to meet specific needs. Traditionally, such customizing has required programming—a skill few teachers possess. *Authoring products* provide an excellent alternative for teachers who need specially designed programs but have limited funds, time, or experience. Those writing these customized lessons are called "authors"— hence, the term *authoring.*

Authoring products give educators a degree of power and control not available in other educational software. This potential ability to individualize computer use makes authoring an exciting tool for all educators. But to take advantage of these capabilities, we recommend that the computer be easily accessible to the teacher—the best arrangement is for the computer to be located in the teacher's classroom.

There are three basic types of authoring products: *mini-authoring programs, authoring systems,* and *authoring languages.*

The three levels of authoring products share a philosophy and some characteristics. *Using Authoring in Education* presents the process and potential of authoring products for student learning and focuses on these available variations. The degree of expertise required varies with the level of authoring. One can simply fill in blanks with content appropriate for a given student or design a lesson from scratch—specifying all its parameters. When a program for a particular skill is not commercially available, authoring makes it possible for educators with different levels of computer experience to create customized lessons.

The material in this book has been organized so that the reader can learn about those types of authoring that are immediately interesting or can pursue other topics to develop a more thorough understanding of the range of authoring products available. Our intent is to introduce the reader to authoring tools that vary in complexity and in the degree of experience required to use them.

A common misconception is that authoring languages, such as PILOT, are the only types of authoring products available. Mastering an authoring language requires considerable computer programming experience, and much time and energy. This misconception has led to the rejection of authoring as a reasonable response to the dilemma of helping teachers write individualized software for students with special learning needs. In response, we have identified a class of authoring tools which do not demand a knowledge of programming. These less complex tools are particularly important because they permit novice computer users to customize simple lessons.

The Organization of This Book

Using Authoring in Education, then, is designed to help teachers become familiar with the concept and use of authoring tools. By presenting examples of classroom applications, including video screens, we show the reader in detail the potential uses for these tools. Explanations of the various authoring categories move from the simplest to the most complex options. Each chapter develops a specific theme revolving around authoring.

Chapter 2 provides background information about the effectiveness of computer-assisted instruction (CAI) with slow or inefficient learners and outlines the difficulties faced by educators trying to use commercially available educational software. This background leads to Chapter 3's introduction to authoring products. This part of the book serves as an introduction to the more technical chapters which follow.

Chapters 4, 5, and 6 describe the three main types of authoring: mini-authoring programs, authoring systems, and authoring languages. This section of the book has been designed to serve as a detailed guide to the use of various authoring products and includes examples of classroom applications as well as information about commercially available authoring tools.

Chapter 7 concerns training in the use of authoring products. It describes the essential considerations for designing training programs for teachers and outlines in detail training workshops for mini-authoring programs and the authoring language PILOT. Chapters 4–7 contain the working material which should serve as an information base for educators interested in using authoring products.

Chapter 8 indicates some of the special features and "extras" which are or may soon be available with authoring packages. Program development, lesson writing, and lesson evaluation are addressed in Chapter 9. Chapter 10 discusses the appropriate use of computers in education, addresses the concerns that the use of authoring tools raise, and proposes the directions that further development of authoring tools may take. A major condition for the further development of these tools is the extent to which schools support this type of software through purchases and staff training.

The appendices include a glossary and resource section. The resource section contains the names and short descriptions of many authoring products, including contact information for obtaining preview copies.

Authoring products hold great potential for specific educational applications: They allow teachers to design and create software which meets the specific needs of individual students. The step-by-step examples and detailed information provided in this book are designed to assist teachers in exploring the benefits of authoring products and in identifying applications for their own situations. Authoring products enable educators to harness the instructional power of the computer, bringing together the reality and the promise of microcomputer technology.

2

Educational Computer Use: Background and Problems

This chapter briefly reviews the effectiveness of computer-assisted instruction (CAI) with special needs populations as well as discusses the problems facing educators when they try to use microcomputers to individualize instruction in their classrooms. These problems are often a result of the incompatibility of software with specific student and curricular needs. Following this discussion is a detailed analysis of the software characteristics necessary for individualizing instruction, particularly for special needs students. This analysis ultimately argues for the use of authoring products to satisfy the need for more flexible, student-focused software.

Computer-Assisted Instruction and Special Needs

Substantial research suggests that computerized tutorial or drill-and-practice programs often have positive results, enhancing student achievement. Dence (1980) has summarized some of the research pertaining to the use of CAI in education; and, based on the studies conducted, CAI seems to be a viable tool through which students can learn. Dence suggests, however, that more extensive research is needed to determine "for whom and under what conditions the use [of] CAI is effective. These are questions that must be answered if educators are to decide when, where, and how to incorporate CAI in their curricula." (p. 54)

Much of the literature on the use of CAI programs with student populations concerns students with special needs. Computerized tutorial and drill-and-practice exercises appear to be more effective for low-ability students than for middle- or high-ability students. In addition, when compared with traditional instructional methods, equal or better achievement scores are obtained using CAI, and in less time (Gershman & Sakamoto, 1981).

Trifilette, Frith, and Armstrong (1984) report encouraging results from the use of a computerized instructional program in mathematics. A comparison of resource room instruction with equal time periods of computerized instruction for two groups of students indicated that students in the computerized instruction groups learned almost twice as many new math skills and had significant increases in achievement levels. Vittello and Bruce (1977) evaluated the use of CAI for teaching addition and shape identification with educable mentally retarded (EMR) students and found that, over a four-month period, the students acquired skills faster through CAI than through traditional methods of instruction. On the other hand, McDermott and Watkins (1983) did not find any significant differences, as measured on standardized achievement tests, between conventional and computer-assisted instruction for learning disabled students. These authors suggest using both methods of instruction in combination and tailoring them to meet individual student needs and preferences.

Thorkildsen (1982) reported that software designed to teach time telling, identification of coins, functional words, sight reading, and directional prepositions have been or are in the process of being field tested. Conclusions drawn from the field tests are:

- teachers are able to use the authoring system effectively;
- some of the instructional formats need to be modified;
- teachers are able to use data to track and reinforce student performance; and
- remedial interventions need to be developed to meet student capabilities at many levels.

An example of complex software designed for students with learning problems is the *Authoring System Supplementing Instruction Selected by Teachers* (ASSIST) (Chiang, Stauffer, & Cannara, 1979). Project ASSIST allowed special educators to plan lessons using an authoring system with a large menu of options. ASSIST was used by 14 teachers for mildly handicapped students, ages 7-16, in the Cupertino, California School District (Chiang et al., 1979). The 14 teachers involved in the project created 975 lessons during the year ASSIST was being used. Many of the lessons involved language arts skills. Evaluation of Project ASSIST indicated that both teachers and students had favorable reactions to the use of this authoring system.

Computerized instruction may also have a positive effect on student adjustment and learning styles. Ryba and Chapman (1983) cite experiences with special needs children using computerized programs which indicate the development of new skills such as planning, sequencing left and right, anticipating events, executing movement combinations with increased motor speed and coordination, and shifting attention among various cues. These authors also believe that student feelings of control and effectiveness over the computer may lead to improved self-concept and self-control. In addition, team cooperation or peer-tutoring activities at the computer may assist in building self-esteem or positive peer relationships (Grimes, 1981).

Finally, Hallworth and Brebner (1980) appear to be describing the special education student when they state:

> Those students who will benefit most from CAI are those for whom the patience and repetitiveness of the computer are of great assistance in their learning, those who require individual attention, those who for some reason have failed to learn in the regular classroom environment, those who feel inadequate and inferior and do not seek help from a teacher for fear of displaying their ignorance, [and] those who do not have ready access to schools. . . (p. 218)

Problems with Software: A Story

Marilyn Simms, district special education coordinator, and Diane, the school system's computer coordinator, are meeting with the nine special education teachers from the district. Each teacher has been asked to share his or her concerns and problems about using computers. The teachers are eager to talk.

> *Barbara*: I'm pleased with the clock and calendar programs we bought. My learning disabled students can tell time more accurately and have improved in spelling the calendar words. Besides, while they

work on the computer, I have time to work with other students who need my personal help.

Dave: I'm afraid things aren't working out as well for my students. My EMR students can't make some of the cognitive leaps that the software requires; it just isn't appropriate for them. The programs progress between levels too quickly. It would be great if there were some way to insert intermediate lessons between the ones already on the disk. The kids are really motivated to work on the computer, but I find I'm spending just as much time with them individually at the machine, explaining how the program works and filling in the missing pieces. It's not the independent activity I hoped it would be.

Sarah: Is there anything we can do for the visually impaired students? They want to use the computers like everyone else, but the print on most of the programs is too small.

Sue: My big problem is finding software that coincides with the goals my students have on their Individualized Education Programs. The programs are either too difficult, skip major steps my students need, or miss the point altogether. I need material that correlates with their educational goals for the year. Otherwise, computer use cuts into the time they need to spend on the goals chosen for them last year.

Mike: The students in my alternative class at the high school really wanted to work on the computer and were excited at first. But some of their friends in the regular class saw the software my students were using. They said the programs were for babies and ridiculed the kids in my class. Now they are demanding "adult" programs. Of course, they can't handle the commercial programs I've seen because their reading levels are much too low.

The preceding describes some of the problems and concerns facing educators, particularly special educators, who would like to use microcomputer software with their students. The Education of All Handicapped Children Act, Public Law 94-142, requiring that all handicapped students must be provided with an educational program appropriate to their needs, forces the special educator who desires to use the positive instructional features of the microcomputer to define these features for each student. Although use of computerized instruction in general appears to have many positive benefits for special needs students, the particular characteristics necessary for any one student or special group of students are often missing from commercially available software.

Software Features
Important for Individualized Instruction

Students who do not learn through regular classroom procedures require variation in presentation modes, levels of instruction, rates of instruction, and modes of response. Other considerations include the reading level required by the software, flexibility in the operation of the software, and the character of the reinforcements used.

Although a selection of these software features may be present in commercially available programs[1], it is rare that they are both available and modifiable in a software package that also contains subject matter appropriate for the student. It is important to understand these features and their general inflexibility in commercially available software in order to recognize the benefits available with authoring products which allow these features to be modified to meet the needs of a range of students or the changing needs of one student.

Presentation Modes

Presentation mode refers to the way in which materials are presented to the student by the computer. On-screen text that is too closely spaced appears cluttered and is often difficult to read. Text size is also an important consideration. Many visually impaired students can use computer programs if the text is displayed in a size large enough for them to see. Complex directions or extraneous information should be avoided. Also, the use of color, animation, and graphics needs to be carefully controlled. A student with a color discrimination problem should not have to depend on color-coded answers. Similarly, an easily distracted student may find that detailed graphics or animation interferes with his or her learning. Finally, special features such as a spoken accompaniment to the program are difficult to find.

Most commercially available educational software does not allow the presentation mode to be modified.

Instructional Levels

To be appropriate for special needs students, software materials must be adaptable to differing ability levels. There may be several students who require instruction in one particular skill, yet their abilities and interest levels may greatly differ. Older students who need remedial work in elementary skills often do not respond favorably to programs designed for young children. Learning styles differ and these differences must be considered when planning instruction for handicapped populations. Some students respond well to detailed presentations and periodic information checks; others need small segments of information with frequent practice.

The term *branching* refers to the ability of a program to modify the instructional level of the presentation based on student responses. Branching, an important feature in good tutorial software, is particularly valuable for special needs students. If the student is making too many errors, or doing exceptionally well, the program automatically "branches" to another section of the lesson, skipping to the appropriate instructional level for the student. Branching may return the student to earlier material for review or may advance the student to more challenging material. Branching allows the lesson to be better aligned with a student's instructional level and previous learning. It also avoids disrupting the student's attention span because inappropriate lesson content is not presented.

Presentation Rates

When reading from the computer screen, students need differing amounts of time to grasp the material before moving ahead. If the program fixes the length of time the material remains on the screen, some students may have too much or too little exposure to the task. Finally, some programs display a full screen, while others show only one word or letter at a time. These varying presentation rates may confuse the student.

In most instances, it is preferable that the student be able to control the rate of the lesson's presentation. Rather than have the screen change in predetermined time segments, the student should be able to advance the lesson presentation by striking a specified key. However, at other times, the teacher may want to vary the rate for specific purposes such as testing. The ideal arrangement allows both alternatives.

Response Modes

The method of response is also very important for special education students. Some students are capable of using a standard keyboard; others have difficulty with it and are helped by programs that allow single-letter responses or simple use of the space bar or RETURN key. Special input devices (speech synthesizers, graphics pads, light pens, etc.) can simplify the response process for particular students.

Reading Levels

One of the major barriers to using software for special education students is the reading level required to use the programs. A student's ability to read the instructions and lesson content are critical to becoming involved with the learning materials. Most commercially available software does not allow the reading level to be altered.

Flexibility of Program Operation

Flexibility is particularly important in special education because student capabilities vary greatly. For example, variability in academic entry level to the software is important. Software should be flexible enough to be used many times by an individual student and by a large number of students. It should not be put aside because the student has learned a particular skill, or worse, because the student is bored. Although storage space on a floppy disk is limited, one diskette should challenge different students by containing a number of different skills, or a variety of difficulty levels for the same skill in order to challenge the same student over time as the student's skill level increases. For the student who learns slowly and needs many repetitions, a program should have several different presentations of the same material. The software should also allow a teacher to insert materials. Alternate forms to develop the same skill are also desirable.

Student or Teacher Control of Presentation and Response Time

It is helpful to have software that allows both the rate of presentation and the response time to be controlled. As discussed above, it is advantageous to have the rate of presentation determined by the student in some instances and the teacher in others. In addition, the software should also allow the teacher to determine the time period during which the student must respond to on-screen requests. This period can be adjusted to meet the differing needs of students, particularly those with handicapping conditions.

Although some commercially available software does allow the teacher to select from a range of options for these settings, in many programs even the slowest speed is often too fast for a student with learning problems. Before purchasing software, determine if the range of options is acceptable for the intended student population.

Number of Problems or Length of Lesson

The teacher needs to regulate the amount of time devoted to particular tasks in order to maintain the student's attention. If the student's attention span would allow for the completion of 20 problems, but after ten problems the program branches to a reward sequence or another task, the software does not meet the student's needs. Time on the task is unnecessarily wasted, and the student is underchallenged.

Type and Rate of Reinforcement

The type of reinforcement presented may be:

- passive—for example, a written message;
- active—for example, a flashing graphic display, a razzing sound for wrong answers, or cheery musical tones for correct answers;
- interactive—for example, presenting the student with a game to play.

Intermittent schedules and varying types of reinforcement are most productive. After using a program a few times with constant reinforcement, most students simply ignore it and get on with the task. Randomization of the type of reinforcing message, with control of how much reinforcement is provided, can help motivate and stimulate the student.

Some software developers overdo or include inappropriate reinforcement. Overuse of reinforcement detracts from the task, wastes time, and becomes boring. Some reinforcements were developed to entice very young children, and some last too long. Both features may make the software unattractive to older students who are learning with below grade level skills. The graphic displays meant to motivate younger children may actually embarrass older students. In addition, if the length of the computer session is limited, reinforcing sequences which require substantial time can be a problem.

Some reinforcers may even motivate the student to answer items incorrectly. For example, if the graphic display for an incorrect answer is as interesting as the one for the right answer, students may produce incorrect answers purposely. The most effective way to deal with incorrect answers is to present very bland, unvarying feedback: Ask the student to try again, give the correct answer, or make the screen blank. In some cases, it is effective to have aversive or tedious feedback for incorrect answers— for example, reroute the student through a tutorial to review information related to the answer.

Students have a natural tendency to test the limits of any program. If the software allows the rate and type of reinforcement to be controlled, the problems described above can be avoided.

Authoring as a Solution

Although computer-assisted instruction may interest teachers, particularly special education teachers, the wide range of student learning needs eliminates the usefulness of much commercially available software. Educators familiar with the commercial software market are aware there are few programs which contain all or even some of the special features described above. Nonetheless, properly programmed, computer-presented lessons can offer a motivating, repetitive method of instruction in basic skills. In those two words "properly programmed" lies the catch. So the search for alternatives begins.

Authoring products were developed to satisfy the needs of educators to have a relatively simple method for constructing customized computer-based lessons. Originally, authoring referred to *authoring languages,* complete programming languages with easy-to-use commands and special built-in features to facilitate the development of interactive tutorial and drill-and-practice programs. *Authoring systems* were then developed to provide more structure for educators developing customized lessons. This type of authoring product provides a template or outline to use for program creation. *Mini-authoring programs* (shells and utility packages) have added yet another dimension to the capabilities of authoring products. Each of the three levels of authoring products is discussed in detail in later chapters.

As we have indicated, commercially available CAI programs often contain many roadblocks for the slow or inefficient learner. Authoring products, particularly authoring systems and languages which are more flexible in their lesson design possibilities, allow the educator to avoid these roadblocks. Even students keeping up in their academic work can benefit from program modifications. Authoring products can be adapted in ways that are often impractical for commercially available programs. In addition, commercial programs are often further constrained by copyright laws or inflexible programming codes.

Authoring products provide the educator with a variety of flexible features which facilitate the construction of computer-based lessons. Various types of authoring products make it possible to utilize one set of instructional information but vary the presentation mode, the rate at which information is presented, the method and rate of student response or input, the level of reading difficulty, and the type of feedback (reinforcement) given to the student.

More and more authoring software is being developed. As both regular and special education needs and interests increase, further adaptations and enhancements will be added to traditional authoring approaches. These include special input and output devices for students with physically handicapping conditions. With these advances, the power of the computer as an instructional tool will continue to grow. Through guided texts, workshops, courses, and user groups, teachers should be given access to resources to assist them in using authoring products, so that they can explore new horizons in the search for ways to unlock the potential of all students.

Notes

1. "Commercially available" is used here and throughout the text to identify software which is available on the commercial market but is not authoring software. Commercially available programs present lessons developed by the software publisher, with lesson content determined by the publisher.

3

Authoring Products: An Introduction

The educational field is filled with numerous programs whose designs are based on different theoretical and practical approaches to learning. Training for special educators stresses technique, methods, and materials rather than content. Not only are there numerous categories of "handicapping conditions," but students within any one category display a wide variety of capabilities and disabilities. Teachers need a complete arsenal of instructional tools to work with any population, and in particular special education students. Although the number of software programs grows monthly, most are directed at the popular market. Few companies are designing software specifically for special education, and even those few cannot be expected to provide programs for the diverse set of students currently receiving special services.

Authoring products allow microcomputers to be incorporated into the existing curriculum to meet individual student needs. The lessons constructed using authoring enable the educator to utilize more fully the instructional power of the computer. However, before discussing specific authoring products, it is important to understand just what authoring is. This chapter answers your questions.

- What is authoring?
- What types of lessons can be written using authoring products?

- What are the basic steps in authoring a lesson?
- Why use authoring?
- What does an "authored" lesson look like in the classroom?

What is Authoring?

Authoring is a term applied to a set of computer programs and languages. These authoring products allow the user to write or "author" software. Authoring may include program design as well as lesson development, and can be done using either a preprogrammed piece of software or a complete programming language designed for educational lesson writing.

Authoring is not a term specific to computers. In fact, any lesson is "authored" at some point or another. The term *authoring* simply refers to the process of organizing and writing a lesson, regardless of the medium.

A lesson's *format*—the way in which the lesson is presented—may involve a variety of instructional tools—computers, textbooks, pictures, films, and records. Furthermore, the manner in which the lesson is presented is a vital part of the lesson's format. For example, a teacher may present new material by telling or by asking, by lecturing or by initiating a discussion. The final structure of the lesson, comprised of both format and content, is designed by the educator to meet the specific needs of the students. The teacher must balance pace, depth, and orientation. Similarly, a computer lesson should demonstrate the same balance, always taking into consideration the student population for which the lesson is intended.

Authoring products enable the computer to be used as an individual teaching tool. The author of a computer lesson can address individual student requirements, accommodate these requirements within the lesson, and adjust the lesson format accordingly. This ability identifies one of the distinct differences between traditional lesson authoring and computer authoring. In the past, teachers have most often authored traditional classroom lessons to meet the needs of a group of students learning in a group setting. Authoring products make it feasible (time and cost effective) to prepare lessons which meet the needs of individual students learning in an individualized setting.

Two other factors clearly distinguish computer authoring from traditional lesson authoring: presentation medium and response medium. With few exceptions, computer lessons are presented via a television screen or video monitor. Although this medium has many unique features, the size and quality limitations of the display are apparent. The two-dimensional surface of the screen is cold and artificial; the video monitor is devoid of texture and emotion. On the other hand, the monitor can present information in a clear, concise manner, and can provide a sense of timing and sequence. It can color, animate, and define patterns. It can even simulate three dimensions.

The way in which the student interacts with the computer lesson, with some notable exceptions, is most often through the computer's keyboard. Using the keyboard requires fairly advanced hand/eye coordination and pattern-recognition skills. Some students may have difficulty with the keyboard, and lesson writers may have to seek another response medium. Alternative input devices are available for those students who have difficulties with the keyboard (see Chapter 8).

Some computer programs address the shortcomings in both presentation and response mediums. Computer systems may be linked to video disk players, robots, or a variety of other items to enhance the presentation of material. Many alternative response devices are available, including special keypads, speech input devices, or touch sensitive screens. A wide range of special hardware is available to address these shortcomings. More and more authoring products and commercially available software will incorporate these advancements.

The Three Types
of Authoring Products

Authoring tools can be classified into three groups: *mini-authoring programs, authoring systems,* and *authoring languages.* Each group approaches authoring in a different way with different results and different possibilities for lesson writing. One can think of building a lesson as being much like building a house. Foundations must be set, the supporting structures erected, and walls built. Plumbing and wiring must be installed; doors and windows must be added. The final structure is designed not only with a specific function in mind but also for a specific setting. The architectural style of the building—the design of its roof; the placement of rooms, doors, and hallways; its color, shape, and size—comprise the building's format. After the building is complete, the furnishings are moved in. In much the same way, lessons are designed and then the specific content is moved in, with a specific function and audience in mind.

Mini-Authoring Programs

Using mini-authoring programs (sometimes called authoring shells) and their related utilities to customize lessons is easy. Mini-authoring programs are like finished buildings: The walls are in place; the author just adds the furniture. This type of product is particularly useful for test and drill-and-practice formats because a wide range of lessons can be developed in a short period of time. In addition, these shell-based lessons are usually centered around a game-like format, and are both easy and enjoyable for students to use. These characteristics make mini-authoring programs particularly valuable in a loosely supervised setting.

Mini-authoring programs, the simplest of the three types of authoring products, are predesigned and preprogrammed lessons which allow content to be changed within the lesson framework. The teacher/author fills in subject matter appropriate to the student's learning task, resulting in a lesson tailored to the student's current knowledge. Thus, mini-authoring programs provide the educator with a fixed framework for lesson writing. These programs are often available in an instructional game-like format and may include graphics and sound in addition to the actual lesson design. The educator needs only to type in subject material as directed by the program in order to create a personalized program with many of the features of prepackaged software programs. In addition, there are other prepackaged instructional programs which include authoring components, allowing the deletion and addition of specific information within the structure of the given program design.

Like commercially available software, mini-authoring programs often emphasize colorful graphics and sound effects. Some manufacturers include several lessons with the software itself. Ideally, mini-authoring programs are fully reproducible and, therefore, have wide mobility and exposure. Unfortunately, the content of these programs is limited to simple, specific questions and answers. Formats cannot be changed. Although the simplicity of constructing computer-based lessons using mini-authoring programs is appealing, particularly for those with limited computer experience, educators may find the range of options limiting.

Master Match and *Tic Tac Show* (from Advanced Ideas Inc.) are examples of mini-authoring programs.

Utility programs are related to mini-authoring programs. Utilities cover a wide range of presentation modes and may include test generation materials, crossword puzzle makers, or word-search designers. Such materials enable the educator to create, in a relatively short amount of time, computer-administered or written format worksheets for student use in reviewing and practicing previously taught skills.

Authoring Systems

The second type of authoring tool, the authoring system, allows the educator far more freedom in lesson development than is available with mini-authoring programs. Authoring systems provide content and can shape the format of the lesson in many ways: The resulting lesson can be more curriculum and student specific. In addition, authoring systems provide many of the features of authoring languages but within a more structured format. The *author* using an authoring system follows computer prompts step by step. Yet, these systems require no programming knowledge: The system automatically uses the information entered to form drills and tests, utilizing the preprogrammed format specified by the teacher/author. Teachers/authors only enter the information they wish to include in the lesson. Systems may allow timed responses, special graphics, hint options, alternate display modes, and internal logic. Systems are generally *menu driven* —allowing the lesson author to design a computer lesson by choosing options from a menu. For this reason, systems are usually easy to learn and use. Record-keeping functions are usually far more advanced than those for either mini-authoring programs or authoring languages. Using our architectural analogy, a system is like a partially completed building.

Private Tutor (from IBM) and *BLOCKS '82* (from the California School for the Deaf) are two examples of authoring systems.

Authoring Languages

Authoring languages overcome the inflexibilities of mini-authoring programs, and, to a lesser degree, those of authoring systems. Authoring languages are true computer programming languages. One of the most common authoring languages for educational purposes is PILOT. PILOT's vocabulary is designed for the task of lesson development. Available for almost all brands of microcomputers, PILOT was written as a language for computer-assisted instruction to be used by educators to design and write interactive teaching and testing programs.

Some of the features of authoring languages include the capability to present text, ask questions, accept full sentence answers, and respond to both anticipated and unanticipated student input. Lessons written using authoring languages can also include branching and student record-keeping options. Authoring languages are usually more difficult to learn because they have special vocabularies and require that the educator/author have some programming skill.

Using our architectural analogy, authoring languages represent building materials: The author must use these materials to build the building, which he or she can then furnish.

Although these three types of authoring products have different capabilities, they share a common purpose. Each provides the educator/author with a simplified method of constructing computer-based lessons to meet the needs of a given individual or situation. The choice of which type of authoring product is most suited to an educator's needs is most often determined by the complexity of the lessons to be constructed and the computer background of the educator/author. As the complexity of the lesson increases, so too do the demands upon the computer skills and lesson development time of the educator/author. Mini-authoring programs require little computer expertise but are limited in their flexibility. Authoring systems are more flexible but do require more lesson development time and effort. Authoring languages offer many options but require a commitment to learn a computer language for programming, albeit one specifically designed for educational purposes.

Types of Lessons

The easiest lessons to write using authoring products are drill and practice or tutorial. *Drill and practice* refers to lessons which present material for review: No new information is included. Instead, these materials are intended for use after the student has received instruction in a skill through some other method. Drill-and-practice exercises present the student with review problems to sharpen skills.

However, good drill-and-practice lessons do more than simply present problems. Microcomputers allow the program designer to expand these exercises by providing the student with immediate feedback to their responses. If the student's response is incorrect, the right answer can be displayed. In addition, the computer can be programmed to keep track of individual student responses. Missed problems can be presented again, and a final score can be tallied. Obviously, these features are beyond the capability of the traditional classroom worksheet.

Tutorial lessons, which teach new materials, are more complex to write but also more interactive. Though the complexity of tutorial exercises depends on their purpose, their general framework is the same. After being presented with information, the student is tested for comprehension. The lesson is often designed to ask frequent questions as the information is presented. In this way, the student is carefully guided through the material.

The special features of the tutorial become clear when the student has difficulty. In a well-written tutorial, all responses trigger some reaction. Correct responses may be praised or accepted as a step toward the next problem. However, when the student makes a mistake, the lesson can branch to a different part. The student's errors can be analyzed, and new teaching can take place. The ability to branch to teaching, testing, and reteaching segments makes the tutorial a powerful instructional tool.

The Basic Steps in Authoring a Lesson

Each authoring product uses a variety of additional features to modify the basic lesson format and accommodate some degree of individualization. Within the basic lesson format, these additional features flavor the computer lesson to meet an educator's specific needs.

Authoring follows some basic steps, particularly in the case of authoring systems. Although each product approaches these steps in a different manner, the sequence is relatively standard.

1. **Instructional Material**: Many products allow the author to present textual information before or during the lesson. This material may be simple test instructions or a complex essay. This feature is particularly important if a lesson is designed to introduce a new topic or concept. However, a text screen need not be a capability of all authoring products. A product may not offer a text screen option but allow questions used in the lesson to display instructional material instead. Usually, this means entering a special code or modifier, an easy task in either case. Some products may require lesson instructions without offering any additional text screen features. Finally, educators/authors should be aware that an *instruction screen* is not necessarily a *text screen.*

2. **Lesson Questions**: Every product has this feature in common. Although some products advertise three or four question formats, most systems provide a structure that allows questions to be formatted in any manner. Generally, question length is limited to less than one screen. One screen is enough room when text is

displayed in normal size; larger-sized text will limit question length.

3. **Correct Response**: This feature is easily overlooked but can dictate a product's practical usefulness. All types of authoring products allow the educator/author to enter an answer which will be considered correct when the lesson is presented. One answer option, however, does not cover other technically correct responses or misspellings. Some products "search" a students's response for the correct answer. Other products allow the educator/author to identify several "correct" or acceptable answers. However, even then, the range is unlikely to include the complete set of feasible responses.

The best option is the *match* feature. Software with this feature "matches" a student's response to an author-designed guide. A wide range of answers can be considered correct if certain letters or groups of letters are present. At the same time, when desired, a rigid guide can be created which allows only a single, correctly spelled answer.

4. **Correct Response Message**: This feature allows the author to specify personalized positive reinforcement for a correct answer. The message is usually limited in size: one or two lines. Anything larger than *Very Good!* or *That's Correct!* may not fit, especially in large type. Products that do not offer this option provide their own positive response messages. Potential editors/authors should check that these responses are appropriate for their students.

5. **Incorrect Response Message**: This message is displayed if a student answers a question incorrectly. Since a question may be answered incorrectly more than once, some products allow optional second or third trial messages. Again, the length of the message may be limited.

6. **Expected Incorrect Response Message**: The author can often predict wrong responses. Some software allows the author to trap these expected responses and to display an appropriate message. For example: "This is not correct, but you are on the right track!" Like correct response messages, the size of the message is limited.

7. **Hint**: Hints may come in many forms. Some products extend the length of an incorrect response message so that the author may use the space for a hint. Other products require the student to ask for a hint or automatically display a hint after a designated number of trials. Hints can be effective for individualizing instruction by allowing teachers to target specific students with special reinforcement.

8. **Branching**: Branching enables the author to set a parameter that can determine the sequence of the lesson material. A teacher may want to skip a series of questions if a student answers one question correctly, or return to a review following an incorrect response.

Branching comes in many forms. Some systems branch to alternative lessons based on a particular response, while others jump from question to question based on the student's identity. Lesson authors can use branching features to customize lessons, even without a target student audience in mind. Advanced branching can also extend the useful life of a lesson, providing fresh material as a student progresses.

9. **Trials**: Most products allow the author to set the number of question trials. This number may be set at the beginning of the lesson, affecting ALL questions, or may be set individually for each question.

10. **Retries**: After a lesson has been presented, missed questions may be asked again. This feature should be optional and the number of trials should be set by the educator/author.

11. **Graphics**: Graphics can be an effective teaching tool. Graphics capability, however, does not necessarily mean graphics development. Some authoring products include graphics, allowing the author to develop those graphics within the software. Others do not include graphics but have the capability of displaying graphics developed with other software and then "loaded" into the authoring product.

Although some lessons require complex, full-screen pictures, the simple line graphics and alternate character sets that many programs provide are easier to use and perhaps more appropriate. Also, it may not be possible to display text over a picture, a capability that is necessary for using graphics as illustrations for questions. Furthermore, while some products may stress the use of graphics in positive reinforcement, others may consider graphics best suited for lesson content.

12. **Question Presentation Order**: In many cases, questions may be presented in sequential or random order. When questions are presented in sequential order, the lesson order is determined by the educator/author. When questions are presented randomly, their sequence changes each time the lesson is run.

13. **Type sizes**: Some authoring products allow the size of the on-screen type to be modified. This feature can be important for the student who benefits from large type. In addition, type size can sometimes be varied within the lesson.

14. **Color**: Color is not widely available, but should become more so in future software.

Why Use Authoring?

As discussed in Chapter 2, the lack of appropriate commercially available software seriously limits the use of the microcomputer in the special education classroom. Since tutorial and drill-and-practice exercises have been used effectively with handicapped students, educators are understandably interested in taking full advantage of software which makes these types of exercises accessible. Authoring products enable educators to construct such computer-based lessons designed for specific student populations and even specific students.

Authoring products have many advantages. Special education students are easily distracted. Using authoring products, the teacher is able to focus the students' attention on relevant stimuli, immediately reinforce correct responses, and provide feedback for incorrect responses. Inverse highlighting, shape boxes, color cuing, underlining, arrows, animation, and sound can be used to draw student attention to relevant information. Although these features are also available in other types of commercially available programs, they have not been invoked to meet the specific learning styles or needs of special students.

Students may also benefit because the computer prevents "second-guessing." Many students are excellent "readers" of the unspoken cues which adults often give. The computer obviously does not provide facial or body cues to the student. Students using computer-based lessons must respond to the information explicitly provided.

However, students do benefit from occasional hints or prompts. With authoring products, teachers can include hints and cues. Later, these hints and cues can be removed, resulting in a modified lesson. Variable practice sequences can be included as a part of the authored lesson so that practice sessions on a skill are discontinued after the student demonstrates mastery.

Students' response rates are also quite variable. Slow-paced students and students who respond impulsively may need the same basic information but require different response times. With authoring products, response times may be varied. For example, the initial response period for a particular piece of software might be three minutes. This time period can be gradually reduced as the student's skills improve. Similarly, overly quick responses can be curbed through use of a delay in the computer's acceptance of an answer.

Feedback needs also differ. Although the ability of the computer to provide immediate feedback is one of its strongest benefits for slow and inefficient learners, the nature of the feedback is equally important. While some students may enjoy the "bells and whistles" found in many commercially available programs, older students may prefer more low-key, written messages. The same academic material may be appropriate for both groups. Lessons for both these groups of students may contain the same content but different types of reinforcement.

In addition, most authoring systems and many other authoring products include management and record-keeping components. The teacher may use these options to allow a student to review his scores. Records can also be kept to assist teachers in tracking student achievement.

Special needs students frequently demonstrate a wide discrepancy between the words they are able to recognize when reading and their comprehension of the material they have read. Some students are "word callers," able to read selections which are many levels above their ability to understand. Others are hindered by a different reading disability and can only read material which is below their intellectual level. By using the branching capabilities of authoring systems and languages, the special educator is able to develop lessons which assist students in the development of new vocabulary and concept awareness, while customizing reading and interest levels for individual students.

Authoring in the Classroom: A Story

How does authoring work in the classroom? Before examining each type of authoring product in depth (Chapters 4, 5, and 6), the application of authoring products to students within the school environment is illustrated in the following scene.

When Joe Mason, the district coordinator for special services, stopped to speak to Tom Bradshaw, Tom was working at the computers with two students. He walked over to see what they were doing. Bill and Janice were both working on money fact drill-and-practice lessons. As Joe watched, he became aware that though the problems, graphics, and sound were the same, the lessons differed in their presentation. After the students left, Tom explained:

> What I've done is tailor the same format to meet individual students' learning-rate needs. Bill has difficulty controlling his impulsiveness. When he's working on an assignment, he tends to put down the first thing that comes to his head. When we tried the computer, the commercial programs were frustrating for him because he would not take the time to read the material or think about the answer, so he made many errors. Janice, on the other hand, has been extremely slow to answer. Usually she takes so long that the other children become impatient and the teacher either supplies the answer or calls on another student to "help out." Janice does need some time to think, but she also needs to be able to try out her skills in a non-threatening environment. Both students are working on the same skills in math but obviously need different presentation formats. I could not find any commercial programs to develope money skills in the way these two had been taught or that allowed for the differences in their learning style needs.
>
> When I heard about authoring products at a computer conference I attended, I decided to look into the idea. There were more choices in the field than I realized, but I decided to use a system called *BLOCKS '82* which had what I wanted. But two other features were even more important. With *BLOCKS '82* I was able to purchase a complete graphics library of 750 pictures. There are 20 categories and the pictures are excellent and waiting for me to use them in the lessons I write. There is an additional option which lets me use pre-drawn shapes or create my own, and an option to use a graphics tablet for drawing. The other feature that caught my interest is the ability to monitor the rate of material presentation and the rate of response.
>
> For Bill, I use an option to control the speed and make the letters and problems appear at a rate his reading teacher helped me to determine. Now the material appears on the screen in keeping with his

reading and comprehension rate. When he responds to a question, he either knows the answer or is aware that he needs to think. Using the feedback and wrong answer options available lets me respond to the types of errors he may make and helps him see why he might have chosen a particular answer.

For Janice, I use a built-in timing option. In the beginning, I just let her sit at the computer on one problem as long as she needed. I made the problems simple, and she started responding. Then I told her the computer was going to start moving things along a little. I set the response rate at the maximum, slightly over four minutes. She waited and waited. It was funny because I had given her a series of problems she knew. When she saw how long the computer would "wait," she went through the series quickly. She then asked if we could make the computer faster. She has gotten almost competitive with herself, asking me to decrease the response time. She is now down to ten seconds on most material, and her classroom teacher says she is volunteering to answer in class. One other thing I did for Janice was to avoid negative feedback. When she didn't respond, the computer just printed a message such as "Let's try a different one." She never felt pushed to try something she wasn't sure of.

This has turned out to be a great tool for me. As you can see, I can write lessons that tie in with my student's curriculum needs, include necessary graphics, and are consistent with their special learning needs. I'm often able to use the same material and just vary the presentation speed, as I did for Janice and Bill. I couldn't have done the same thing as quickly or simply any other way, and I'm convinced that using the computer has helped my students make important gains.

This example demonstrates the use of one type of authoring product, in this case the authoring system *BLOCKS '82*. By taking advantage of the special capabilities of the computer and the authoring system, Tom was able to develop materials designed to meet the specific needs of his students. Authoring provides educators with a tool which allows them to capitalize on the capabilities of the microcomputer while providing students with individualized instruction. Authoring allows a school to develop software that fits into and supports existing curricula.

4

Mini-Authoring Programs

Of the various types of authoring products available—mini-authoring programs, authoring systems, and authoring languages—mini-authoring is the most *user friendly*. Mini-authoring programs, and their related utilities, supply the classroom teacher with ready-made lesson formats. These programs are easy to understand and their application to the curriculum is usually obvious.

Briefly described in the previous chapter, mini-authoring programs are drill-and-practice exercises which are complete in all but content. It is the ability to modify or create content which makes the mini-authoring program so appealing. No programming skill is required: Each format is complete and the program can present material, solicit student responses, determine the correctness of those responses, and keep student records. Some programs also allow the correct answer to be displayed during the lesson. Frequently included are such features as graphics, sound, color, and animation. Sample exercises, complete with content, are usually available with mini-authoring programs, but they are not appropriate for every situation. The appeal of a mini-authoring program is that all the educator needs to do is enter the information requested, namely the subject matter, and a professional-looking customized lesson is immediately available.

Mini-authoring programs are designed to be easy to use. Educators can learn them more quickly than authoring systems or authoring languages, and they are more time efficient than programming from scratch. The directions for using the authoring portion of a mini-authoring program appear on the computer screen, in accompanying printed documentation, or both on the screen and in a manual.

Mini-authoring programs are most effective when used to reinforce learned materials. Students who need to practice and reinforce rote skills particularly benefit from the types of lessons created using mini-authoring programs.

Most commonly, educators use mini-authoring programs to provide students with another mode of learning to review subject matter learned using another instructional tool. Subject areas such as math, spelling, grammar, science, and social studies can be easily included in the mini-authoring framework. Teachers can also use these programs for small group or class "team" practice. Parents may use mini-authoring programs as a homework incentive. Older and more capable students can even develop their own materials to review for tests, etc.

The variety of mini-authoring programs available provides the educator with many presentation formats. Generally, mini-authoring programs use a game-like format—an approach which is already familiar and non-threatening to students and which capitalizes on characteristics identified as "intrinsically motivating" in computer games: challenge, fantasy, and curiosity (Malone, 1980).

For some applications, however, mini-authoring programs may be too limited. Lesson management or record-keeping capabilities are generally unsophisticated, usually taking the form of straight scores. Although formats vary among programs, each software package usually has only one scenario. The rate of presentation and other factors cannot always be modified. Designed primarily for drill and practice, mini-authoring programs do not contain the branching or tutorial capabilities available in both authoring systems and authoring languages.

Mini-authoring programs vary in the features they contain and are best used as *templates* for lessons or exercises. This Chapter provides examples of program use as well as excerpts from selected mini-authoring programs. These examples indicate both the skill and time required to use these programs, and assist educators in determining if mini-authoring programs are best suited to meet their needs. Two related types of software, utility packages and modifiable programs, are also discussed.

The Appendix to Chapter 4 contains a detailed "walk-through" of an actual mini-authoring program.

Mini-Authoring at Work: A Story

Linda Hold and Kathy Benson are learning disability resource room teachers. Kathy has used microcomputers with her students for two years. Linda has had a computer in her resource room for six months, and is seeking Kathy's help.

Linda: I'm really fed up with the pressure I'm getting from the main office. The director wants all the kids in the resource room to use the computer. The research on drill-and-practice software has him convinced that they're just what we need. I have no argument with using computers, but I can't find the right software. I did find a couple of okay things for math, but I haven't been able to find anything at all that corresponds to our reading curriculum. The classroom teachers are adamant about wanting the mainstreamed students to be able to read and define the vocabulary words for the books they're using, but the publisher hasn't produced any software for that series and none of the commercial programs have the right words. I talked to Ed, the sixth-grade teacher who uses BASIC in his math classes. Even he admitted that writing flashy programs takes lots of time and effort. You know how my students are—they want bells and whistles and fun. I just don't have the time at night to learn how to program and write my own software. There's already so much paperwork. If I had release time, it might be different, but I'm not going to spend any more time than I already do making individual worksheets and dittos.

Kathy: I know how you feel. I got really angry myself during that first year until I found out about authoring products.

Linda: I've heard about them, but don't you still have to learn how to program? What about graphics and animation?

Kathy: Wait a minute! There's an entire range of authoring products—mini-authoring programs—that might be perfect for you. And they don't take any more time than making up a worksheet. I call them "shells" because these programs come with the complete format for a lesson. All you do is follow simple directions and put in your own content. They can be used like worksheets. The structure or shell is already there, including graphics or animation. You customize them to whatever subject you want. Of course, they're more attention grabbing and motivating for the kids. My students really like using them!

An Example of a
Mini-Authoring Program

Master Match (from Advanced Ideas Inc.) is a typical mini-authoring program, used here to introduce the general operation of a mini-authoring program.

Master Match is based on the concentration or memory-game format. A series of numbered boxes, hiding information, are turned over two at a time by the player. If the two boxes match, the player receives a point and continues. Non-matches give the next turn to another player. The students playing the game see the lesson content exactly as it was typed in by the teacher/author. They then direct the computer to "turn over" the numbered boxes.

After loading *Master Match* into the computer, an initial menu is displayed.

> Press   Press
> RETURN   ESC
> to play   to quit
> the game
>
> Press S to create or change a subject

Pressing the *S* key displays:

> Put the MASTER MATCH diskette into the
> drive, type 'Y' and press RETURN.
> (Press ESC now to return to the game.)

Typing *Y* <Return> causes a new message to appear on the screen:

> Please type an EXCLAMATION POINT (!) to continue.

These multiple steps leading to the authoring portion of *Master Match* are designed to prevent teachers/authors from accidentally entering the editing sections. The next screen contains the Author Work Menu:

1. CATALOG of subject areas
2. CREATE a *new* subject area
3. CHANGE an *old* subject area
4. EDIT the *current* subject
5. SAVE the current subject
6. DELETE a subject from disk
7. FORMAT a new subject disk
8. RETURN to the game

Choose a number:
(then press the RETURN key)

If Option # 2 is selected (*Create a new subject area*), two squares appear side-by-side on the screen. Each has space for up to 108 characters in a display twelve characters wide and nine characters high. Between the two large squares is a smaller rectangle labeled *key*. The lesson content is entered in these two large squares. All the commands for moving the cursor and entering text are also displayed on the screen.

Match Set	Use ctrl-B to change box
Number 1	Press ESC when finished
→ : move right	ctrl-A : Alternate set
← : move left	ctrl-S : Show alternate
ctrl-K : move up	ctrl-I : Insert space
ctrl-J : move down	ctrl-D : Delete letter
	ctrl-C : Clear box
	ctrl-R : Restart

The material the teacher/author enters in the two boxes corresponds to the material the student sees when playing the game.

Master Match has the added feature of a *key* which allows the teacher/author to coordinate different match sets which could have the same answer. For example, if the objective is to classify foods, there may be four fruits, four vegetables, and four dairy products in the set. Obviously, the student should be able to match any two of the fruits, without having to worry about which ones the teacher typed in together. The *key* allows the teacher/author to identify a key word which the computer uses to search for acceptable matches. In this example, all fruit names (i.e., grape, apple, pear, and cherry) should match interchangeably. If the teacher/author types the word *fruit* into the *key* box at the bottom of the screen for each set of fruit words, any pair combination will be accepted as a match.

Another special feature of *Master Match* is the alternate character set. This is a set of different letter and figure styles which can be used to create a subject area. When an alternate character set is used, the keys on the keyboard do not print the standard letters. Rather, a special character, such as an italicized letter or a graphic shape, appears. *Master Match* contains a few alternate character sets which allow use of italics and foreign language characters, as well as some graphics. These character sets can be very useful for developing lessons for special purposes—such as drawing outlines of counties, states, or countries; or writing lessons for English as a Second Language (ESL) students.

After the information is entered in the Author Work Mode, the lesson is run. In *Master Match,* an animated owl emcee appears on the screen below a grid of numbered squares (Figure 4-1). The owl "asks" the student to select squares by typing numbers. The information on the screen in the squares is the same material entered by the teacher/author.

Figure 4-1

Master Match is typical of many mini-authoring programs. It does not take long to input the information and the finished lesson looks professional. The program appeals to students because it is familiar—they recognize it as another computer game, complete with flashing lights, point accumulations for correct answers, and a sober message from the owl for incorrect responses.

Mini-authoring programs such as *Master Match* combine excitement and challenge, and reinforce material presented with other instructional tools. Although other mini-authoring programs use different game formats, they share the feature of enabling the teacher to become an author and construct customized computer-based lessons for students.

Features of Mini-Authoring Programs

Mini-authoring programs differ in specific format but have many features in common. In general, such programs appeal to educators for a number of reasons.

1. They are easy to use.
2. They are flexible and can be used for a variety of students.
3. They appeal to students.
4. They usually contain characteristics useful for special populations.
5. They can be easily incorporated into existing curricula.

Ease of Use

Factors which result in ease of use are:

- on-screen directions,
- accompanying printed documentation, usually a manual, and
- menus.

As can be seen in the *Master Match* example above, one of the most important aspects of a good mini-authoring program is ease of use. Most mini-authoring programs include directions that are simple to follow, often displayed directly on the computer screen. These directions are also frequently detailed in the accompanying printed documentation or manual.

In addition, some of these programs are "menu-driven": They provide a list of options for selection. A *menu* makes selection simple by listing on the screen all the options available at various points in the program. Menus serve to prompt or guide the author. Usually, the selection of options is made by keyboarding a single key. The Author Work Menu (above) for *Master Match* illustrates this single key response mode.

Such user-friendly programs simplify the authoring process for educators. Menus also reduce the amount of time involved both to learn how the program works and to enter new information to customize the program. Although most mini-authoring programs are sold with printed documentation, educators usually find it more efficient and less complicated to follow on-screen directions. The combination of good printed documentation and menus helps make these programs easier to learn and use.

Mini-authoring programs make it possible to "do while learning"— Periods spent becoming familiar with the programs can also be productive. The teacher/author often has a sense of accomplishment when finished, since the end product is a lesson which is immediately usable. Since only specific material related to a given educational objective is entered, the overall entry time is relatively short. Modifying previously entered material is also simple. Compared to the time needed to write original programs or locate and preview commercially available software, mini-authoring programs can expedite the development of usable educational programs and provide a viable alternative source for appropriate computer-based lessons.

Flexibility for Student Use

Mini-authoring programs are flexible. They

- capitalize on the appeal of the computer game format;
- use a selection of graphics, animation, and immediate feedback; and
- allow multiple modes of play—student against student, team against team, student or team against computer, or student against self.

Most mini-authoring programs stress rote skills typically covered in drill-and-practice exercises, much like workbooks. However, mini-authoring programs capitalize on the appeal of the computer by imbedding these exercises within a challenging and fun game-like format. The resulting instructional game is appropriate for a variety of students. Games appeal to many children so this format capitalizes on the students' interest. The use of graphics, animation, and immediate feedback are characteristics common to mini-authoring but missing in comparable traditional instructional tools.

Another important feature of mini-authoring programs is the opportunity for the teacher or student to determine the mode of play. The choice can be to play against the computer (self-competition), against another classmate, in a team against the computer, or in a team against another team. When playing against the computer, the self-challenge allows students to work on improving personal scores and setting new goals without outside pressure. Gaining confidence on a program and with its material can assist such students in eventually using the programs with other classmates. For other players, peer challenges are more valuable and enjoyable. With mini-authoring programs, it is possible for partners or whole teams to play against each other. This option can be helpful for students who resist games with peers. In addition, for certain students, having the opportunity to share a computer game with another student or teach someone else how to play can do much toward building self-esteem and peer respect. The variety of modes of play makes it possible to meet the needs of students who enjoy competition and challenge as well as the needs of those who require more privacy and time to develop skills. This type of individualization is particularly valuable for slow or inefficient learners.

Special Character Sets

A few mini-authoring programs, including *Master Match*, contain special character sets applications. These sets allow the teacher/author to include graphic displays or pictures and special words. Diacritical markings may be included for lesson content in languages other than English. Teachers working with ESL students can make excellent use of this feature. Special character sets may also be useful for students with special needs or in special settings such as preschool. Computer lessons to develop basic language and math concepts, such as same/different and other relationships, can be designed. Mini-authoring programs can also be used to create vocabulary and item-matching lessons for older special needs students in life-skills courses. Special character sets can result in more appealing lesson presentations as well as expand the types of lesson content.

Incorporation into the Curriculum

A final advantage gained through the use of mini-authoring programs comes from the ease with which these programs may be adapted for inclusion into the curriculum. The resulting software can be directly correlated with a student's educational plan because the actual practice material is generated by the teacher/author. Information entered by the teacher/author can be used by students to reinforce and practice material specific to the curriculum. Since many of the mini-authoring programs use a motivating game-like format, they can be adapted to a variety of educational settings. Uses include traditional classroom periods, resource room periods, "free-time" activities, before and after school periods, and behavioral or work reinforcement. Mini-authoring programs also provide a time-controlled and motivating activity for students with short attention spans who require variety during a class period.

Using the Authoring Section of Mini-Authoring Programs

The unique feature of mini-authoring programs, and of all authoring products, is their ability to be customized by the teacher/author. The graphics, animation, and program itself remain unchanged. Only the actual material, such as spelling words or math problems, is actually modified. The modification of the program is accomplished by following step-by-step instructions. These directions are usually printed on the screen, as well as in accompanying printed documentation. Usually, the modification process is achieved either by answering questions presented on the computer screen or in the printed documentation (prompts for authoring) or changing data lines or statements in the program itself (modifiable programs). To explain these processes more fully, descriptions of the use of these basic types of program modification follow.

Screen or Documentation Prompts for Authoring

Recently developed mini-authoring programs contain relatively clear instructions for guiding the teacher/author through the process of program change. The most common approach consists of question-and-answer sequences between computer and teacher/author. Information is entered into the program by responding to questions on the screen. Usually, descriptions of the questions and an explanation of what these prompts mean are included in the accompanying printed documentation. For example, in a game on antonyms, the computer might use the prompt *What is the first word?* After the teacher/author has typed in the first word and <Return>, the screen might next prompt with a statement such as *What is the opposite?* After the teacher/author has entered the response, the computer would then direct him or her to enter another pair until all desired word pairs had been entered.

As indicated earlier, the obvious advantage to this type of program is the ease of use. Authoring this lesson requires absolutely no programming skill. The teacher/author is led through the complete writing process, and merely fills in the lesson content. The following example illustrates the simplicity and ease of the process.

Game Show (from Advanced Ideas Inc.) is an example of a particularly user-friendly mini-authoring program.

The format of *Game Show* is similar to that of the TV game show, *Password.* Two players, two teams, or an individual can play the game. The goal is to guess a word or phrase based upon clues and hints given by the game partner, a role played by the computer. The game starts after players type in their names and select a topic area by responding to questions printed on the screen. The computer displays a word from the topic area and presents clues to each player in turn. Correct answers result in points for the responding team, complete with cheering and an animated waving arm from the computer partner. Incorrect guesses shift the turn to the other team. Another clue is given by the computer, and the second team has a chance to guess. The exchange continues until a team answers correctly or all clues for a given word have been used. As many as ten clues per word or phrase can be given, and topics can be of varied length.

Many mini-authoring programs contain several subjects, already entered. Although software varies, there is often space on the original disk for new material to be added. However, it is usually a good idea to prepare several additional data disks for storing new subject files. Directions for preparing a blank disk are frequently included in printed documentation. In *Game Show,* for example, directions for preparing a new subject diskette are included in the text on the screen as well as in the printed documentation which comes with the program.

Authoring a lesson by following screen or printed documentation prompts is straightforward. In *Game Show,* the teacher/author begins by loading the program disk into the computer. The *main menu,* consisting of a list of numbered options from which to chose, then appears on the screen.

1. Play Game Show
2. Build or Change a Subject Area
3. Quit

Before authoring a lesson, it helps to "play" a lesson using one of the preprogrammed subjects. A quick run-through gives the teacher/author a clear picture of what the students see in a lesson after the modified material has been entered. To play the game, chose Option #1 (*Play Game Show*).

To begin customizing subject areas, or files, select Option #2 (*Build or Change a Subject Area*), by pressing the number 2 key and <Return>. An on-screen message then requests that the teacher/author *Press the Shift Key and* <Return>. This sequence allows the computer to determine if any upper/lower case shifting modifications have been added to the computer. Throughout, the teacher/author needs only to follow the requests/directions displayed on the screen.

The next screen instructs the teacher/author to *Insert the Proper Subject Area Diskette*. At this point, the teacher/author can use a disk with prerecorded files or replace the original *Game Show* disk with a blank disk. A new menu appears on the screen:

1. Catalog of Subject Areas
2. Create a New Subject Area
3. Change an Old Subject Area
4. Delete a Subject Area
5. Make a New Subject Diskette
6. Return to Main Menu

Selecting Option #5 (*Make a New Subject Diskette*) and pressing <Return> causes the computer to print the question: *Do you want to make a new subject diskette?* Since the answer is yes, the teacher/author types *yes* and presses <Return>. At this point, the computer displays a warning:

* * * WARNING * * *
MAKING A SUBJECT DISKETTE WILL ERASE
ALL PROGRAMS AND INFORMATION ON THE DISKETTE.
DO YOU WISH TO CONTINUE?

The process which prepares a blank disk so that it can be used to store information erases anything currently on the disk. This warning reminds the teacher/author to be sure the disk being used does not contain important information. The teacher/author confirms his or her desire to continue by typing *yes* and pressing <Return>. One more prompt, *Insert Blank Diskette into Drive 1* appears on the screen. This is one last demand for verification before erasing the disk. Pressing the <Return> key then begins the disk preparation process. The light for the disk drive goes on. When the light goes off, the disk is ready to be used.

It is not necessary to prepare a disk each time a new subject area is going to be created. One disk contains a fair amount of space, and multiple subject files may be created and saved before it is necessary to prepare a new disk. When the disk is full, the computer prints an informative message on the screen, and does not allow additional files to be saved on the disk. At this point, having prepared a new subject disk at an earlier time saves the teacher/author from interrupting a session to do so. It is advisable to always have a spare or two ready.

Option #2 is selected to *Create a New Subject Area*. The computer screen now prompts the teacher/author to enter the lesson content, "walking" step-by-step through the process of adding new words and clues. The first prompt appears as: *Target Word # 1*.   The computer waits for the teacher/author to enter the first word. At this time, spelling errors may be corrected. Although words may also be changed at a later point, corrections are most easily made when content is first entered.

After typing in the first target word and pressing <Return>, the computer prompts: *Clue 1*. At this point, the user types in the first clue which relates to Target Word #1. Pressing <Return> advances the program to the second clue, and so forth. Up to ten clues may be entered for each target word in *Game Show*. Pressing ESC (the escape key) moves the user forward to the next target word. (The use of ESC and <Return> are clear in the program instructions.) Clues and target words are limited to one complete line. If the teacher/author tries to exceed the limit, the computer displays a message concerning the length.

A special feature of *Game Show* allows the teacher/author to specify more than one possible answer. Using a comma between answers serves as a cue to the computer to accept either answer as a correct response. This feature allows the teacher/author to predict alternative correct answers which students might give and have the lesson count these answers as acceptable.

When all target words and clues have been entered, the file of information can be saved on the data disk for use with the complete program. In order to save the information, more on-screen prompts need to be followed. After pressing ESC twice, a new Edit Menu appears:

ADD, EDIT, LIST, DELETE, SAVE OR MAKE (A SUBJECT DISKETTE)

To save the new subject file, the teacher/author types *save* and presses <Return>. The computer next asks for a title for the new subject. This new title is added to the list of available subjects. After entering a name and pressing <Return>, the computer indicates that the file is being saved. After the file has been saved, the Work Menu reappears.

Other files can be created or altered by choosing other program options from this menu, or the teacher/author can return to the Main Menu.

Obviously, on-screen or documentation prompts simplify the authoring process making it possible for individuals with little computer experience to create instructional games which not only appear professional but also use material tailored to meet individual student and curriculum needs.

Mini-Authoring Using Program Alteration

Another type of mini-authoring program is modified by changing the data lines within the program listing itself. In this method, it is helpful if the teacher/author has some familiarity with programming, although those with little programming experience can make the changes easily enough. An example helps to clarify how such changes are made.

One of the best known mini-authoring programs of this type is *The Shell Games* (from Apple Computer Inc.). *The Shell Games* is a set of *shells*, including formats for matching words and phrases, true-false, and multiple choice. One of these shells is *Match Machine*.

Match Machine creates two columns of information on the screen which can be matched according to corresponding numbers and letters. The program provides the teacher/author with the format for entering the topic to be covered, the headings for each of the two columns, the matches themselves, and extra answers that won't match. In order to fill in this information, the teacher/author must type program lines using a format specified in the accompanying manual. When the student uses the program, he or she sees the information presented in columns with directions to select matches. Although not as easy to use as mini-authoring programs utilizing the on-screen prompts, data statement modification is still uncomplicated and not difficult to learn.

The first step is to load *Match Machine*, following the on-screen directions. When the directions *Press the Space bar to Begin* appear on the screen, the teacher/author instead presses Control-C (holds down both the Control and the C keys simultaneously). Pressing <Return> now exits the program and makes it possible to modify the actual program lines. In all *The Shell Games* programs, the quiz information is stored beginning on line number 9010. The sets of matches are stored in memory locations called *string variables* and designated using traditional programming terms. Following the directions in the manual, the teacher/author retypes the lines of information, replacing current quiz items with new items. The format for entering this information is very specific and must be carefully followed, or the program will not run correctly. A typical set of program lines follows:

```
9010 D1$="DAYS OF THE WEEK,DAY&ABBREVIATION,
SUNDAY&SUN.,MONDAY&MON.,TUESDAY&TUES."
9011 D2$="WEDNESDAY&WED.,THURSDAY&THURS.,
FRIDAY&FRI.,SATURDAY&SAT."
9012 RETURN
```

The lesson is displayed on the screen as two columns of choices.

DAY	ABBREVIATION
0 - SUNDAY	A - SAT.
1 - MONDAY	B - WED.
2 - TUESDAY	C - MON.
3 - WEDNESDAY	D - THURS.
4 - THURSDAY	E - SUN.
5 - FRIDAY	F - FRI.
6 - SATURDAY	G - TUES.

TRY TO GUESS A MATCH!
PLEASE ENTER A NUMBER FROM 0 TO 9
AND A LETTER FROM A TO G AND PRESS
<RETURN>

It is possible to increase the difficulty of this exercise by including more definitions (column 2) than items (column 1). This avoids students using the process of elimination.

Although this type of authoring format is different from screen prompted programs, modifying the program is no more difficult to use. Some educators are initially intimidated by the appearance of the program lines, but this response is easily overcome. Educators with computer programming background will find this type of modification procedure particularly easy to understand.

The Shell Games includes *The Shell Games Editor* which provides an alternative method for modifying the program. Program lines can be altered using screen prompts and detailed printed documentation.

The Shell Games: A Story

Margie Mason, former director of Project MASS (Microcomputer Assistance for Special Students) in Charleston, Illinois, has described the use of *The Shell Games* (Mason, 1983). At the time the games were used in Charleston, all students in Illinois were required to pass a test on the constitutions of the United States and Illinois, and no special allowances were made for learning disabled or mildly retarded students. Prior to Project MASS, many of these students repeatedly failed the tests. Teachers in the Project found their own programming skills too limited and advanced programming too time consuming, so they searched for commercially available programs. They decided to use *The Shell Games* to create drills containing factual questions on the Constitutions. Questions could be written at the students' own reading levels and structured for their understanding.

The results of the project were most encouraging. The students enjoyed the game format and were able to progress at their own rates. When the formal testing was done and results returned, it was discovered that the mildly retarded class had averaged higher scores than the regular students. Drill and practice in the special format had really worked!

Related Software Packages

Other categories of software packages, related to mini-authoring although not actually mini-authoring programs, can assist teachers in preparing material for student use. The two most common are utility packages and modifiable programs.

Utility Packages

Utility packages are related to mini-authoring programs and are used to develop dittos, worksheets, or tests. *Puzzles and Posters* (from the Minnesota Educational Computer Consortium) is an example of a utility program.

Puzzles and Posters is a set of individual programs (*Word Search, Crossword Puzzle, A-Maze-Ment,* and *Posters and Banners*) which includes procedures for creating crossword puzzles, word searches, mazes, posters, and banners. By following on-screen directions or using the manual, teachers/authors are able to enter and edit their own information to meet individual student and curriculum needs. The following description of the process for designing a word- search worksheet demonstrates how easy authoring is with this software package.

When *Puzzles and Posters* is first loaded, a menu of several options appears. The first program on the main menu is *Word Search. Word Search* allows the user to create and print a list of words as a word-search puzzle. This list may be stored on the disk, or used only during the current computer session. It is necessary to have prepared (initialized) a data disk to store the list. If a data disk needs to be prepared, the teacher/author is instructed how to make one. After the data disk is ready, the Word Search Menu appears on the screen. It contains these options:

Word Search Menu

You may:
1. Create a new list
2. Edit a list/Print a puzzle
3. Delete a list
4. Return to main menu

Which number?

After selecting Option #1, another menu appears:

Create a New List

You may:
1. Create a temporary list
2. Create a permanent list on a data diskette

Which number?

A new list for *Word Search* can contain up to fifty words. Each word is limited to a length of no greater than fifteen characters. Words are entered one at a time, and the teacher/author presses <Return> after each word.

When all the desired words have been entered, the teacher/author presses <Return> again. This signals that the list is complete.

The editing procedure for correcting any mistakes depends upon whether the list is temporary or permanent. In the Temporary List Mode, a screen prompt asks after each word: *Do you want to make any changes?* A *Y* response allows the user to re-type the word; an *N* response advances the program to accept a new word. In the Permanent List Mode, lists can also be edited after they have been created. This allows the teacher/author to modify one word list to meet other needs, rather than having to create an entirely new list.

When all the words have been entered, prompts allow the teacher/author to select the word arrangement. Words may be arranged horizontally, vertically, diagonally, and in inverted order.

To construct a word-search puzzle using a temporary list, the teacher/author selects the word arrangement and presses <Return>. The prompt on the screen then asks: *Do you want to use the entire word list for the puzzle?* If the answer is *N*, the screen changes to a delete mode. Arrow keys move a marker from word to word. Any word the teacher/author wants deleted is highlighted when the space bar is pressed. Pressing <Return> removes the word from the list. When all deletions are completed, a sample puzzle is shown on the screen and the teacher/author is asked if this word-search puzzle should be printed. An *N* response causes another puzzle to be printed with the same words. The new puzzle may be of the same type or a different type. If the same type of arrangement is chosen, the words will be rearranged so that the word-search puzzles are not identical. In this manner the same words can be used to generate several puzzles, each with a different word arrangement. Any words that do not fit into the puzzle are shown, and the teacher/author decides whether or not to print the puzzle.

When the arrangement is acceptable, the teacher/author responds with a *Y* to the prompt: *Do you want to print this puzzle?* The teacher/author is then stepped through a printing process which requires that certain decisions be made.

1. The teacher/author can add a title to the word-search puzzle, if desired, by following screen prompts.
2. The program asks the teacher/author if an answer key should be added.
3. The teacher/author is reminded that a ditto master can be used in the printer.
4. The teacher/author is asked how many copies (up to nine) should be generated.

5. The teacher/author is instructed to prepare the printer. The printer should be connected to the computer, the power turned on, the select or on-line button correctly set, and paper or a ditto placed in the machine.

6. The word-search puzzle is printed. When using tractor feed paper, the title, puzzle, and a list of words are printed on one page, then paper is automatically advanced, additional copies are printed (if indicated), and the answer sheet is printed on a separate page. When using dittos, the printer stops after each page and waits for a new piece of paper to be inserted. When the printing is finished, the teacher can choose to make another word-search puzzle, return to the main menu, or exit the program. One additional feature of this program allows the teacher/author to access any special character sets (such as large print or bold-face type) which are available on a particular printer.

The process for creating a word-search puzzle from a permanent list varies slightly from the procedure for a temporary list. After selecting Option #2 (*Create a permanent list on a data diskette*), the computer prompts the teacher/author to place a data diskette in the drive. The teacher/author is then asked for a list name and prompted to enter each of the words to be included in the word list. Words can be edited immediately or later. After entering the word list, an editing screen appears:

Edit a list

You may:
1. See and print a list of entries
2. Add entries
3. Delete entries
4. Change entries
5. Change title of the list
6. Print the puzzle
7. Return to Word Search menu

Which number?

These options allow a variety of changes to be made to the current list. The word-search puzzle can be printed now or later. When printing later, the teacher/author must first select Option # 2 from the Word Search Menu (*Edit a list/Print a puzzle*). This option displays a catalog of the lists on the data disk. The list to be printed is then selected from this catalog. The printing process is described above.

The time involved in producing worksheets such as crossword and word-search puzzles is greatly reduced by using a utility program. The various options allow flexibility in individualizing puzzles. It is possible to use the same word list for several different students, and to vary the word arrangement. In addition, the word lists created for *Word Search* and *Crossword Puzzle* can be used interchangeably. The ability to create a word list to be printed later allows a teacher/author the freedom to construct puzzles on computers without printers. Since schools often have one printer for several computers, this ability to separate the creation and printing steps can be important.

Utility programs, then, offer educators another set of tools for developing dittos, worksheets, and tests with customized content.

Modifiable Programs

Another type of mini-authoring program is one which can be modified by the teacher/author. Modifiable programs are generally in the drill-and-practice format. Although these software packages arrive with predetermined vocabulary, it is possible to edit the content or add content.

Special Needs Volume I—Spelling (from the Minnesota Educational Computer Consortium) contains special features which allow the teacher to use prestored spelling drills or create new ones. By following directions in the accompanying teachers' manual or answering on-screen questions, the teacher/author is able to add words, customizing lessons for students. Material from other classroom activities (current reading projects, etc.) is easily utilized. In addition, this program utilizes input devices which make it appealing for the physically handicapped.

New words appear within the framework of the drill-and-practice exercise, in this case multiple-choice fill-in-the-blank lessons. A square "marker" moves at a preset pace from one answer to the next. The student responds by pressing any key on the keyboard or moving a game paddle when the desired choice is surrounded by the square. The ease of response increases the range of students able to use this program.

Although this program was originally designed for spelling, any material which can be placed within the preprogrammed format can also be used. For example, science, social studies, reading, or even math information could be used in this program.

Comparison with
Other Authoring Programs

The wide variety of mini-authoring programs available meets many needs, for both educators and students. These programs are generally easy to use, and can be adapted to classroom needs more quickly and easily than can other forms of authoring products. The variety of presentation modes and graphics make the lessons appropriate for a range of students. The drill-and-practice format provides essential practice for students who require extensive repetition, review, and reinforcement of skills.

The game approach is non-threatening for students and may capitalize on the characteristics which Thomas Malone (1980) has identified in his research as "intrinsically motivating" in computer games—challenge, fantasy, and curiosity. The utility packages and programs with modification features provide further sources for educators looking for prewritten programs which allow easy adaptation to learning needs. These types of programs are valuable in many different settings with students who have a variety of learning problems, whether they are in regular education classes, remedial classes, or special needs settings.

For some applications, however, mini-authoring programs may be too limited. Generally, these programs include limited management and record-keeping features. Although a variety of formats is available, most mini-authoring programs have only one format. The rate of presentation and other factors cannot always be modified. Finally, these programs are designed to construct drill-and-practice exercises, and do not contain the branching and tutorial capabilities available with authoring systems and authoring languages. If the educator's needs can be met through drill-and-practice instruction games, then mini-authoring programs have much to offer.

Appendix to Chapter 4
A Mini-Authoring Program: Stepping Through the Process

Tic Tac Show, (from Advanced Ideas Inc.) is an example of a mini-authoring program. *Tic Tac Show* uses an animated quiz show host, exciting sound effects, colorful graphics, and the strategy of a tic-tac-toe game. The program includes preprogrammed lesson content in 14 subjects as well as authoring capabilities to construct customized lessons. Additional preprogrammed subject disks can also be purchased.

After loading the *Tic Tac Show* program disk, the main menu appears on the screen:

Tic Tac Show

1. Play Tic Tac Show
2. Build or Change a Subject Area
3. Quit

CHOOSE A NUMBER:
(WHEN DONE, PRESS RETURN)

Playing *Tic Tac Show*

When looking at a mini-authoring program for the first time, it is very helpful to know what students see during a lesson. Selecting Option # 1 (*Play Tic Tac Show*) causes the game screen in Figure 4-2 to appear.

Figure 4-2

This introductory screen is displayed until the teacher/author presses
<Return>. Next, a series of questions appears. Each needs to be
answered before proceeding.

1. The first question refers to the sound which can accompany the les-
    son. A simple yes or no response turns the sound on or off. Having
    control of this feature is useful because sound motivates some stu-
    dents but distracts or disturbs others.
2. The player's name is then requested. The name is then displayed in
    the first square below the quiz show host shown on the screen. If
    correct, the student presses <Return>. The next question asks if
    anyone else is playing. A positive response results in a request for
    the second name and a negative response inserts the word *COM-
    PUTER* for the second player.
3. An opportunity to read the instructions for the game is offered next.

4. The player is then instructed to insert the proper Subject Diskette and press <Return>. In this walk-through, no new subject areas have been created so the player leaves the program disk in the drive and presses <Return>. The name of the subject file to be used is then requested. If *Catalog* is typed, all subjects available on the current disk are displayed on the screen. The player then presses ESC (the escape key) and types the number associated with the desired subject. The game then begins.

The first player picks a number on the tic-tac-toe gameboard; a question appears on the screen related to the selected topic; and the player types in the answer. If the answer is correct, the space on the gameboard "goes" to the player. At the same time, the player giving the correct response is also given a point on the scoreboard. If the player's answer is incorrect, the correct answer is displayed and the box on the gameboard is awarded to the opposing player. In this case, no points are awarded to either player on the scoreboard.

The game continues in this fashion until one player scores a "Tic Tac Toe" or all the squares are taken. Even in a draw game, there is still a winner. In this case, the points accrued on the scoreboard are used to determine the winning player. At the close of a round, the players can play again; different players can take their places; the subject area can be changed; or the players can stop playing.

Authoring a Lesson

Selecting Option #2 (*Build or Change a Subject Area*) in the main menu initiates a lesson-writing session. The session begins with screen directions.

To continue press down the SHIFT key
and press RETURN

The next screen requests a Subject Area Diskette. The original master *Tic Tac Show* disk has some room available, but it is usually wise to store new lessons on a blank initialized disk.

The next screen is a new menu:

WORK ON A SUBJECT

1. Catalog of Subject Areas
2. Create a New Subject Area
3. Change Old Subject Area
4. Delete a Subject Area
5. Resume the Current Subject
6. Make a New Subject Diskette
7. Return to the Game Menu

CHOOSE A NUMBER:
(then press RETURN)

To create a new subject area, select Option #2 and press <Return>. The editing commands are then displayed, accompanied by a frame.

EDIT COMMANDS

ctrl-C : Erase Text
ctrl-I : Insert Space
ctrl-D : Erase Letter
ctrl-X : Erase Line Return : Next Line
← : Move Left
→ : Move Right

To continue, press ESC.

Text written within the frame will be displayed later when the student "plays" the game using this subject area.

To construct a lesson to practice the abbreviations for days of the week, the following steps are used.

For Question #1, the teacher/author moves the cursor down the frame three lines by pressing <Return>, typing *What is the abbreviation for Monday?* and pressing ESC. Next, the prompt *CORRECT ANSWER* appears in inverse letters in the lower left corner of the screen, with the cursor blinking below. The teacher/author types *Mon.*, and presses ESC.

The screen then clears, displaying a new frame labeled *Question # 2.* When all questions have been prepared as described above, pressing ESC a second time, without entering any information in the current frame, moves the teacher/author to the Edit Menu.

ADD, EDIT, LIST, DELETE, SAVE OR MAKE (A DATA DISKETTE)
—
SAVE must be used to return to work menu

Saving an Authored Lesson

Before saving a lesson in *Tic Tac Show*, a new data disk can be initialized. Assuming one has already been prepared, the initialized data disk is placed in the drive and the door is closed. After typing *Save* and pressing <Return>, the following appears:

SAVE A SUBJECT

Should this lesson be presented
Randomly or Sequentially (R/S)?

Selecting a random presentation helps to ensure that students are learning the abbreviations and not just memorizing sequences. (For other topics in which questions build upon previous questions, a sequential presentation is used.) For this example, select *R* (for *random*) and press <Return>. The computer then displays:

Minimum number of wild cards is 2.
How many wild cards in this game (2-9)?

The *Tic Tac Show* gameboard has nine spaces. Since the days of the week require using only seven of the spaces, the remaining two spaces must be filled—either with additional questions during the authoring section or with "wild cards." Wild cards are placed randomly. When a player picks a location holding a wild card, the slot is "free" and the player's mark is placed in that spot, but no points are awarded. For this example, the teacher/author selects 2.

The sequence to save the lesson then continues.

> Type the subject name to be saved
> (Type CATALOG to see current subjects)
> (UP TO 19 CHARACTERS)
>
> To see the Work Menu press ESC.

Typing *ABBREV. OF DAYS* names the file. After pressing <Return>, the message *SAVING ABBREV. OF DAYS* appears and the file is stored on the disk. The teacher/author is then automatically returned to the Work on a Subject Menu.

Playing an Authored Lesson

To see how the game looks with the new subject area, select Option #7 (*Return to the Game Menu*), and *Tic Tac Show* is ready to be played using the new content.

This lesson, once created, can be used at any time. To do so, the original master disk for *Tic Tac Show* must be loaded and then the data disk inserted when a subject area is requested.

Summary

Clearly the steps to both author and "play" a lesson using a mini-authoring program like *Tic Tac Show* are simple and straightforward. Although the format is fixed and the lesson presentation lacks the flexibility available with authoring systems or authoring languages, mini-authoring programs are valuable because they offer educators who have limited time and no programming knowledge the ability to construct professional-looking computer-based drill-and-practice lessons with content customized to meet their students' needs.

5

Authoring Systems

Mini-authoring programs (discussed in Chapter 4) provide the educator with relatively easy-to-use formats to construct customized drill-and-practice exercises. As teachers using computers become more experienced, however, they frequently want to "do more." This desire can be satisfied by authoring systems. Authoring systems have greater flexibility and more precise customizing features than mini-authoring programs.

What is an authoring system? Why and when would a teacher choose to use this type of authoring product rather than the simpler and less time-consuming mini-authoring program? An explanation of authoring systems, some examples, and a "walk-through" (Appendix to Chapter 5) should help answer these questions.

An authoring system provides the teacher with a flexible format for both drill-and-practice and tutorial lessons. Using any subject matter, the teacher can first present a picture, written text, or both; and then ask questions about them. Unlike the conventional ditto, however, a lesson written with an authoring system has several motivating features. The teacher can take advantage of the computer's graphics abilities, including color. Text can be highlighted to emphasize specific information. Most important, the student can receive immediate feedback regardless of his or her response. Correct answers are praised, and incorrect responses can be immediately followed by review material.

An authoring system, then, does more than a mini-authoring program. It offers more than simple testing or drill-and-practice exercises. Rather, authoring systems begin to utilize the interactive features of the computer, turning teacher-designed lessons into real teaching tools.

Authoring systems have many benefits. They have more flexibility and a greater range of subject matter than mini-authoring programs. Authoring systems allow beginning programmers to construct lessons which look very professional. In addition, the authoring task is greatly simplified because the directions are usually presented on-screen in an easy-to-follow, step-by-step format.

The typical authoring system consists of a predesigned set of "pages" or *templates* which follow a set pattern of presentation. For example, the authoring system, *BLOCKS '82* (from California School for the Deaf), mentioned at the beginning of Chapter 3 and detailed in the Appendix to this Chapter, uses a series of presentation, answer, and feedback screens or "pages." In this authoring system, the teacher/author enters text, a picture, a question, and or a combination of these three on the *text screen*. Next, the correct answer (or answers) to the question is entered on the *right answer screen*. Feedback for the correct answer (or answers) is then entered on the *right answer feedback screen*. Following the correct answer and associated feedback information, incorrect answer information is entered on a series of *wrong answer screens*. Each wrong answer screen is followed by a *wrong answer feedback screen* which the teacher/author can use for reteaching, hints, etc. Other more sophisticated authoring systems have built-in capabilities for providing additional instruction after correct or incorrect responses by *branching* to other lessons or other sections of the same lesson for more extensive reteaching or review segments.

Why and when to use an authoring system as opposed to a mini-authoring program is best answered on the basis of the student's educational plan. If the teacher wants to use the computer for more than simple drill-and-practice lessons on factual material, authoring systems should be considered. Authoring systems allow the educator to develop tutorial lessons in which the written material, pictures, responses, and corrections are created for a specific student or population. In such a tutorial lesson, the student is presented with information and then questioned regarding the information. If the student answers incorrectly, the lesson can offer sophisticated wrong answer messages and/or *branch* to present the student with review material—in essence reteaching the particular skill. The reteaching segments can be simple or involved, and can contain testing segments themselves. If the student has difficulty within one of the reteaching segments, more branching can occur. This process can be as simple or involved as the teacher wishes.

For the special needs teacher who wants a lesson which will tutor students, the authoring system offers a cost-effective and time-efficient method of computerized instruction. Furthermore, authoring systems contain several features which are especially useful for special needs students. Such generally available features include good record-keeping, lesson management, branching, graphics, and hint capabilities.

An Authoring System: A Story

Cindy Heath speaks about her experience with an authoring system:

> . . .so what I'd like to do this afternoon is describe briefly how I use the *Author I* authoring system with my special needs students, and point out those features which I find particularly helpful.
>
> As I explained, I usually use the same format for all the computer lessons I write. At first, I thought that the lack of variety might be a problem. Instead, I have found that just changing the subject matter makes the format seem like new to my students.
>
> One positive feature I did not anticipate actually resulted from the sameness of the format. My EMR students have a lot of trouble changing from one textbook or workbook to another. Learning new formats and new directions can sometimes take a whole morning. With the computer lessons I have designed, this isn't a problem. Once I introduce the system, my students know how to select or type an answer, how to move from screen to screen, and how to move back to the text. It was really wonderful the other day when I went to check on one of the students, and he told me I could help someone else because he knew how to "run the thing." His confidence with the computer has made it easier for him to try new subject matter—and the other students seem to find the similarities reassuring.
>
> There are some other features in my format that I also find helpful. For example, there are three ways to record student responses. A particularly useful one for me lets me have the computer save my students' answers. Later, I can access their answers to see exactly what they are saying and how they are saying it. This is really helpful for some subjects. Recently, I found out that one of my students reverses the labels for adjectives and adverbs. Until I saw the consistency in her answers, her English teacher and I had not realized just why she was making the errors she does. Now I can spend some individual time with her sorting out the definitions and parts of speech so she won't have this problem.

Cindy has found other features of *Author I* (from Tandy Corporation/Radio Shack) useful. Students with limited typing skills find the use of the single character-option in the multiple-choice format easy to use. A sliding answer option offers another alternative for those who have difficulty using the keyboard. In this answer mode, a marker moves under several possible answers, and the student selects the correct answer by pressing <Return>.

Another feature of this authoring system is the "Glossary," a computerized dictionary of words the students might need to know. Definitions and demonstration sentences can be stored for easy reference. If the student requests a word that is not in the dictionary, it is simple to add it. The glossary is also useful for introducing new vocabulary and helping students become more familiar with the concept of referencing material.

Cindy's instructional efforts are particularly helped by the student feedback and lesson branching features. Developing a lesson for her students on spelling the months, Cindy demonstrated the *hint* feature of *Author I*. Her lesson is designed to be both an initial tutorial and drill-and-practice lesson on spelling the months. Following a text screen about the need to learn these words and another screen displaying the year, the students begin work on recognizing and eventually spelling the words through various exercises which include matching, missing letters, scrambled letters, and total recall. With *Author I*, Cindy is able to produce positive feedback for correct answers, and a different message or no message for incorrect answers. The number of tries allowed can even be specified before the item is counted as "wrong." Cindy continues.

> I especially like the hint option. I can type in any clue or message that I want my student to see when a mistake is made—and I can even indicate how many errors can be made before the hint appears. I can even include "triggered" hints. As you know, there are many spelling errors that are common when students are learning to spell the months. I can anticipate those errors I think will occur, and have the computer print a hint related specifically to each particular error. For example, my students frequently misspell *February*. One of the triggered hints looks for the spelling *Febuary* and brings the student's attention to the missing *r*. I can include as many of these hints as I want. I can even include a hint for errors I haven't anticipated.

Another feature, *branching*, allows Cindy to provide immediate reteaching for students who make specific errors. If the student consistently repeats one type of error, falls below a predetermined score, or has difficulty with a new concept, the lesson can be designed to branch to another section or lesson designed to develop skills in the weak area. Cindy elaborates.

> I have also authored a lesson for my oldest and most advanced students to practice writing checks. The lesson presents all the information and responses necessary for a student who is reviewing and practicing the skill. However, sometimes students become confused or forget related information from an earlier lesson. That's when I can use the branching feature called a Control Page in *Author I.* With this feature, based on any condition I state, I can go to any other part of a lesson for review or instruction. Not only can I "call up" any section of the current lesson but also any section of any other lesson on the disk. For example, if a student forgets how to spell the months while writing checks, I can branch to the earlier lesson on spelling the months. Being able to write routines for branching really helps me meet individualized instructional objectives.

Other aspects of this authoring system include graphics capabilities and a management system. The record-keeping section tracks student scores, lesson use dates, and the number of times each student has used a particular lesson. Student answers can be saved and student scores can also be averaged. Particular students can be prevented from repeating or even using a particular lesson. The management section also allows the teacher/author to determine whether or not a student should have the ability to exit a lesson at any point or be forced to complete a specific sequence.

An authoring system, as described above, requires more teacher time and effort than the mini-authoring programs of Chapter 4. Accompanying the increased time and effort are other benefits: in particular more flexibility in constructing computer-based lessons for students.

The next section details the process involved in using the authoring system, *Author I* (from Tandy Corporation/Radio Shack). The Appendix to Chapter 5 "walks-through" another system, *BLOCKS '82* (from California School for the Deaf).

Authoring a Lesson with an Authoring System

Written documentation is very important when using an authoring system. The directions must be easy to follow, or the process becomes too time consuming. A good authoring system is easy to use. Directions for writing lessons using authoring systems are usually in two locations: in the written documentation accompanying the software package and on the computer screen. Directions printed on-screen are usually in the form of *menus,* or lists of available options. By responding to the questions printed on the screen, the teacher should be able to author sophisticated lessons for the classroom.

In the past, many authoring systems have been written for Apple computers. Today, more and more authoring systems are becoming available for other brands of computer as well. The system discussed here, *Author I,* illustrates how authoring systems work and reminds Tandy Corporation/Radio Shack (TRS) computer users that there are authoring systems available for them.

As advised in the discussion of mini-authoring programs, the most useful first step for a teacher/author is to use the software as a student would. *Author I* begins with this step in mind. The written documentation contains sections which lead the teacher/author through a simulation of three of the phases of the authoring system:

1.   taking a lesson;
2.   setting up a student score file; and
3.   creating a lesson.

These three segments are also prerecorded on disk, so that the teacher/author actually performs many of the authoring steps and has the opportunity to "learn by doing." By progressing through the segments, the potential author develops a clearer picture of the purpose, capabilities, and limitations of this authoring system. The simulations, called "walk-throughs," are arranged to allow the potential author to use an already "completed" lesson and set up record-keeping units for specific students before "creating" a lesson. Having a clear picture of how the finished lesson looks when students use it is very helpful in the "creating" or authoring stage.

Initially, the written documentation for *Author I* describes how this authoring system uses the computer keys. This information helps the teacher/author adapt to the computer keyboard. Keyboard use is particularly important for changing, correcting, and revising material after it has been entered. Understanding how special keys or function keys are used by an authoring system (or any piece of software) facilitates using that software.

After the teacher/author has completed the simulation described above, the *Author I* program disk should be loaded. This disk contains four program options or modules:

1. TEACH—to present a lesson
2. STUDENT—to work with a student score file
3. AUTHOR—to create or edit a lesson
4. PRTVERF—to print or verify a lesson

Since creating a lesson is the desired outcome, the teacher/author types *Author* and presses <Return>. This loads the module used to create or edit a lesson. A message then asks the teacher/author to *Enter LESSON name*. If the name is new, a prompt appears, and the computer sets up a new file for that lesson. Once the lesson name is entered, a menu appears providing choices to:

> A to ADD PAGES
>
> B to REVIEW AND EDIT PAGES
>
> S to SAVE LESSON
>
> E to EXIT

Since a new lesson is being created, the teacher/author selects *A* to add pages. A new menu then appears on the screen. At this point, the teacher/author can choose to add a *Text Page*, a *Question Page*, a *Glossary Page*, a *Control Page*, or to *Exit*. By selecting the single letter code and pressing <Return>, the teacher/author continues the process.

Text Pages

Assuming the teacher/author selects a Text Page, the screen becomes a blank "page" (see Figure 5-1). On the left edge of the screen and along the bottom are white "bars" which serve as edge markers. The page number is at the bottom of the screen, below the line. The area above the bottom line is used by the teacher/author to create the "page" the student will see. This page can contain words (text), pictures (graphics), and special characters.

Information Section

The area to the left of the left-edge marker is used by the teacher/author to mark special points in the lesson. For example, the teacher/author can mark parts in the lesson for *branching.* When other parts in the lesson need to be referenced at certain points, they can also be indicated in the left margin. Finally, the left margin can be used to designate "stop" sections: This feature allows the teacher to prevent students from backtracking past a certain point in the text. If, for example, the student is being asked to recall an item, the teacher can prevent the student from "flipping" back through the computer "pages" to find the answer. This feature is valuable, particularly in testing situations.

By using the cursor keys, the teacher/author can enter text or other information on the screen. Pictures can be entered using the graphics mode and cursor keys. Simple line drawings can be created. Special character sets are also available for some computer models and can be used to enhance the pictures created in the graphics mode.

A character set is a specially designed set of characters or shapes which allows the teacher/author to draw or write in special ways. For example, it is possible to design a lesson for ESL students using special character sets to print the diacritical marks needed for specific foreign languages. The diacritical marks are designed and stored as a special character set.

Some authoring systems have special or alternate character sets already available, while others allow the teacher/author to develop new ones as needed.

To complete the first part of the lesson, the teacher/author continues to use as many Text Pages as necessary until the information to be taught in the lesson has been entered.

Questions Section

To add a question, the teacher/author types the question on a Text Page, indicating where the student should respond by placing a prompt (>) at the selected location. *Author I* contains three possible question formats: single-character responses, multiple-character responses, and multiple-choice responses. Single-character responses are useful for multiple-choice and true/false questions. Multiple-character responses require the student to type an answer of two or more characters.

The multiple-choice response format is the easiest to use and very helpful for special needs populations. In this mode, the teacher/author places several possible answers along the bottom of the screen. When the student runs the lesson, he or she moves the cursor along the bottom of the screen under the possible answers and simply presses <Return> when the cursor is positioned under the desired answer.

Figure 5-1

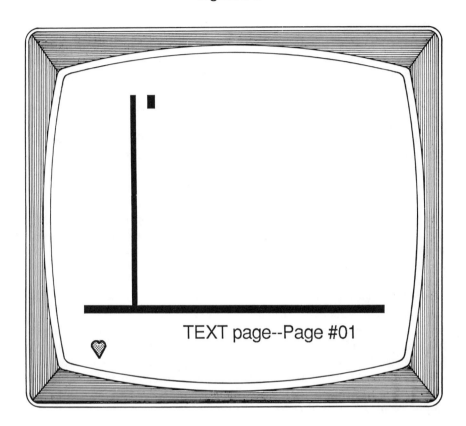

Question Pages

Once the information and question has been entered on the Text Page, the teacher/author returns to the menu and selects the *Question Page* option. On this "page" or screen, the teacher/author indicates how responses should be evaluated and determines the feedback for various answers. In other words, this page is used to determine whether the student has the correct answer as well as provide help if the answer is incorrect.

The Question Page has both an *answer* and a *hint* section.

Answer Section

The answer section of the Question Page appears first. Here, the teacher/author indicates the correct answer to the question. There are sixty-two spaces to record information so more than one acceptable answer can be listed.

Using a special key to designate the format, multiple-choice responses using the sliding-cursor format can also be entered. Another area on the screen allows the teacher/author to indicate that a single key is all that is needed for the student's response. The computer then evaluates the response after only one key has been pressed. If this special section is not marked, the computer waits for the student to press <Return> before evaluating the response.

The Question Page answer section also prompts the teacher/author to determine the number of tries the student will be allowed before the computer counts the response as incorrect. For example, if the authoring system is being used to present test material, it is most likely the teacher/author would specify that the student have only one try, maintaining traditional testing style. At other times, it is appropriate for the student to have several chances at attempting to answer a question. Special needs students, in particular, tend to benefit from the opportunity to try a second time. The hint section of the Question Page (see below) can be used to assist students in repeated answer attempts.

Author I also allows the teacher/author to weight questions. If the teacher/author wishes certain questions to carry more "weight" in the final score, the score can be modified. *Author I* modifies scores using a percentage rating. In addition, the student's exact responses to specified questions can be saved on disk. During the authoring process, the teacher can indicate that student responses to specified questions should be saved on the disk. After the student has used the lesson, the teacher can review the student's answers and, thus, track the type of errors being made.

Comprehension can also be checked, and it is possible for the teacher to determine how material is being processed by the student. This allows the teacher to pinpoint misinformation. By discovering what material is unclear or confusing to students, teachers are better able to assist them in further study.

Author I provides the option to prepare positive and negative feedback messages. These messages are prerecorded and will be generated randomly by the computer if the teacher/author does not create his or her own original positive feedback messages. The teacher/author can also request that no feedback be given. If negative feedback messages are desired, they must be specified. The negative messages will appear only after a predetermined number of tries. The teacher/author specifies the number of attempts allowed in the *tries* area of the *answer section*. There are no prerecorded negative messages in the *Author I,* guaranteeing that inappropriate feedback is not used and allowing feedback to be tailored to meet the learning and emotional needs of the students.

Hint Section

When the *answer section* of the Question Page has been completed, the teacher/author has the option of adding special clues to assist a student who is having difficulty with a specific question. These clues or hints can be as general or specific as a teacher/author desires. For example:

> Question: *In which state is Boston?*
> Hint: *It is an East Coast state.*

The *hint section* of *Author I* is easily accessed by the teacher/author during the authoring process and automatically appears in accordance with the teacher's designs. The teacher/author can determine when a hint will appear by indicating the number of tries.

There is also an option for "triggered" hints—hints or clues which appear when the student's answer matches a particular incorrect response or "trigger." For example, suppose the student's answer to the above question is *Massachusets*. Anticipating this particular misspelling of *Massachusetts*, the teacher/author can provide a triggered hint such as *You are very close. Watch the spelling!* Triggered hints only appear when the student gives the anticipated incorrect answer.

Although the space for a hint is limited, it is possible to branch to another section and use that section as a hint. To carry the above example further, the teacher/author may want to show the student a map of the New England states with Boston highlighted. This map could be a useful hint for the student. However, the standard space for a hint is too limited to allow a map or picture to be drawn. Using branching features, the teacher/author can prepare a lesson segment in which the map is drawn. This segment is in another part of the authoring system and can be accessed from the hint section when needed. After displaying the map hint, the authoring system automatically returns to the original question.

The Text Pages and Question Pages make up the major portion of most drill-and-practice or tutorial lessons. Two more options which exist in *Author I* allow for greater flexibility.

Glossary Pages

Glossary Pages allow the teacher/author to store any word and its definition. To include an entry, the teacher/author selects the Glossary Page option at the main *Add* menu and is then shown a blank screen with prompts for a word and a definition. The teacher/author types any word, which can be up to twenty characters in length using upper- and lower-case letters. Moving to the definition prompt, the teacher/author types any definition up to two lines of fifty-one characters each in length.

Glossary Pages can be added at any time during the creation of a lesson, since they are not arranged in any particular order and do not appear during a lesson unless the student specifically requests a word by typing a question mark and that word. This means that the teacher/author can create a customized dictionary of terms for a particular topic. Particularly valuable is the easy access which characterizes Glossary Pages. Students are more likely to use such readily available on-line information during the lesson as opposed to external reference materials.

Control Pages

The Control Page option of *Author I* allows greater flexibility in developing a complete tutorial. Control Pages can be used to define two types of *branching*: unconditional and conditional. *Unconditional* branches occur every time a student reaches a specific Control Page within a lesson. *Conditional* branches occur only when specified conditions are met.

When preparing a Control Page for an unconditional branching sequence, the teacher/author selects the *always* option, by placing an x in the appropriate box. When this option is selected, the system always moves in a particular direction when it encounters the Control Page.

Use of Control Pages can also be conditional. In this case, the teacher/author indicates that a certain action should occur only if an antecedent condition has been met. To continue using the Boston example, if the student misspells *Massachusetts* twice, the system can branch to a small spelling unit. This is a conditional branch which the teacher/author identifies by filling in blanks after the *IF* and *THEN GO TO* phrases on the screen. Questions, answer labels, or group designations can all be used to indicate branching. These terms all refer to different methods of labeling or indicating separate segments of the authoring system. The system will then go to or branch to the section of the text specified. This feature can be used in a variety of ways. For example, a student doing extremely well could "skip" over other similar problems to a more advanced section or to testing sections. A student having difficulty can be branched to an easier section or review material.

Control Pages can also route the system to other programs written in BASIC or machine language. This capability makes extensive program development possible but is designed for proficient programmers. For most purposes, educators using authoring systems would not use this feature. However, if a teacher/author wanted to include a routine from another program—for example, graphics from a public domain program—then it would be possible to access that program from *Author I* using the Control Pages.

Other Features

It is important to realize that the finished lesson is never actually "sealed." The teacher/author can return to review and edit an existing lesson at any time, simply by loading the *Author* module and typing the lesson name at the prompt.

Another important feature of many authoring systems is the inclusion of a predesigned record-keeping file which records student progress. One of the four *Author I* modules, *Student,* provides easy-to-use record-keeping which allows the teacher/author to work with student score files. Following the written documentation and prompts on the screen, the teacher is able to add, delete, change, or view student files.

Supplying students with passwords helps maintain privacy for student records. Once a student's name has been entered for a lesson, the computer will keep track of the number of times the student uses it, the date of the last time the student used it, and the total score. The time taken to work through a section is also recorded. There is also space for two complete sets of specific answers, making it possible to review the precise answers given by any student.

Other special features of the *Student* module include the ability to "overlay," "average" and "lock-out." With the "overlay" option, the teacher/author allows the student to use the lesson as many times as desired; but only the most recent score, time, and two sets of answers are recorded. The computer selects this option automatically, unless the teacher/author designates otherwise. The "average" option averages the scores and times of repeated trials. The "lock-out" option prevents a student from using a particular lesson more than once, making it possible to exclude some students from certain lessons or to predetermine the number of trials a student will have on any lesson.

An Authoring System at Work: A Story

Obviously, authoring systems are more powerful than mini-authoring programs: They allow greater flexibility and an increased ability to develop
more sophisticated instructional lessons. Mini-authoring programs are well
suited to drill-and-practice exercises and allow teachers to adjust to the
needs of their students. The general framework of most authoring systems
leads directly to the design of tutorial lessons. The following describes how
a teacher authored a lesson for learning disabled students using a system
such as *Author I.*

Dropping by Mark's resource room after school, his fellow teacher Sam
finds him at work on the computer. Mark has begun to develop a tutorial
lesson on word problems for his students. From observation in the classroom, he determined that his students are making errors based on errone-
ous cuing techniques. He has been unable to find any commercially available programs which approach working with word problems in a manner
which is helpful for his students. Mark is also anxious to use the computer
as a "third-party" instructor. He knows that his students often try to
"read" him in order to second guess at correct answers. And, like many
special needs teachers who have been working with the same group of students over a period of time, Mark wants to disassociate himself from the
learning process periodically to determine more accurately just what the
students have learned.

Mark loads a disk in the drive of his computer system, selects one of the
lessons he authored, *Word Probs # 1,* and selects the option to work on a
Text Page. As Sam watches, Mark describes how he authors a lesson.

> Here's my first word problem:
>
>> There are three boys in the car.
>> There are two girls in the car.
>> There is one dog in the car.
>> How many children are in the car?
>
> Above the text I can use the cursor keys to draw a long converti-
> ble car and stick figures to represent the children and dog. At the bot-
> tom of the page, I can type in the question I want my students to
> think about:
>
>> In this question, you are asked to find the number of _____ .
>
> I then move to the answer section and enter the answers *children,
> boys and girls, girls and boys, kids.* For any of these answers, I can direct
> the computer to give a short *Well done* phrase before going on. I also

want to give clues to those students having difficulty, so I type in several hints. Knowing my students, I am aware of some of the common errors they make and can provide appropriate hints. One probable error is misspelling the word *children*; so I want any response beginning with *ch* to cause the computer to react with the message: *You seem to be on the right track, better check your spelling.* The same message can also appear for misspellings of girls and boys. I am able to designate this type of error using special characters in the authoring system. For answers with *car* or *dog* in them, I redirect the student's attention to the last line in the problem and ask them to try again. If the student makes three errors, the computer branches to a little side segment in which I use arrows and underlining with additional text to bring their attention to the last line of the problem. Then the computer returns to the next step of the lesson.

On the next screen, I ask the students to look at each line of the problem to determine if the information presented is necessary for the final answer. By using a graphics figure to point to each line, the computer can ask the students line by line if the material is relevant. Correct answers are quickly rewarded, and the student moves on. Incorrect answers result in additional hints similar to this:

> The problem asks about the number of children.
> Does this line tell about children?

When the students answer these questions, they are directed to a screen in which they exclude the inappropriate information. Typing the letter which appears before the sentence is sufficient. Again, the computer rewards correct answers.

I can develop the lesson further to have the students specify which operation they need to perform, determine the problem, and reach a solution. After this teaching segment, I give them several more problems, each with branching for incorrect responses and reward screens for correct responses. The last part of this unit has three problems with no branching or hint sections. That part is my test segment and shows me which students understand the process.

Using an authoring system gives me the flexibility to have individual students working on one important skill, while I work with other students in the room on other tasks. Besides, the authoring system keeps track of the students' scores and also records their actual responses. That means that I can look at this information later in the day and make decisions about what material each student should work on next.

The kids at this grade level really avoid word problems, but they also want to work on the computer. Using the computer for word problems is great: I can capitalize on my students' enthusiasm for playing on the computer in spite of their dislike for doing word problems.

I get the most out of my students' attention and the most out of my time.

I'm pleased that we have an authoring system because it's easy to use and doesn't require any programming skills on my part. Constructing these lessons takes longer than simply making a worksheet; but my worksheets only have problems written on them, and I have to be there to go over every step. Using the computer lets me use the same material for several students, without having to be there. I rarely have two students at the same skill level in one class, so having an authoring system is really important to me.

Summary

The use of an authoring system allows the educator to develop software tailored for a specific curricular or student learning need. The examples and descriptions in this Chapter should help clarify the scope and use of authoring systems. The applications are many. In addition to use in teaching and practicing skills, authoring systems provide excellent formats for creating testing materials in a wide variety of subjects. The expanded record-keeping features are also valuable. By recording not only student scores but also the specific answers, the record-keeping module provides the teacher with the information necessary to restructure lessons and develop concepts further in additional lessons or correct and modify the current lesson to meet student needs.

In authoring systems, graphics can be developed specifically to meet the needs of each individual lesson. The material can be presented in a manner which imitates some of the instruction the students receive in class. Feedback can also be adjusted for a specific age group or student. Branching and tutorial instruction, capabilities not generally available with mini-authoring programs, make the range of applications for authoring systems greater than for mini-authoring systems. Authoring systems, not mini-authoring programs, should be used if special material needs to be presented to a student in a tutorial framework, and the motivational and record-keeping capabilities of the computer are important for the student and teacher.

Of course, there are problems connected with using authoring systems. The greater freedom and flexibility in designing lessons means an increase in the amount of time required to learn these authoring products and the time needed to write usable lessons. While mini-authoring programs allow educators to write lessons quickly by simply entering content, authoring systems require more authoring time, though less than that required for an authoring language.

A teacher needs to weigh the advantages and disadvantages of using an authoring system for a particular educational need. Central to the decision are the teachers' level of computer experience, and time and energy. Authoring systems can result in highly appealing and very flexible lessons customized to meet both student needs and teacher record-keeping requirements.

Appendix to Chapter 5
An Authoring System:
Stepping Through the Process

To illustrate further the use of an authoring system, this Appendix "walks through" the process of authoring a lesson using *BLOCKS '82* (from the California School for the Deaf). *BLOCKS '82* allows the teacher/author to combine images, labels, and text (see Figure 5-2). Each image, label, and accompanying text (questions, answers, and feedback) is a *block*, hence, the system's name. A special feature of *BLOCKS '82* is an extensive graphics library of predesigned pictures which can be used in constructing lessons. As the process unfolds, the advantages of such a library will become apparent.

   BLOCKS '82 runs on Apple II, II+, //e, or //c computers with at least one disk drive. As with any other authoring product, it is a good policy for a teacher/author to begin by "playing" a lesson in order to see how the program behaves from the student's perspective. *BLOCKS '82* encourages this practice by including a *Lesson Sampler* designed to guide a new author through a progression of lessons, introducing *BLOCKS '82* in the process.

Authoring a Lesson

BLOCKS '82 requires separate disks for student activities ("playing" a lesson) and authoring activities. To author a lesson, a teacher/author begins by placing an empty Author Disk into the disk drive and booting up the system. The *BLOCKS '82* Level One Menu is then displayed on the screen.

CSDF BLOCKS '82   LEVEL ONE MENU

1 CATALOG
2 ADD A NEW LESSON
3 LOAD AN OLD LESSON
4 RESUME CURRENT LESSON
5 SAVE CURRENT LESSON
6 DELETE A LESSON
7 QUIT

COMMAND (1-7):

If the Author Disk is not empty, another screen is displayed which identifies the temporary lesson currently on the disk and asks the teacher/author if he or she wishes to (1) continue working on the current lesson or save it for student use on a Lesson Disk, or (2) erase a current lesson. After deciding the fate of an already existing lesson, the teacher/author is presented with the Level One Menu above.

To author a lesson in *BLOCKS '82*, the teacher/author selects Option # 2 (*Add a New Lesson*) from the Level One Menu. A possible screen lay-out, which can be modified, is then displayed.

Defining the Text Area

The text area can be any size rectangle placed in any area of the screen. The remainder of the screen is used for graphics. If the displayed layout is acceptable, pressing the space bar freezes the rectangle in place.

If another layout is desired, pressing <Return> causes a $90°$ angle to appear on the screen. This angle represents the upper left corner of the rectangle reserved for text. This angle can be repositioned by using game paddles, a joystick, a Koala Pad, or the *I, J, K,* and *M* keys. Pressing the space bar (or small button on other input devices) freezes the corner into place. The lower right corner of the rectangle is relocated in the same manner. Having now redefined the text area, the remainder of the screen is available for graphics and/or labels.

Options for Lesson Presentation

The next screen, the Block Display Choices, indicates the various options for lesson presentation. These options are set in a *default* mode which can be changed as needed. The default values are generally appropriate for initial lesson design. However, as the teacher becomes a more sophisticated author, these options allow extensive individualization of lessons.

INDISTINGUISHABLE U/L CASE	
DISTINCT U/L CASE	
UPPERCASE ONLY (I/D/U)	I
TEXT SIZE, BIG OR SMALL (B/S)	B
COLOR (W/P/G/B/O/R)	W
ERASE GRAPHICS ON BLOCK EXIT (Y/N)	Y
PRINT SPEED (0=FAST, 1=MED, 2=SLOW)	0
SEQUENTIAL OR RANDOM (S/R)	S
TRIES PER QUESTION (1-5)	3
SHOW ANSWER AFTER (1-5) TRIES	2
STUDENT RESPONSE TIME (1-255) SECS	60

OR	AND	AND THEN	WORD END	ALL END
,	&	@	^	#

ESC TO GO ON →

Each of these items determines how various aspects of the final lesson appear.

1. *Capitalization*: Letters can be capitalized or upper- and lower-case. The first choice, *indistinguishable u/l case,* allows the most freedom— The answer is correct if the letters in the student response match those in the recorded response, regardless of the capitalization. If *distinct u/l case* is selected, the student answer must match the teacher answer letter per letter, including appropriate capital and lower-case letters. (This option is useful for lessons using proper names, i.e., cities, states, etc.). The third option, *upper case only,* causes all student answers to be automatically capitalized. This option is helpful for students with particular types of learning disabilities since the letter on the keyboard looks like the letter on the screen.

Figure 5-2

2. *Text size* refers to character size. There are both big and small upper- and lower-case letters. Small characters are the standard monitor size. Big characters are double the standard size. This option should be set for the size most used in the lesson, since sizes can be intermingled.

3. *Color*: Most lessons are written with white letters but *BLOCKS '82* allows the use of other text colors—purple, green, blue, orange, and rainbow (a cycle of the four non-white colors). Color can also be changed during editing so that particular words or phrases can be colored for emphasis. If the text size is small, color should be left in the default setting (white) because the combination of non-white color and small text size is not readable.

4. *Erase graphics* clears the screen as the program moves to a new display area or *block*. Generally, when moving to a new display area,

the teacher/author is choosing to load new images and labels. However, there may be instances in which it is desirable to retain the old graphics when exiting a block. This option is most likely to be useful if features (timing, number of tries, etc) are being changed but content is remaining the same.

5. *Print speed* controls the rate of presentation of the text on the screen. This setting affects the rate during authoring as well as lesson presentation. For this reason, it is advisable to author lessons at the fastest setting (0) and then later edit the lesson to slow the speed, if necessary, for lesson presentation.

6. *Sequential and random* determine the order in which information is presented to the student. The first block created is not affected by the random command, allowing the teacher/author to place directions and other important information so that they will be presented at the beginning of play. Sequential causes the questions to be presented in the same order as written by the teacher/author. Random causes the order of the blocks making up the lesson, as well as the questions within each block, to be scrambled.

7. *Tries per question* allows the teacher/author to control the number of times a student can answer a question incorrectly.

8. *Fixed or comeback* is an option in the random mode only when more than one try per question is allowed. When the fixed mode is used, the question appears for the number of tries allowed and then is not repeated in the lesson. Comeback mode results in missed questions being presented again after all other questions in the block have been completed.

9. *Show answer* allows the teacher/author to set the point at which the correct answer will be displayed during the lesson. The default displays the correct answer after the second try and then allows the student one more attempt so that the student can experience a sense of success with the question. To allow the student to see the correct answer after every try, specify *1*. To avoid having the student ever see the correct answer, make the number of tries per question smaller than the number of tries after which the correct answer will be displayed. (If multiple correct answers have been specified, only the first is displayed with this feature.)

10. *Student response time* allows the teacher/author to determine the length of time between the appearance of the prompt for the student response and the appearance of the wrong answer message.

11. *Answer line delimiters*: These symbols are used by the teacher/author when keyboarding answers and cannot be used by students to answer questions. These symbols are displayed among the *Block*

> *Display Choices* because they can be changed to meet the needs of specific lessons. For example, a math lesson might include commas in the correct answers (i.e., 10,000). To avoid the program "reading" these commas as *or*, the teacher/author would substitute another character (i.e., *) for *or*.

After changing the default settings or accepting them as they stand, the teacher/author presses ESC. (ESC is used throughout *BLOCKS '85* to signal the completion of tasks.)

Images and Labels

Now the screen displays the message *Load Image*. The program is ready for a picture or graphics image to be loaded from the graphics disks which are available with *BLOCKS '82*. After placing the correct Graphics Disk in the drive, the teacher/author loads the image desired by typing the exact name of the image. Typing *Catalog* displays a list of images on the disk. After it is loaded, the picture can be moved to the correct spot and frozen there by using the same methods used to position the text area. The teacher/author can continue to load images until all the pictures are on the screen in the desired locations. When finished, the teacher/author presses ESC.

Now, the message *Use Paddles to Locate Beginning of Label* appears at the bottom of the screen. (Of course, the other alternative input devices described above are also acceptable.) The arrow on the screen represents the point at which the label will begin. The teacher/author moves the arrow to any spot outside the text-area rectangle to type a label. After "freezing" the current location of the arrow, the teacher/author types the label. This sequence can be repeated as many times as desired. After all the labeling is completed, pressing ESC saves the graphics image onto the disk. (Labels should not be typed within the text area rectangle because they will be overwritten when the text is keyboarded.)

Writing the Questions and Identifying the Answers

The teacher/author is now ready to begin writing the questions in the lesson. The graphic image(s) and label(s) just defined will be associated with all questions written (one or many) until another Display Area is defined. The image(s), label(s), and associated question(s)/answers/feedback compose the *block*. When authoring a lesson, the teacher/author establishes a new *block* whenever subsequent questions should be displayed with a different picture, label, or other option.

The prompt for the first question is now displayed at the bottom of the screen: *Text of Question # 1*. This means that the teacher/author can begin to type the first area of text. If the text requires more than one screen, holding Control-P moves ahead to a clean screen (page). It is possible to type up to nine pages of text for each information/question section. The question must be included as part of the text. (Color changes can be added during editing to emphasize specific words or phrases.) When finished, the teacher/author presses ESC.

The computer now prompts *Right Answer for Question # 1*. The teacher/author types in the answers which should be considered correct. These answers are separated by commas which indicate "or" in *BLOCKS '82*. Other delimiters can be used to specify how "exact" answers must be. The most desirable answer should be listed first because it will be used in the Show Answer After (1-5) Tries segment of the lesson. Once again, when the task is completed, the teacher/author presses ESC.

BLOCKS '82 now prompts for feedback. After *Right Answer Feedback for Question # 1* appears on the screen, the teacher/author types in a positive reinforcement message for the student. Once again, pressing ESC signals that the task has been completed.

BLOCKS '82 now prompts *Wrong Answer # 1 for Question # 1*. At this point, the teacher/author can identify a specific expected wrong answer or a range of wrong answers. It is a good policy to use this opportunity to define the most often expected wrong answer. After keyboarding the wrong answer, the teacher/author presses ESC. This elicits another prompt *Wrong Answer Feedback # 1 for Question # 1*. The teacher/author can use this area for reteaching by responding directly to the wrong answer just identified. Again, color changes can be added during editing to draw attention to specific words or phrases.

After pressing ESC, *BLOCKS '82* prompts *Wrong Answer # 2 for Question # 1*. Keyboarding a space causes the computer to identify all answers other than the correct one(s) and Wrong Answer # 1 as incorrect. Obviously, many other incorrect answers can also be accommodated in more specific terms as well. Pressing ESC to signal the end of the answer causes a new prompt to appear: *Wrong Answer Feedback # 2 for Question # 1*. Once again, the teacher/author can use this opportunity to provide a hint, reteach, etc. Pressing ESC automatically moves the teacher/author to the prompt *Wrong Answer # 3 for Question # 1*.

This sequence of numbered wrong answers and their feedback continues until the teacher/author ends it at the beginning of a new numbered cycle by pressing ESC without keyboarding a response. The teacher/author can include as many wrong answers as he or she wishes. Escaping from a completely empty wrong answer causes the entire question with all its associated answers and feedback to be saved to the Author Disk.

After Question # 1 has been saved, the prompt *Text for Question # 2* appears. The teacher/author thus continues in the same manner through the desired number of questions (with their associated answers and feedback). Escaping the sequence after leaving a new question blank causes the Level Two Menu to appear.

> CSDF BLOCKS '82   LEVEL TWO MENU
>
>   1 LIST QUESTIONS
>   2 ADD (DISPLAY AREA OR QUESTION)
>   3 INSERT (DISPLAY AREA OR QUESTION)
>   4 COPY (DISPLAY AREA OR QUESTION)
>   5 EDIT (DISPLAY AREA OR QUESTION)
>   6 DELETE (DISPLAY AREA OR QUESTION)
>   7 RETURN TO LEVEL ONE
>   (TO SAVE LESSON FOR STUDENT USE)
>
>   COMMAND (1-7):

At this point the teacher/author can add a new *block*, (load a new image, type new labels, and write another set of questions/answers/feedback associated with the new graphic.) To do this, select Option #2 for *Add Display Area or Question*. A choice is then requested between display area or question. *Display Area* refers to adding another block. *Question* permits more questions to be added to a previously written lesson, allowing the teacher/author to construct partial lessons and return to them later. In this example, the teacher/author would select Display Area to create another block. The teacher/author can add as many blocks of images, labels, and questions as desired. When through, the teacher/author selects Option #7 (*Return to Level One—To Save Lesson for Student Use*) in the Level Two Menu.

Saving a Lesson

Selecting Option #5 (*Save Current Lesson*) in the Level One Menu results in a series of requests for information concerning the lesson to be saved. This step is designed to assist other teachers (and as a reminder for the author) in determining what is included in the lesson. This information, composing the Header for the Lesson, consists of lesson name, subject area category, school level, school name, author, date, and a description of the lesson. It is helpful that a lesson need not be complete to be saved. This allows teachers to author a lesson in multiple sessions. After the Header is complete, *BLOCKS '82* instructs the teacher/author which disk to place in the drive so that the lesson can be saved.

Before finishing for the day, it is a good idea to load the newly created lesson into the computer and "play" it as a student would. In this way, any errors in presentation, spelling, or design can be found and corrected before students use the material. Changes and corrections are accomplished by selecting Option #5 to *Edit (Display Area or Question)* in the Level Two Menu. Computer prompts assist in the editing process. In general, the editing process is similar to the authoring process, except that the text and graphics are already on the screen so only those changes desired need to be keyboarded. After any changes, the modified lesson needs to be saved. Subsequent re-saves do not require a new Header to be prepared, although changes can be made in the old Header.

Summary

This is a quick explanation of an authoring session using one type of authoring system, *BLOCKS '82*. *BLOCKS '82* is a particularly nice authoring system. The inclusion of a graphics library greatly simplifies the author's task and enhances the presentation of lesson material. In addition, *BLOCKS '82* offers many features to individualize lessons and provide lesson management (planning) and record-keeping while still being easy to learn. The following menu indicates the options available in the lesson planning segment of *BLOCKS '82*.

AUTHORING SYSTEM LESSON PLANNER

1　LIST STUDENTS IN CLASS
2　ADD A STUDENT TO CLASS
3　REMOVE A STUDENT FORM CLASS
4　COPY LESSON PLANS TO STUDENT FILES

   5 LIST LESSON PLANS
   6 ADD LESSON PLANS
   7 INSERT LESSON PLAN
   8 EDIT LESSON PLAN
   9 DELETE LESSON PLAN

  10 LIST STUDENT SCORES
  11 LIST TEACHERS ON DISK
  12 ADD A TEACHER
  13 REMOVE A TEACHER
  14 QUIT

There are some major differences between mini-authoring programs and authoring systems. Authoring systems are more flexible, but require more time and skill. This increased flexibility makes authoring systems well suited for both drill-and practice as well as tutorial lessons. Authoring systems also include more sophisticated lesson management and record keeping options. As the educator's interest and expertise develop, new avenues can be explored. An educator can create a range of sophisticated lessons using an authoring system without outgrowing the system.

6

Authoring Languages

After exploring the capabilities of the other two types of authoring products (mini-authoring programs and authoring systems) in Chapters 5 and 6, it is time to consider authoring languages. This Chapter illustrates the use of authoring languages and examines the major characteristics of the language PILOT. Because all authoring languages are designed for the same purpose, the popular and common authoring language PILOT is used as a model for examples and descriptions. In addition to the examples of program text within the Chapter, the Appendix to Chapter 6 contains three short but complete lessons written in PILOT by a special education teacher.

Authoring languages are the most flexible—and the most complex—of the family of authoring products currently available. They demand more of the teacher/author—more skill, time, and effort—but they also allow the teacher/author to construct more complex individualized lessons with a greater choice of features than either mini-authoring programs or authoring systems. Authoring languages make fully individualized and customized lessons possible. Because authoring languages are designed primarily for the development of computer-assisted instruction, programs written using these languages are usually referred to as *lessons* and the persons writing these lessons are called *authors*.

The Right Language

The design of computer languages differs according to their purpose. For-tran (FORmula TRANslator) was designed for scientific data analysis and related computations. COBOL (COmmon Business Oriented Language) was designed for data processing in business. BASIC (Beginner's All Pur-pose Symbolic Instruction Code), designed to be all purpose, is relatively easy to use. Authoring languages were designed for the development of computer assisted instruction, particularly tutorials, and were not intended for "general-purpose" programming tasks. PILOT (Programmed Inquiry, Learning or Teaching Language), the most commonly used authoring language, is a complete programming language and is available for most microcomputers found in educational settings.

Thus, by definition, each programming language is designed to include special characteristics which enhance its use for its intended purpose. Features suited for one type of use are often obstructive if the programmer tries to use them to develop programs for purposes they were not designed to meet. These problems often become evident when developing software for classroom use. The following describes the search for an appropriate task-specific language.

Determining Which Language: A Story

Having attended a one-week workshop on the programming language BASIC, Jill, the resource room teacher, was attempting to develop a tutorial lesson for her social studies students. She had run into some difficulties and had taken her problems to Betty, one of the programming teachers at the high school.

> My biggest problem with BASIC is finding a way to avoid count-ing misspellings as errors but still reinforce close approximations to the terms the students are learning. In BASIC, it's necessary to use state-ments to capture any conceivable combination the students might give. The program I'm working on has gotten hopelessly cluttered because I've written so many statements to catch all the acceptable misspel-lings I can think of. I'm sure I haven't even anticipated all the possi-ble answers. I really don't want answers counted as incorrect simply because I didn't think of all the acceptable alternatives.

After listening to Jill's dilemma, Betty suggested a different programming option.

> When I ran into similar difficulties, I looked into the possibility of using another programming language. I now use a language specifically designed for writing classroom lessons. I use PILOT for the type of tutorial lesson you're describing. Let me show you how easily the problem you're having can be dealt with using PILOT.
>
> One of the most useful commands in PILOT is *Match*. It allows me to designate the type of answer I expect from my students. I can specify exactly how I want the answer spelled. Best of all, it's easy for me to identify partial spellings or certain misspellings as acceptable answers.
>
> For example, suppose in your lesson you are looking for the answer *MASSACHUSETTS*. If you are concerned with spelling, then BASIC can handle this answer with no problem. However, if you want to give credit for partial spellings and misspellings—even ones you can't completely anticipate—then you have to write a statement for each in BASIC and make sure that you catch them all. Doing that takes a lot of time. And, of course, the more you type, the more typing mistakes you can make.
>
> Now let's look at PILOT. With PILOT you can use the Match Command. By using the Match Command, you can specify certain types of answers. For example, you can tell the computer to accept anything starting with an *M* and followed sequentially by an *S* and a *T*. This means even a phrase or sentence will be accepted. This capability makes the lesson seem more "natural": Students can almost "talk" with the computer. So in this case, a student could answer *MASSACHUSETTS, MASACHUSETS, I THINK IT'S MASSA-CHUSETS*, or even *IT'S MASUCHEWSITS*.
>
> If this allows too much variation, it can be changed. You are the programmer and you determine the range of acceptable answers. PILOT just lets you define the range with a lot less effort then BASIC.

BASIC vs. PILOT

One frequently raised issue is whether an authoring language (usually PILOT) is the most appropriate programming language for teachers to use to author classroom lessons. Many teachers have attended workshops or introductory courses on microcomputers or have computers at home on which they have "played around." The language for most of these activities is BASIC, Beginners All-Purpose Symbolic Instruction Code. BASIC is a popular language because it is available for almost all computers and is included in the original purchase price with most microcomputers.

BASIC has several features, such as an advanced computational capability, which are more awkward to use or don't exist in PILOT. On the other hand, BASIC does not include other features available in PILOT. Because PILOT was designed as a programming language to be used in the development of instruction, its special features (detailed later in this Chapter) allow lessons to be authored in a relatively short time. The lessons developed using PILOT also tend to be of a better quality than those created in the same amount of time by individuals with the same level of experience using BASIC.

However, there are no hard and fast rules, and each teacher/author must decide which language is best suited for him or her based on time, skill, and desired outcome. That interactive tutorial instruction is the goal of PILOT use should always be kept in mind when determining which language to use.

The following, based on the story above, illustrates some of these differences as it compares a small lesson segment in both PILOT and in BASIC. The instructions *T* for *Type*, *A* for *Accept*, *M* for *Match*, *TN* for *Type if No*, and *TY* for *Type if Yes* are detailed later in the Chapter.

In PILOT, the segment appears as follows:

```
T:BOSTON IS THE CAPITOL OF WHICH STATE?
A:M:MASSACHUSETTS!MASACHUSETS!MASUCHEWSITS
TY:YES, BOSTON IS THE CAPITOL OF MASSACHUSETTS.
TN:NO, BOSTON IS THE CAPITOL OF MASSACHUSETTS.
```

In BASIC, the same program looks this way:

```
10 PRINT "BOSTON IS THE CAPITOL OF WHICH STATE?"
20 INPUT D$
30 IF D$ = "MASSACHUSETTS" THEN PRINT "YES, BOSTON IS THE
CAPITOL OF MASSACHUSETTS."
40 IF D$ = "MASACHUSETS" THEN PRINT "YES, BOSTON IS THE
CAPITOL OF MASSACHUSETTS."
50 IF D$ = "MASUCHEWSITS" THEN PRINT "YES, BOSTON IS THE
CAPITOL OF MASSACHUSETTS."
60 PRINT "NO, BOSTON IS THE CAPITOL OF MASSACHUSETTS."
```

For this type of answer checking and interaction, the PILOT lesson is obviously shorter. BASIC does not have a statement which functions with the ease of PILOT's Match Command. Matching parts of words is very difficult in BASIC. PILOT's features give it more flexibility in lessons calling for linguistic responses. In addition, PILOT is able to accept sentence or phrase answers through its answer window.

When deciding which language to use, the teacher/author needs to determine the final goal of the lesson. Knowing the type of lesson content (math, language, etc.) and being familiar with the characteristics of the available programming languages should equip the teacher/author to select the programming language best suited to his or her needs, skill, and time.

Uses for an Authoring Language

Authoring languages such as PILOT were designed to be used in the development of computer-assisted instruction. These languages contain special features which facilitate the development of computer-assisted instruction. Authoring languages can be used for many types of CAI, including science and social studies simulations (Conlon, 1984). However, the design of authoring languages most readily facilitates the writing of tutorial rather than drill-and-practice lessons. Although drill-and-practice and testing lessons can also be constructed with authoring languages, it is usually more practical to use mini-authoring programs or authoring systems—both of which are well suited for these types of lessons, require less teacher/author commitment, and allow a fair amount of individualization. Authoring languages are the best solution when computer materials tailored to specific curriculum objectives are not available, and mini-authoring programs and authoring systems do not provide enough flexibility.

Using Authoring Languages
for Curriculum Purposes: A Story

The following situations represent ways in which an authoring language, such as PILOT, can be used to meet students' educational needs effectively.

Ann is a teacher in a self-contained class for educable mentally retarded adolescents and has requested that Sue, the computer coordinator, visit the classroom. Although Ann was initially enthusiastic about the potential uses of computers with her students, the classroom computer had now been relegated to an isolated corner where it sits unused. Ann explains.

At first, my students were fascinated by the computer and could hardly wait to use it. However, I have become disenchanted. The drill-and-practice exercises are fun for the students but give little or no feedback to help them when they are wrong. I want to include the computer in my teaching, but only if it really helps with instruction. I don't want my students just using it to play drill-and-practice games that don't even reinforce the right answer.

There is very little educational software for our computer, and I am really interested in finding tutorial lessons on subjects relevant for my students. I need lessons for the skills I am trying to teach. I've found a few pieces of commercially available software I like, but they always turn out to be for a different brand of microcomputer. Unfortunately, our computer seems to be geared more toward the video game market than the classroom.

Through the ensuing conversation, it became obvious that Ann needed lessons which would develop skills based on the everyday situations her students encountered. Lessons which reinforced previously introduced material were helpful, but her students needed more than straight drill-and-practice exercises: They needed to be able to see correct responses graphically displayed. Ann's requirements could be easily met by the use of the computer's branching capabilities combined with clean and simple graphics.

Since Ann had some experience with beginning programming, Sue decided to mention the capabilities of an authoring language such as PILOT.

Your brand of computer has an excellent version of PILOT. The graphics section is similar to turtle graphics in LOGO and is quite easy to use. You could construct you own computer-based lessons depending on each student's needs and include all the instruction and branching you want. I'm willing to spend some time with you going over how to use PILOT. I'm sure that we can create some useful lessons. Why don't you decide on a particular student or group, and a specific topic? Then we'll write a lesson while you learn.

Because of the modular design of her classroom management system, Ann could make time available during the day for tutoring in PILOT. Working together, she and Sue were able to develop a tutorial lesson covering restaurant vocabulary. When students responded incorrectly, the lesson branched to check if the problem was with the vocabulary word or because they didn't understand the question. How students responded to questions in these branching sections of the lessons determined what subject content would be next.

The lesson covered practical skills that the students faced in their community. They were frequently on their own at small local restaurants for dinner and would only order those items they knew were offered. In order to avoid revealing their inability to understand the menu, they would eat the same thing every dinner rather than ask what else was available. By using the new lesson, students were able to practice, in a non-threatening environment, the skills they needed. They had the additional advantage of working independently.

Ann was particularly impressed with the graphics section of this version of PILOT. Using the LOGO-like commands made drawing simple. She was able to create pictures which corresponded to the actual settings and menus. Later, class time was spent with actual menus. Her students were much more comfortable trying "the real thing" in front of their peers because they had already tested their knowledge first by using the non-threatening computer-based lessons. The students seemed proud of their new skills and their increased independence. Both parents and students were happy with the lessons and their results.

Ann's goal was tutorial instruction. For this reason, she found the capabilities and design of PILOT especially well suited to her needs. Using PILOT, she was able to create several "reality-based" lessons for her students. She found PILOT met her needs: The special features it offered and the relative ease of its use allowed her to write the particular lessons she needed more easily than she could have with BASIC. In addition, she felt that including graphics displays for her students was essential, and the PILOT graphics simplified the task. In particular, important features such as the Match Command for branching in tutorial instruction made the use of PILOT almost mandatory. In addition, Ann found that she was able to write the lessons she wanted more quickly using PILOT than BASIC—a particularly important consideration for her.

Using an authoring language in this situation has many advantages. It avoids the constraints of the school budget: Purchasing the PILOT language disk gave Ann the power to develop a wide variety of lessons. Its special commands and graphics capabilities reduce the time spent authoring lessons from what it is with other, less-specialized programming languages. Authoring languages make it practical, in terms of cost, time and effort, to produce highly individualized lessons, thereby capitalizing on the computer's appeal to the students.

Using Authoring Languages
to Meet Individual Student Needs: A Story

The principal has asked Eileen to assist with a situation new to their school. In keeping with the district policy of mainstreaming special education students in the least restrictive environment, the pupil personnel director had enrolled Jim Foreman in their school. He was to receive special assistance from Eileen in academic subjects but to participate as much as possible in the regular classroom. Jim was visually impaired and was unable to read from any of the standard textbooks. Until this time, Jim had used a "reader": Either his parents or a volunteer read material to him. He had learned to read using large-print materials and over-sized hand-printed sheets. The junior high school curriculum was making this system unworkable. The complexity and volume of school work demanded that Jim be able to access more material independently, without depending on someone else. The ideal would be a system which allowed him to use the materials in the standard junior high school curriculum.

Eileen knew from testing sent by the school psychologist that Jim understood vocabulary commensurate with his grade level and that he was able to read words at grade level when they were visually accessible to him. However, the print size of the material at the junior high level was smaller than that of the lower grades. In addition, worksheets, homework assignments, and tests were often teacher-designed dittos. These types of reading materials were definitely not visually accessible for Jim. The issue was how to meet Jim's needs within the constraints of staff time, financial considerations, and available resources.

It was clear that Jim would be able to assimilate some information during class because the curriculum had a heavy emphasis on discussion. In addition, the school system already owned a non-computer large-text reading machine and had decided to "hire" an older honors student to read homework assignments to Jim. However, there was still a need for tests, worksheets, and homework papers to be made available to Jim. Since these types of assignments required response time from Jim, it was felt that use of a reader would not be efficient. In addition, the importance of Jim's sense of independence was recognized. It was determined that machines which enlarge print on the computer were not the solution: They were too expensive and would not provide the interactive aspects which Eileen wanted for Jim.

Through a grant the previous year, Eileen had purchased a microcomputer for use with remedial math students. A course at the local university on computers in special education had exposed her to the use of authoring products. Eileen felt confident that she could create a character set of over-sized letters so that the print on the computer screen would be large enough for Jim to read. Now to develop the lessons. . .

Jim was extremely enthusiastic when he was shown Eileen's lessons and heard her plan. He had envied other students their time on the computer and was excited about the independence the computer could provide for him.

Eileen's plan was simple and easily implemented. Using the authoring language PILOT, she created interactive worksheets and tests which used the material from the regular curriculum. After using the non-computer large-text reading machine or a reader to study material, Jim loaded a disk into the computer and selected the appropriate lesson from the over-sized menu. Jim had learned the position of the numeric keys on a pad, and all the lessons used for worksheets contained multiple-choice responses which were numbered. The material displayed on the screen used the special over-sized character set Eileen had been able to employ in PILOT. Jim simply read the material on the screen and made selections using the numeric keys. Incorrect answers invoked the branching capabilities of PILOT, routing Jim to a tutorial section of the lesson which dealt with the particular skill causing Jim difficulty. When Jim missed material in a particular area three times, the screen directed him to a specific page in his text. Jim then placed the book under the non-computer reading machine to restudy the material. In this way, Jim was able to complete assignments and receive tutorial instruction fairly independently. For work requiring non-multiple-choice responses, Jim used a tape recorder and handed in the tapes to his teachers.

Jim found this arrangement quite satisfactory. Not only was he working independently and at his own pace but also he was no longer so dependent upon others to provide him with their time. In addition, Jim gained confidence with the computer, which boosted both his self-esteem and his position in the eyes of his peers.

The next step in Eileen's plans is to teach Jim to touch type using large print on the screen. The combination of Jim's ability to type and the special over-sized character set will allow Jim to use the computer, rather than a tape recorder, for non-multiple choice responses.

PILOT has enabled Jim to work with the standard junior high school curriculum of his peers while gaining control over his learning pace. By decreasing his dependance on outside assistance, PILOT has made it possible for Jim to keep pace with the increasing complexity and volume in the curriculum.

Eileen found the use of the Match Command in PILOT particularly valuable in meeting her goals for Jim's learning system. BASIC would not have allowed her to produce lessons as flexible and responsive to Jim's needs, let alone lessons with the over-sized special character sets available in PILOT.

Using Authoring Languages
with a Student/Author: A Story

Although originally designed with the teacher in mind, PILOT can also be used by students as a programming language. PILOT commands are easier for students to remember than commands in other programming languages: The commands are meaningful and easy to type. PILOT is structured to present information, ask questions, and "respond." These are the tasks that students are required to perform in school, and they frequently use these same techniques when interacting with their peers.

How can PILOT be used to enhance the learning situation for special needs students?

Three words—frequency, intensity, and duration—form the basis of many special needs teaching techniques. Repeating tasks, using as many modalities as possible, and increasing the time periods of study are steps familiar to special educators. What do these items have in common with PILOT?

The whole basis for drill-and-practice exercises centers around the capability of the computer to repeat material indefinitely. Tutorial lessons advance the process one step further, allowing the student to interact with the lesson content.

In some cases, students should be encouraged to write their own lessons using PILOT. Using PILOT to write simple drill-and-practice exercises can provide students with more complex and complete experiences. From an educational standpoint, a larger variety of skills can be tapped.

In order to write a lesson that works correctly, students need to sequence material. Special needs students often have weak sequencing skills. The computer's capacity for immediate feedback can assist some students in developing an understanding of sequence and logic.

When students write their own drill-and-practice exercises, they must do some research first. In order to develop lessons which other students can use, the student/author needs to be confident that he or she is "teaching" information that is correct. In normal circumstances, an assignment to prepare a test or worksheet on facts about the states in the United States might elicit little enthusiasm from students. For a variety of reasons, students in special needs settings are particularly reticent to tackle such tasks. Reading and writing are difficult for many special needs students, and these students avoid these tasks as much as possible. However, the computer is a very motivating tool, and special needs students are not immune to this allure. Using the simple structure of PILOT and its editing features, a student can design a lesson for another student to use. In this way, the student/author is studying and learning the material needed to make the lesson factual but this studying and learning is less distasteful because it is embedded in a larger, more appealing task.

Learning to program a computer gives a student insight into more than sequencing. When students write even the shortest lesson, they see that the computer responds to them and what they are doing. The computer only does as it is directed—and suddenly the special needs student has control over something in his or her environment. For many special needs students, programming a computer is their first experience with this sense of control.

More important than control over an object is the change that can occur in peer relationships, and the effect of this change on a student's self-esteem. The following scenario typifies the personal growth that can result through learning to use an authoring language such as PILOT.

> Sam was in the learning disabilities resource room for instruction in math. As a seventh grader, he was very self-conscious about going to the "dummy" room. Yet he really wanted to learn and hoped each year that the concepts which eluded him would finally be within his grasp.
>
> Last year, his resource room teacher had purchased a computer and bought some prepackaged software for drill-and-practice activities. Sam enjoyed using the computer but wanted to be able to do something more. His teacher, Ms. Hiller, had a copy of the authoring language PILOT for the computer and suggested they work together to write a lesson that would tutor Sam in the vocabulary of geometry, an area he needed for his regular math class. Sam was excited about the idea of "programming," although the subject matter wasn't his favorite. They set to work.
>
> Sam found the commands in PILOT easy to understand and remember since the letters stood for the functions and used the first letter of the function. Typing in the terms and definitions with Ms. Hiller's assistance was even part of the instruction. Sam read the words to Ms. Hiller as she typed. They used the editing features of PILOT to correct any errors she made, and to rearrange the visual lay-out of the screen. As Sam and Ms. Hiller used the editing commands in PILOT, Sam was taking his first steps to learning basic word processing concepts.
>
> After working together to write some lessons using PILOT, Ms. Hiller approached Sam with a proposition. The fifth grade math teacher, Mr. Galloway, wanted to talk to Sam. Some of his students were going to be working on an independent geometry unit for extra

credit, and he thought Sam's lesson would be a good introductory lesson for them. Though Sam was unsure how he felt about the idea, he agreed to meet with Mr. Galloway.

When Mr. Galloway saw Sam's PILOT lesson, he expressed real enthusiasm. "This lesson looks just perfect, Sam. I'd really like to use it. I especially like the pictures you drew on the screen that demonstrate each of the terms. Just one question. Have you thought about adding a picture to go with the score at the end of the lesson? Some of the younger students might really like that."

After Mr. Galloway left, Sam talked with Ms. Hiller. "I've got an idea, but I don't know if it'll work. And I'd need your help until I get good. Does this PILOT we're using let you make pictures that move around? See, what I was thinking was that I could make a sort of game, like the ones at arcades: You get to shoot things down if you get so many right. That would make this a lot more fun. Can I do it? We could work on it together, like we did before."

"Well, Sam, I don't know. This version of PILOT has something called 'sprites' but I haven't done anything with them. It sounds like we can make shapes and move them around but it will mean a lot of time before or after school."

"I'll come, if it's okay with you. Can we start tomorrow? Mr. Galloway said he'd need something in a few weeks."

So Sam and Ms. Hiller embarked on a new adventure. Ms. Hiller spent a weekend tackling the sprite section of the PILOT package with the manual, a computer, and a friend who had some programming experience. By Monday, she was ready to start with Sam.

Sam had worked out an idea of what he wanted to see on the screen. Ms. Hiller had explained that sprites were shapes he could design and then move around the screen. With their version of PILOT, eight sprites could be moving around at one time. Sam decided to call his animation section the *Black Hole.* The center of the screen would have a dark shape, which was the black hole. The sprites would race across the screen. When they passed over the hole, the student playing the game would have to press the space bar to grab the sprite and pull it into the black hole. There would be only one chance per sprite, and some would be worth more points than others. To make it tie in with the lesson, Sam decided that each unit would have eight questions, and the student would get one sprite for every right answer.

Ms. Hiller and Sam found themselves really engrossed in the project and were able to finish the reward section in time for Mr. Galloway's students.

Sam almost got cold feet about letting other students look at his lesson, but he had made an agreement, and the lesson went to Mr. Galloway's room. The results were more exciting than any of them had counted on. The students in Mr. Galloway's room could hardly wait to use the lesson—and, of course, the section with the black hole was the most popular. They worked to get as many correct answers as possible. Soon students from other classes were asking if they could play, and word of Sam's skill as a programmer spread around the school.

Ms. Hiller was delighted with the results. Sam became more confident, and the new status he had with his peers boosted his self-esteem. He gained some insight into how computers function and has become more structured in his own projects and assignments. In addition, the editing commands were a great introduction to word processing concepts. Sam even decided to take a touch typing class so that he can enter his own programs!

As this example illustrates, there are several tangible and intangible benefits related to the use of an authoring language such as PILOT with special needs students. These students benefit from a logical step-by-step procedure. The allure of working on computers spurs some reluctant students to try new material. The process of writing a program is in itself a double instructional tool—both on computer use and on the information used as the lesson content. Editing familiarizes the student with word processing and can serve as an added impetus to learn typing. For many special needs students, the impetus to learn typing skills can help alleviate difficulties encountered with pencil and paper tasks. And self-confidence and esteem, so important to healthy development, can be positively influenced through peer reaction.

Another possible application of PILOT is in peer tutoring situations. Students who write lessons for other students to use might also teach their peers, younger students, or even adults to use PILOT to write their own lessons. Again, the effects on learning and on self-esteem can be quite positive.

PILOT is not only for teachers. It is not simply a language for writing drill-and-practice or tutorial lessons. When placed in student hands, the effects of PILOT can be far-reaching.

Other Applications

In the three different situations described above, special circumstances combined to create environments in which the use of an authoring language met specific needs. When considering the use of authoring products as part of an instructional plan, each individual situation should be carefully analyzed. When student, teacher, or curriculum objectives require special adaptations, an authoring language can be a better choice for constructing high-quality flexible computer-based lessons than mini-authoring programs or authoring shells.

Since authoring languages differ, including versions of PILOT, it is recommended that a teacher/author review the written documentation which accompanies the language disk to determine if the special features available in that authoring language meet the author's programming needs.

PILOT

First developed in 1968 by Dr. John A. Starkweather and his colleagues at the University of California at San Francisco, PILOT is a specialized computer language. PILOT (Programmed Inquiry, Learning or Teaching Language) was designed as a tool to be used in developing computer assisted instruction, particularly interactive tutorials. Because of its specialized purpose, PILOT is able to perform many tasks typically associated with drill-and-practice and tutorial software with greater ease than other computer languages. This special capability also limits PILOT's applications. If the programming task is to design an interactive tutorial, drill-and-practice, or test lesson, PILOT may well offer one of the most expeditious routes to high quality lessons. Some forms of simulation programs, especially in the area of science and social studies, are also well suited to the use of PILOT (Conlon, 1984). The simplicity of the commands and the special structure inherent to the authoring language PILOT enable the teacher/author to develop interactive tutorial lessons of high quality more quickly than with other programming languages.

There are several versions of PILOT currently available: At least one, and sometimes more than one, are available for the different brands of microcomputers typically found in schools today. "Common" PILOT forms the basis of most PILOT packages. Many similarities exist among the versions of PILOT. The major differences among versions center around special features such as record-keeping and management capabilities, sound, graphics, and the use of various peripherals. For example, some versions of PILOT allow the use of devices such as light pens, graphics pads, speech synthesizers, and video disk technology. These special aspects need to be considered when selecting which version of PILOT to use. These considerations have a particular impact on the use of an authoring language with special needs populations and are discussed later.

Some versions of PILOT are menu driven, providing on-screen lists of options. Many versions also contain "help" screens, or sections of text that can be called up easily when the user is having difficulty. These features are particularly useful for referencing commands. In addition, written documentation accompanies most PILOT packages. Books detailing the commands and functioning of PILOT are easily available.

PILOT, although a programming language, is not difficult to master. The written documentation and/or on-screen menus which accompany most PILOT language disks are usually complete and offer step-by-step instruction for designing and writing a tutorial lesson.

Authoring Lessons with PILOT

Just as spoken languages have certain structures which determine their usage, PILOT also has systematic rules. Although there are not nearly as many of these rules in PILOT as there are in languages such as English, Latin, and Russian, it is important to understand the framework in which PILOT operates.

In PILOT, directions are given to the computer by using *statements*. Each statement is a *command* for the computer to follow. These statements are placed together in a logical sequence to create a program, usually called a *lesson*. When the computer is instructed to "run" the program or lesson, it begins at the first statement and moves through the statements, performing each as it occurs. The programmer or author writes and orders the statements to create the lesson the student sees when the lesson is run. It is helpful to think of a lesson as a set of instructions, much like directions for using a new piece of equipment. In this case, the teacher/author is giving the computer directions to follow. That, in essence, is what programming is all about.

A simple analogy should help those new to programming to understand the framework used in PILOT. PILOT is a language and as such is composed of statements, which are akin to sentences. These statements must follow certain rules of presentation or "syntax." Sections of lessons can be grouped, much as thoughts are grouped in paragraphs. A finished program or lesson can be viewed as a completed written work.

Of course, it's not quite that straightforward. Authoring languages do have rules, and there are conventions for constructing good lessons using authoring languages. But understanding the process and the various commands is not difficult. By learning the basic commands in PILOT, it is possible to acquire a feeling for the logic and structure of the language. Once familiar with the process, teachers can determine whether it is appropriate to allot time to learn PILOT.

Program Line Structure

PILOT lessons consist of a series of program lines. Each program line is a statement or command. Every statement or command in a PILOT lesson contains three sections. On the left is the instruction for the computer to follow. Immediately following the instruction is a colon. Following the colon is the text or information to be acted upon. The colon signals the division between the instruction and the material or text to which the instruction refers. For example:

T:This is a sample program line.

In this line, the *T* is the instruction, in this case meaning *Type*. The sentence *This is a sample program line* is the material which the computer is being told to *Type*. The colon divides the two sections of the command. To make the computer follow the directions in this sample program line, the teacher/author keyboards *Run* <Return>. The screen displays:

This is a sample program line.

In this way, the teacher/author enters program lines (statements, commands) and then checks the program by typing *Run*.

Most versions of PILOT limit the number of characters allowed on a program line. This limitation helps prevent the screen from becoming too crowded with information.

The Type Command

The Type Command provides the teacher/author with a method for creating a legible screen. One of the most important features to consider when preparing software for special needs students is the visual impact of the material. Making the lesson clear and appealing to the eyes of a student can be a time consuming process but it is essential for maximum impact and effectiveness. The Type Command, demonstrated above, allows the teacher/author to present text on the screen. Blank lines can be inserted between text lines by using the Type Command without any text after the colon. Inserting these blank lines is not time consuming and can add to the clarity and appeal of the visual presentation.

Thus, the program lines:

> T:Hello there.
> T:
> T:I am speaking to you in PILOT.

after typing RUN, appear with a space between them.

> Hello, there.
>
> I am speaking to you in PILOT.

The Accept Command

A lesson that only prints words on the screen has little more to offer than a standard textbook. Computer languages are, by definition, interactive. Authoring languages are designed to allow the interaction between computer and student to occur in a relatively open and natural manner. The Accept Command demonstrates this feature.

In order to interact with the student, the computer needs to be able to request and then respond to information. This process is sequential, as are all processes on the computer. The lesson, usually through a Type Command, asks a question or solicits information from the student. The computer needs to be able to wait for the answer, store the answer somewhere, and then do something with the information. The Accept Command, using the instruction A, performs the first part of this sequence: Waiting for the answer.

In the form,

> A:

the computer waits for the student to answer. After typing the answer, the student must press <Return> to signal the computer that the answer is complete.

For example:

> T:What is your name?
> A:
> T:Well, I'm glad you're here today!

In this example, the answer given by the student is simply accepted by the lesson. It is neither stored nor evaluated.

However, there are times when the teacher/author wants to store the information typed by the student and use it again later in the lesson. The use of a student's name is a common example of this. Students particularly enjoy seeing their names on the screen. Personalizing a lesson by using a student's name can be very motivating, particularly for some special needs students. In order to store typed information so that it can be retrieved later, the information is given a label. These labels are called *variables.*

Variables

After waiting for the answer (*A*), the computer sometimes needs to store that answer. Variables, sometimes called string variables, are used for this purpose. The term *variable* means that the information in a storage location can change each time it is used. For example, a lesson that only stores the name of the first student using it will not interest many other students. Having the lesson address them with the incorrect name might even make them angry. With variables, each time a new student uses the lesson, his or her name is stored and used as long as he or she remains on the computer. An expanded version of the short segment begun above follows.

> T:What is your name?
> A:N
> T:Well, N, I'm glad you're here today!

When this lesson is used by a student named Bill, the sequence on the screen looks like this:

> What is your name?
> Bill
> Well, Bill, I'm glad you're here today!

Now, throughout the lesson, any time the variable name *N* is used, the word *Bill* appears on the screen. Later, if Sue Williams uses the lesson and types her name in response to the question *What is your name*, the computer will place the words *Sue Williams* in the memory location where *N* appears. *Sue Williams* then replaces any name stored earlier. Now, throughout the lesson, the words *Sue Williams* will appear whenever the variable name *N* is used.

A common analogy to the variable name, in this case *N*, is a mailbox where letters are the information stored in the box. However, only one set of information can be stored in one mailbox or variable location at a time.

The important concept to understand is that it is possible to input information into the computer when a lesson is running and have the computer "remember" that information so that it can do something with it. There are times when a response needs to be remembered and used again, as in the case of a student's name. Other responses only need to be stored for a short period of time within a lesson segment, and so do not need a special variable name. Another type of statement, the Match Command, demonstrates the difference.

The Match Command

Once a student has responded to a question on the computer screen and the computer has accepted the response (A), the lesson must analyze and act upon the student's response. The Match Command, using the instruction M, is designed to handle responses.

The Match Command is one of the most unique statements in authoring languages. It allows the computer to respond differently based on a match. A typical sequence is:

1. A question is asked by the computer.
2. The student types in a response.
3. The computer compares (tries to match) the typed answer with the teacher's/author's answers recorded earlier.
4. The computer responds differently depending on whether or not the typed answer "matches" the prerecorded answer(s).

Again, an illustration:

```
T:WHAT IS THE FIRST DAY OF SCHOOL?
A:
M:MONDAY
TY:YES, WE START SCHOOL EACH WEEK ON MONDAY.
TN:NO, THE FIRST DAY IS MONDAY.
```

In the above example, the student is asked to type in the first day of school. The response *MONDAY* causes the lesson to go to the next line. *TY* stands for *Type if Yes*. The Type if Yes text is displayed if the student's answer and the answer in the Match Command are the same. If the answer does not correspond to that in the Match Command, then the *TN,* or *Type if No* Command is executed. This interactive process is illustrated by "running" the program lines above.

WHAT IS THE FIRST DAY OF SCHOOL?
MONDAY
YES, WE START SCHOOL EACH WEEK ON MONDAY.

WHAT IS THE FIRST DAY OF SCHOOL?
I THINK IT'S WEDNESDAY.
NO, THE FIRST DAY IS MONDAY.

In this example, the student must spell *MONDAY* correctly in order to have the answer considered as correct. If spelling is the purpose of the lesson, then this feature is important. If, on the other hand, a variety of responses is acceptable, there needs to be more flexibility in possible answers. There are several adaptations to the Match Command which provide this flexibility by employing special punctuation. The punctuation marks allow the teacher/author to specify the acceptability of a variety of answers. The particular punctuation marks vary depending on the version of PILOT being used.

T:WHAT IS THE FIRST DAY OF SCHOOL?
A:
M:MONDAY!MON.!MON

In this example of the Match Command, the *!* represents the word *or.* The above example identifies three possible answers which will be accepted by the computer as correct and result in a positive response. It is also possible to require that two or more answers appear somewhere in the response.

Another punctuation mark, the asterisk (*), allows for variability in spelling of student responses. In the example below, the use of the asterisks in the Match Command allow the student to respond with any spelling that uses an *M*, *N*, and a *D* in that order. Thus, *MUNDAE* would be accepted as a correct response.

> T:WHAT IS THE FIRST DAY OF SCHOOL?
> A:
> M:M*N*D

The Match Command can be used to accommodate a range of other variations as well. Possibly one of the most exciting features of the Match Command in PILOT is the capability of accepting phrase or full-sentence answers. Lessons written in BASIC usually require a precise answer. With PILOT, students can respond using a single word, phrases, or full sentences. This is possible because the Match Command uses an answer "window." Thus, when the answer to a question is *MONDAY*, as in the example above, the Match Command directs the computer to look for the word *MONDAY*. The word can appear by itself or with other words. This allows a student to respond in a variety of ways to the question *WHAT IS THE FIRST DAY OF SCHOOL?*

- THE FIRST DAY IS MONDAY.
- MONDAY IS THE FIRST DAY OF SCHOOL.
- I'M NOT SURE, BUT I THINK IT'S MONDAY.
- MONDAY.

All of these responses are acceptable because the word *MONDAY* appears in each.

The advantages of this type of varied response are many. Students do not need to worry about the exact wording of phrases (unless the Match Command so specifies). More importantly, students can respond to the computer naturally without using stilted expressions which are typical in lessons written in other computer languages. For teachers stressing the use of complete sentences, grammar, and vocabulary, the ability of PILOT to accept a variety of complete-sentence answers is invaluable. Too often, students use single-word responses. The Match Command in PILOT can be used to encourage the use of complete phrases and sentences. Special education teachers and language therapists find this feature particularly valuable.

It is also possible to change Match Commands to fit individual student needs and progress levels. For example, students just learning the days of the week can be allowed a more flexible response option (by using asterisks in the Match Command, for example), while students completing a unit on days might be limited to exact responses. This flexibility allows the teacher to use the same basic information and tailor the lesson to meet a variety of student needs.

The Type if Yes and Type if No Commands

In some lessons, the teacher/author wants to provide extra information based on the student's response. Continuing with the example above, perhaps the teacher wants to target a few days of the week which the student might be expected to pick erroneously. The following example demonstrates a method for dealing with this type of situation using the Type if Yes and Type if No Commands in PILOT.

```
T:WHAT IS THE FIRST DAY OF SCHOOL?
A:
M:SUNDAY
TY:NO, SUNDAY IS THE FIRST DAY OF THE WEEK,
TY:BUT WE DON'T GO TO SCHOOL THEN.
M:SATURDAY
TY:SATURDAY IS THE FIRST DAY OF THE WEEKEND.
M:MONDAY
TY:YES, MONDAY IS THE FIRST DAY OF SCHOOL.
TN:NO, MONDAY IS THE FIRST DAY OF SCHOOL.
```

The new commands, *TY* and *TN*, stand for *Type if Yes* and *Type if No*. These commands instruct the computer to look for a match to the student's response. If the match is found, the *TY* text will be printed on the screen. When a match is not found, the *TN* text is displayed.

In the example above, the lesson advances to each succeeding program line, looking for an answer to match. If the student answers with *SUNDAY*, then the computer displays *NO, SUNDAY IS THE FIRST DAY OF THE WEEK, BUT WE DON'T GO TO SCHOOL THEN.* If the student's answer is not *SUNDAY*, then the computer bypasses all three lines, looking for another match. The computer continues to search through the program lines, in order, until it finds a match or reaches the last Type if No Command.

The Jump Command

Suppose the teacher/author wants to have a student repeat a problem if the answer was wrong the first time. PILOT has a Jump Command, using the instruction *J*, which allows this type of branching.

```
T:WHAT IS THE FIRST DAY OF SCHOOL?
A:
M:MONDAY!MON.!MON
TY:YES, MONDAY IS THE FIRST DAY OF SCHOOL.
TN:NO, THAT IS NOT QUITE RIGHT. TRY AGAIN.
JN:@A
```

This example uses *JN* (*Jump if No*). Notice the *@A* in the last program line. This indicates that the computer will jump to the most recently executed Accept Command (*A*) in the lesson. Here, an answer other than *MONDAY, MON.* or *MON* will result in the feedback message *NO, THAT IS NOT QUITE RIGHT. TRY AGAIN.* The student then has another chance to enter the correct answer. A sample screen appears as follows:

```
WHAT IS THE FIRST DAY OF SCHOOL?
SUNDAY
NO, THAT IS NOT QUITE RIGHT. TRY AGAIN.
MONDAY
YES, MONDAY IS THE FIRST DAY OF SCHOOL.
```

Of course, as this lesson is now written, a student could continue to go around in a loop indefinitely, providing incorrect answers and being directed to try again. There are other features of the authoring language PILOT which allow the teacher/author to control the number of attempts a student is allowed or asked to make. It is also possible to keep track of student responses as well as final scores. These capabilities enhance the lesson being developed. If the teacher is interested in using PILOT to author interactive tutorials, it is worth his or her time to master the record-keeping capabilities.

The simple sample examples given above illustrate the capabilities and complexities of programming with an authoring language. The manuals that accompany authoring language disks and the books currently available on the use of specific languages, specifically PILOT, are good resources for the beginning author.

Graphics

Graphics refers to the insertion of pictures, charts, and other drawings into the lesson. Most versions of PILOT allow the use of some graphics capabilities. Many systems use a coordinate-point system, which requires that the teacher/author specify the precise locations on the screen where drawing should take place. The programmer visualizes the screen as a grid and specifies points along the x and y axes. This type of graphics screen is similar to the graphics systems used in other programming languages such as BASIC. The use of graph paper in the pre-computer preparation stages of lesson development helps to simplify the task for the teacher/author.

Other versions of PILOT allow the use of special character sets embedded within the language or microcomputer. These character sets are groups of graphics symbols which can be joined together to create pictures and shapes. Each key on the computer keyboard can be programmed to represent a different shape. These shapes or character sets are entered into the lesson by typing the representative keys on the keyboard.

Some brands of microcomputers, such as Commodore, make use of a special graphics feature called *sprites*. Sprites are shapes which can be created by the teacher/author and then programmed to move so as to result in animation effects. This special feature can add a great deal to the quality and motivational impact of the lesson on students. Such special features do, however, require the commitment of extra learning and programming time on the part of the teacher/author.

Still other versions of PILOT allow the use of simple LOGO-like commands to manipulate the cursor on the screen. By using directions such as "forward," "back," "right," and "left," the cursor can be moved about the screen, leaving a trail behind as it moves. This capability turns the screen into a modified sketch pad, enabling the teacher/author to draw simple drawings and charts. Although easier to use than some other graphics features, this approach takes time to master and has limitations of its own.

Thus, when selecting an authoring language, the prospective author should consider the type of graphics capabilities available. Some models of computers have limited offerings, while others have a broad range from which to choose. Some languages have a greater range of graphics or use graphics more flexibly than others. The potential author must consider not only the ease of use but also the overall benefits of graphics from the perspective of both the model of computer and the specific authoring language.

Lesson Management with PILOT

At times, the terms *special education* and *record keeping* seem synonymous to teachers. Use of a diagnostic-prescriptive model of teaching requires careful records be kept of all student responses to lessons. Each response, or set of responses, to individual lessons can be used to develop and identify subsequent lessons. The tutorial flavor of PILOT makes it possible to author lessons which contain both diagnosis and prescription. The necessity that special education teachers have a record of individual student responses and scores demands some method for systematically documenting and tracking student progress. Various authoring languages, and various versions of PILOT, handle this requirement in different ways.

The record-keeping method most common to versions of PILOT is the use of a data file. Using *variables* and storage locations, the teacher/author can set up separate data files for each student in the class. These data files can be designed to contain student scores and answers. This framework requires that the teacher/author write a subroutine, or small program, within the larger lesson. This subroutine handles the record-keeping aspects. A few versions of PILOT, such as SuperPILOT (from Apple Computers, Inc.), have additional record-keeping commands built into the language. With SuperPILOT, by simply using the instruction K for *Keep*, the teacher/author is able to store answers, scores, and even comments typed in by the student throughout the lesson. SuperPILOT also manages cumulative student records automatically. The contents of each data file can then be reviewed whenever the teacher chooses.

The ability to keep track of student scores is useful. But the ability to record specific responses for later evaluation is even more important, especially in special needs settings. Identifying the differences in built-in management features can help determine the potential usefulness of a given authoring language for a given classroom need.

Summary

As discussed, the third category of authoring products, authoring languages, is the most complex and demands most of the teacher/author. With this complexity and demand comes the potential for more individualized and flexible computer-based lessons. The author is the programmer when using an authoring language—and, as the programmer, the author decides exactly which form the lesson will take.

Authoring languages are the best solution when computer materials tailored to specific curriculum objectives are not available, and mini-authoring programs and authoring systems do not provide enough flexibility. Having decided to employ a programming language rather than a mini-authoring program or authoring system, the teacher/author must then decide which programming language best meets his or her instructional needs. There are some general guidelines which assist in making this decision.

The decision is most often made on the basis of the features available with the programming language rather than the time commitment. Authoring languages, such as PILOT, were designed for the development of computer - assisted instruction. Unlike general all-purpose programming languages, authoring languages include features particularly well suited to lesson development. These features simplify the teacher's/author's tasks, in particular accommodating selective "answer checking" or "matching" of responses and the inclusion of graphics.

Generally, if a teacher/author is interested in developing and creating original drill-and-practice or tutorial lessons for classroom use, an authoring language should be considered.

Appendix to Chapter 6
Some Examples of PILOT

This Appendix includes three simple sample lessons written in PILOT: *Numberguesser, Mad-Libs Speech,* and *Do You Know Your States?* These lessons are representative of the variety of applications and commands available in PILOT. These lessons are practical and complete, but shorter than most programs used in classrooms. Although the lessons in this Appendix are written in Apple SuperPILOT (available from Apple Computer, Inc.), the commands work with most versions of PILOT available for common microcomputers.

These lessons are intentionally short so that interested readers can keyboard them on their own machines. It is recommended that the reader use these lessons to experiment with the various commands and program sequence.

The learning process in this Appendix begins with loading the authoring language PILOT into the computer.

The Numberguesser: A Classic

The following program is common. Almost everyone who has played a game on the computer has tried to "guess" the number the computer is "thinking." Teachers familiar with BASIC or Logo should be able to compare the commands and logic of different versions of the number-guessing game. Those new to programming should find the sequence of steps in this lesson informative. Students always seem to enjoy this game, and don't seem to realize they are engaged in logic and problem solving.

Numberguesser

```
D:F$(20)
PR:U
T:Hello! Let's play Number Guesser!
T:I'll think of a number, and you guess.
*Again
T:
T:The number I'm thinking of is between
T:1 and 100. What is it?
T:
C:X = RND(100)
A:# G
T:
TH(G>X):Your guess is too high.
TH(G>X):Try again!
J(G>X):@A
T:
TH(G<X):That's too low! Try again.
J(G<X):@A
T:
T(G=X):Great! You got it!
TH(G=X):Want to try another?
A:$F$
M:Yes!Y!Y*!Sure!OK!
JY:Again
TN:Okay. See you later!
W:60
E:
```

Mad-Libs: An Approach to Parts of Speech

Children enjoy the commercial tablets called "Mad-Libs" containing pre-formatted short stories which are missing various adjectives, adverbs, nouns, and verbs. To play, the person with the commercial tablet asks another player to supply an appropriate word: "Give me an adjective" or "How about a verb?" The answers are placed in the designated blanks in the preformatted text, and the resulting story can be quite amusing. Since students are familiar with the format, and tend to enjoy it so much, the Mad-Libs format has worked well in computer-based lessons as a method to practice parts of speech. The following SuperPILOT lesson makes use of the same format for this purpose.

Mad-Libs Speech

```
D:V$(20)
D:N$(20)
D:J$(20)
D:D$(20)
D:P$(20)
D:B$(20)
D:C$(20)
D:Q$(20)
D:L$(20)
T:This is a Mad-Lib.
T:
T:You will be asked for parts of speech.
T:
T:All of your words will be used in a
T:story at the end. One more thing.
T:The words should be twenty (20)
T:letters or less. Okay? Okay.
T:
T:Here we go!
T:
T:Type a verb ending in "ing".
A:$V$
T:
T:Now, give me a noun.
A:$N$
T:
T:Great! Now, how about an adjective?
A:$J$
T:
T:All right. Now, I'd like a word that
T:describes a noun.
A:$D$
T:
T:Next, enter a present tense verb.
```

```
A:$P$
T:
T:Give me a noun.
A:$B$
T:
T:You're doing well. Now, how about a
T:verb ending with "ed"?
A:$C$
T:
T:Another past tense verb, please.
A:$Q$
T:
T:Let's finish with a noun that
T:names a place.
A:$L$
T:
T:
T:Now, I'm going to use your words in a
T:sentence. If you used the correct
T:parts of speech, it may be silly,
T:but it will sound correct!
T:
T:I was $V$ along the road when I came
T:
T:to a(n) $N$ . It was all $J$ and $D$ .
T:
T:I bent down to $P$ it. Suddenly, a
T:
T:$B$ $C$ out! I $Q$ all the way
T:to the $L$ !
W:60
E:
```

An Interactive Quiz in Pilot

The last lesson is an example of an interactive quiz. The assumption is made here that the student has been exposed to the lesson content prior to playing this game on the computer. Prepared slightly differently, this program could become a tutorial—providing the information first, and then testing the student later.

Do You Know Your States?

```
T:How well do you know your states?
T:
T:Let's find out!
T:
T:You will get three guesses before the
T:computer will have to tell you.
T:
T:Good luck!
PR:U
T:
*STATE1
T:
T:
T:Which state is the "Golden State"?
A:
M:CALIFORNIA!CA!CALIF!CAL*
TY:Great! Here's the next one.
JY:STATE2
T1:The state flower is a golden poppy.
T2:The capital is Sacramento.
T3:I'm thinking of California.
JN3:STATE2
JN:STATE1
T:
*STATE2
T:
T:
T:What state is known for sunshine?
A:
M:FLORIDA!FL!FLOR*!F*R*A
TY:Good. Florida is a sunny place.
JY:STATE3
T1:Hint 1: This state is on the Gulf of Mexico.
T2:Hunt 2: Everglades National Park is there.
T3:The state is Florida.
JN3:STATE3
```

```
JN:STATE2
T:
*STATE3
T:
T:
T:Which state is the fourth largest?
A:
M:MONTANA!MT!MON*
TY:Montana has lots of open space!
JY:STATE4
T1:Hint 1: One of this state's beautiful
T1:parks has 60 glaciers.
T2:Hint 2: Helena is the capital.
T3:I'm talking about Montana, Big Sky!
JN3:STATE4
JN:STATE3
*STATE4
W:60
E:
```

Obviously, this lesson could continue with questions for all fifty states. The format allows for some misspelling or recall errors, and lets students try three times before the computer reveals the correct answer. The lesson can be modified so that it tracks the number of initial correct responses. It is also possible to include more sophisticated branching and provide more information about each state. This sample lesson should be considered as a simple outline which can be expanded or modified as the situation requires.

7

Training

Perhaps the most important issue raised by the use of microcomputers in schools is training. To use computers effectively in the classroom, teachers need to feel comfortable with computers. To feel comfortable, teachers must be familiar with the operation of the computer itself, know how to use a variety of software packages, understand how to integrate computers into the curriculum to support their students' learning efforts, and be able to trouble-shoot unforeseen problems. Meeting these criteria is especially important when teachers use authoring products to construct computer-based lessons.

This Chapter introduces many of the variables in training teachers/authors to use authoring products. Starting with a general philosophy of the purpose of training, it discusses the objectives of training and presents formats for workshops on mini-authoring programs and authoring languages. Also discussed are follow-up training experiences and the use of "coaching" as a model for teacher assistance.

The use of authoring products—mini-authoring programs, authoring systems, or authoring languages—places more demands on the classroom teacher than most other curriculum materials. For example, when new textbooks are purchased for the social studies curriculum, the accompanying teacher's guide and student workbooks provide step-by-step instructions for using the material. Authoring products do not include corresponding guides indicating how to integrate computer lessons into the curriculum. Furthermore, computers are not as simple to use as standard textbooks. Teachers are accustomed to using teacher's guides and textbooks. Designing, developing, and implementing their own computer assisted instruction is unfamiliar.

Training helps teachers become comfortable using computers, and is essential for an educationally sound, well-integrated classroom approach which utilizes the computer as an instructional tool.

When developing a training plan, the type of authoring product—mini-authoring program, authoring system, or authoring language—should determine the structure of the training. Learning to program in an authoring language such as PILOT takes substantially more time than learning to use a menu-driven authoring system. Mini-authoring programs require the least amount of training and follow-up practice time.

What is accomplished through training? Ideally, a training session or series of sessions should equip teachers with the information necessary:

1. to determine when and for what an authoring product should be used,
2. to ask informed questions, and
3. to use the authoring product to create simple lessons for classroom use.

Objectives for Training

To be effective, training must be accompanied by objectives—a list of purposes and expected outcomes—so that individuals being trained are aware of the training goals. Objectives also serve as a set of criteria for determining the effectiveness of the training in achieving its desired outcome. What are some of the major objectives to be achieved through training sessions for authoring products?

1. Participants should understand the rationale, advantages and disadvantages of the use of customized CAI in the classroom.
2. Participants should be able to outline the steps of a specific lesson.
3. Teachers should be able to use authoring products to construct usable student lessons containing a variety of subject matter.

4. At the conclusion of training, when a computer-based lesson has been authored, participants should know definitely where the lesson they have authored fits within the curriculum.

The Rationale, Advantages, and Disadvantages of Computer Assisted Instruction

Participants should understand the rationale, advantages, and disadvantages of the use of customized CAI in the classroom. Why and when to use computer-assisted drill-and-practice or tutorial lessons are important questions. As discussed in Chapters 2 and 3, there are situations in which student or teacher needs are met by the special characteristics of computer assisted instruction. The need to have customized, curriculum-related materials available is also a reason to use authoring products.

Outlining Computer-Based Lessons

Participants should be able to outline the steps of a specific lesson and delineate the objectives to be accomplished by the student using the computer lesson. The subject material to be included in the lesson should be identified and sequenced, and must be consistent with the lesson's objectives. The complexity of the lesson outline will differ depending on the level of authoring product.

In general, the objective for mini-authoring programs tends to be reinforcement and practice of material that has already been learned (drill-and-practice exercises). Most mini-authoring programs require that the teacher/author collect the lesson content and enter it. Some allow minimal format design. Mini-authoring programs do not require that the teacher/author know how to program. Since the *shell* of the lesson is predesigned in a mini-authoring program, the teacher/author must work within the variety of available lesson structures. Authoring systems provide more flexible lessons but still require the educator to keep the objectives of the lesson in mind, and sequence each page accordingly. Like mini-authoring programs, authoring systems often impose some restrictions on lesson format. The tutorial approach, using branching, is common in authoring systems. The use of an authoring language, such as PILOT, requires that the educator develop a flowchart—a step-by-step layout of the framework and "flow" of the program/lesson. A flowchart can be a very useful guide for both lesson development and the evaluation of lesson effectiveness.

Constructing Computer-Based Lessons

Teachers should be able to use authoring products to construct usable student lessons containing a variety of subject matter. This is the major goal of training—to enable the participant to use the authoring product. The amount of time needed for training and practice differs greatly depending on the type of authoring product and each teacher's/author's level of experience.

Mini-authoring programs require the least amount of training time to achieve some proficiency in constructing lessons. Although a few experienced teachers might be interested or willing to instruct themselves, most teachers find a "walk-through" training session very helpful. This session usually takes the form of a short lecture and demonstration followed by hands-on time allowing the teacher/author to use the mini-authoring program. A $2\frac{1}{2}-3$-hour session is usually sufficient for participants to develop some degree of comfort using a mini-authoring program to construct lessons. Familiarity with one mini-authoring program makes it possible for most teachers/authors to use other mini-authoring programs with very little orientation.

Achieving proficiency in constructing lessons using authoring systems requires substantially more training time, usually more than one session. Teachers/authors need time to learn the general framework of the authoring system, as well as the various commands for editing, paging, branching, and other lesson characteristics. The first session should cover system background, instruction, and practice. Subsequent sessions should focus on system use to meet specific classroom needs. Since the process of software development is ongoing, periodic sessions (such as staff in-service days) should be scheduled throughout the year. These later training opportunities provide teachers/authors with time to develop lessons as well as ask questions and clarify issues about the authoring system as they become more adept with it.

Learning to use an authoring language such as PILOT to construct lessons is a time-consuming process. The basic commands in PILOT can be presented, practiced, and understood during a two-day workshop. However, constructing lessons using an authoring language demands significant pre-planning, outlining, and programming time. It is often wise to encourage these teachers/authors, and speed the creation of lessons authored with a language, by providing release or paid time for lesson creation. The total time required to construct a lesson depends on the teacher's/author's experience with computers, his or her motivation, and the variety of features used in the lessons.

Integrating Computer-Based Lessons

At the close of the training, when a computer-based lesson has been authored, teachers/authors should have a definite idea of where the lesson they have authored fits in the curriculum so that they can integrate it into classroom use. The teacher/author should leave training sessions with specific ideas for possible lesson applications—individual and group instruction, testing or review, lessons for students who have been absent, etc.

Guidelines for Training Sessions

Though the formats of the workshops for the various types of authoring products differ, the workshops also have some things in common: "hands-on" activity, low participant-to-machine and participant-to-leader ratios, and relevance and application of the authoring product to the workshop participants' backgrounds. The initial introduction to many new skills can be best achieved through the process of demonstration and guided practice. During a training session on authoring, the workshop leader explains and demonstrates a concept or command and then provides participants with sample exercises and a practice period. During this period, the workshop leader moves around the room, assisting the participants, and answering their questions. In this way, the leader actively monitors the learning and teaching process and maintains an appropriate pace.

In order for practice periods to be effective, the ratio of participants to leader and the number of participants using each computer should be kept low. Depending upon the experience of the workshop leader, groups of 10–20 participants are small enough to allow some individual attention from the leader and large enough to provide a variety of approaches and questions from the participants. Groups which are too large are often forced to move at the pace of the slowest-moving member. Smaller groups allow the workshop leader to provide more individualization.

Similarly, it is preferable that no more than two persons use one computer. A one-on-one ratio is ideal but not always possible. To place more than two workshop participants at a computer at one time means that neither will have much hands-on practice time.

Workshop participants should leave the training session understanding the practical applications of the authoring product and how it meets their particular classroom needs, and with the skills necessary to begin independently using the authoring product. If time permits, which will vary depending on the level of authoring being taught, it is helpful to provide the opportunity within the training session for teachers/authors to begin developing their own lessons using the authoring product. Teachers/authors who are able to leave a workshop with material which ties into their curriculum goals and is immediately usable are more likely to apply the new skills learned during the workshop. When a teacher sees the positive student response to a computer-based lesson he or she has authored, he or she will be motivated to continue authoring additional computer-based lessons.

Another important factor is the workshop leader's background and educational expertise. The leader should be able to work with educators and should understand the issues and concerns facing teachers in the classroom. Furthermore, the leader must be familiar with the specific authoring product(s) being used in the workshop. Ideally, the workshop leader should have used each authoring product to author lessons and used those lessons with students. Leaders from many backgrounds, such as industry or business, may be technically capable but not sufficiently aware of teachers' concerns. Communication is often most open when the workshop leader has a background similar to the teacher trainees.

Examples of Training Workshops

How might a typical authoring workshop proceed? Following are outlines of two workshops—one on mini-authoring and the other on the use of PILOT. Both outlines were derived from workshops which were run to introduce educators to these authoring products. Using these outlines, educators or administrators should be able to organize workshops to introduce teachers to either of these two authoring products. It is assumed that the reader will modify these workshop outlines to meet the needs of other workshop participants and leaders. The outlines are included here to give the reader the framework for training sessions, thereby setting new teachers/authors more quickly upon the path to constructing customized computer-based lessons.

An Introduction to Authoring Products, with an Emphasis on Mini-Authoring Programs: A Workshop

This mini-authoring workshop requires 3–4 hours. The explanation and demonstration sections take approximately 1½ hours with the remaining time devoted to hands-on experience and guided practice. If, after the workshop, the teachers return to their classrooms with the software, a longer training period allows them to prepare lessons which can be used the next day in their classes. If the workshop is intended as an introduction, and multiple copies of the mini-authoring program are not immediately available, then a shorter time period allows teachers to become familiar with the software and provides them with enough practice to determine whether the authoring product is useful in their classroom setting. Ideally, participants should be able to borrow the software used during the workshop when they return to their classrooms.

It is usually a good policy to encourage workshop participants to bring classroom materials—workbooks, textbooks, etc.—with them. In addition, the workshop, as outlined, should provide the following materials:

- one computer, with at least one disk drive, and monitor for each (or every two) participant(s);
- one demonstration computer with a large-screen monitor;
- samples of authoring products: several mini-authoring programs, an authoring system, and a version of the authoring language PILOT;
- multiple copies of the primary mini-authoring program being demonstrated (one for each computer being used in the workshop);
- if applicable, copies of mini-authoring programs to be distributed to workshop participants for use after the workshop concludes;
- a sufficient number of blank data disks—some formatted prior to the workshop.

I. Introduction
  A. Workshop objective: background, demonstration, and hands-on practice in using mini-authoring programs
  B. Rationale for using authoring products
     1. Need customized software for subject area or student needs
     2. Professional programmers too expensive

      3. Teachers require easy-to-use packages
      4. Students respond positively to personalized lessons
      5. Takes advantage of motivational power of computer
  C. Types/levels of authoring products: mini-authoring programs, authoring systems, authoring languages
      1. Mini-authoring programs
         a. Simplest and most limited type of authoring product
         b. Usually drill-and-practice exercises
         c. Use predesigned templates or "shells," into which teachers/authors insert lesson content
         d. Require little more time and planning than is needed to construct traditional dittos
         e. Subcategories: utility packages and modifiable programs
         f. Examples: *Tic Tac Show, Master Match,* and the *Game Show* (all from Advanced Ideas, Inc.)
      2. Authoring systems
         a. More complex and flexible than mini-authoring programs but less complex and flexible than authoring languages
         b. Drill-and-practice or tutorial exercises
         c. Allow significant teacher/author control of special features (presentation mode, presentation rate, response mode, response rate, type and frequency of feedback, etc.)
         d. Usually include easily accessed graphics
         e. Examples: *BLOCKS '82* (from California School for the Deaf) and *Author I* (from Tandy Co./Radio Shack).
      3. Authoring languages
         a. Most complex and flexible type of authoring product
         b. A complete programming language designed for the development of computer-assisted instruction
         c. Best suited for tutorial lessons
         d. Make possible extensive graphics, branching, and record keeping
         e. Examples: numerous versions of PILOT

 II. General guidelines for becoming familiar with a mini-authoring program
  A. "Playing" the lesson
      1. Review written and on-screen documentation on how to play the lesson (Many mini-authoring programs come with a sample lesson.)

  2. Play a lesson to see it from the student's perspective and to become familiar with the format, pace, sound, graphics, and general set-up

 B. *Format* or *initialize* a data disk (following directions in documentation)

 C. Follow directions on-screen and in written documentation to create a customized lesson

 D. Play the newly constructed customized lesson

 E. If necessary, revise the newly-constructed customized lesson

III. Walk-through a specific mini-authoring program—the *Game Show*

 A. "Play" the *Game Show* using the large-screen monitor

 B. Create a set of problems for a lesson (Be sure to use a variety of problem types so that workshop participants see samples from several disciplines such as math, English, reading, and science.)

 C. Demonstrate the use of at least one alternate input or output device

 D. Define and demonstrate a utility package

  1. Related to mini-authoring programs but tend to be more test/worksheet oriented—usually designed to produce a printed product, similar to a ditto, for classroom use

  2. Demonstrate a utility package— *Puzzles and Posters* (from Minnesota Educational Computing Consortium)

 E. Define and demonstrate a modifiable program

  1. Related to mini-authoring programs. Include preprogrammed lessons which can be used as are or modified by the teacher/author

  2. Demonstrate a modifiable program— *Special Needs Vol. I - Spelling* (from Minnesota Educational Computing Consortium)

* BREAK *

IV. Hands-on practice

 A. Go over computer procedures, verifying that all participants are familiar with equipment, how to turn the hardware on and off, and how to handle disks

 B. Distribute blank disks

 C. Distribute mini-authoring program disks and documentation

 D. *Format* or *initialize* blank disk to be used for lesson

 E. "Play" a sample lesson to familiarize workshop participants with the mini-authoring program

    F. Review how to construct a lesson using the mini-authoring program

    G. Circulate around the room as workshop participants begin to construct their own lessons (Assist as necessary. Encourage participants to try lesson content in several different subject areas.)

    H. Make other mini-authoring programs available for hands-on practice and encourage participants to try at least two packages

    I. Summarize advantages and disadvantages, strengths and weaknesses of mini-authoring programs used in workshop

V. Closing

    A. Question-and-answer period

    B. Wrap up with concluding remarks

    C. Evaluate workshop (usually written)

    D. Indicate whether follow-up training and/or coaching are available

    E. Identify other available resources—personnel, groups, software libraries, etc.

    F. Indicate ordering information for mini-authoring programs

    G. Indicate policies for borrowing mini-authoring programs used in workshop.

This introductory workshop has four basic objectives:

1. to introduce briefly the three levels of authoring products,
2. to acquaint participants with the functioning of a mini-authoring program,
3. to allow participants to visualize applications quickly, and
4. to begin constructing simple lessons with assistance.

To capitalize on the workshop, the demonstrated mini-authoring programs should be made available to the participants so that they can experiment outside the context and time constraints of the workshop. This individual experimentation can serve as a prelude to follow-up training sessions for interested participants.

An Introduction to the
Authoring Language PILOT: A Workshop

The following outline is a sample format for a two-day workshop on PILOT, the most common authoring language. The version used for this workshop demonstration is PILOT for the Commodore 64 computer. Although other versions of PILOT differ slightly with regard to editing, graphics and animation, and record-keeping capabilities, the basic commands and concepts are similar. This workshop outline is intended to serve as a model for workshops using other versions of PILOT.

The first day of this PILOT workshop is designed to acquaint the participants with PILOT: Its potential, features, structure, simpler commands, and operation. More elaborate features are introduced and practiced on the second day.

Once again, it is a good policy to encourage workshop participants to bring classroom materials—workbooks, textbooks, etc.—with them. In addition, the workshop, as outlined, should provide the following materials:

- one computer, with at least one disk drive, and monitor for each (or every two) participant(s);
- one demonstration computer with a large-screen monitor;
- sufficient copies of PILOT so that there is one for each computer being used in the workshop;
- a sufficient number of blank storage disks—some formatted prior to the workshop;
- workshop handouts—as referred to in the outline; and
- if applicable, copies of PILOT to be distributed to workshop participants for use after the workshop concludes.

Day One of PILOT Workshop

    I. Introduction
        A. Workshop objective: present background and rationale for use, introduce commands, provide hands-on experience using the basic elements of programming in PILOT
        B. Introduce participants, as necessary, to computer model being used
        C. Discuss different versions of PILOT; pros/cons of each

   II. Background on PILOT
        A. PILOT = Programmed Inquiry, Learning or Teaching

    B. Developed in 1968 by John Starkweather at University of California Medical Center at San Francisco

    C. Not an all-purpose programming language: Designed for the development of computer-assisted instruction, primarily tutorial or drill-and-practice lessons

    D. Review differences between authoring languages, authoring systems, and mini-authoring programs

III. Getting Set Up

    A. Demonstrate loading procedures (Clarify the need to "load" the authoring language in order to program. Not necessary to load the authoring language to run lessons once they have been authored.)

    B. Discuss modes (4 modes in Commodore 64 PILOT)

        1. EDIT to create or edit lessons
Simultaneously strike *RUN/STOP* and *E* (*RUN/STOP–E*)

        2. RUN to execute lessons (to make the lesson "go")
Simultaneously strike *RUN/STOP* and *R* (*RUN/STOP–R*)

        3. IMMEDIATE to execute individual program lines immediately (The program line is executed as soon as <Return> is pressed.)
Simultaneously strike *RUN/STOP* and *I* (*RUN/STOP–I*)

        4. COMMAND to load, store, and print the lesson
Strike *RUN/STOP* while in any of the other modes

    C. Practice language operation

        1. Become familiar with the screen associated with each mode and return to Command Mode from all other modes

        2. Warning: *RUN/STOP–I* can erase lesson being programmed

        3. Clear memory: Simultaneously strike *SHIFT* and *CLR/HOME*

        4. Restore default colors with F2 function key

        5. Exit from PILOT and return to machine BASIC with F8 function key

IV. PILOT Format

    A. Each program line is a command and is composed of several parts
Example: *TS(x* < *2)*:This is just a sample.

        1. *T* is the "opcode," the operation or what the computer is supposed to do. *T* tells the computer to *Type* the words.

2. *S* is the modifier, modifying the opcode. *S* tells the computer to clear the screen.
3. *(x < 2)* is a conditioner. It stipulates that the operation should only occur if the stated condition is met. *(x < 2)* tells the computer that *x* must be less than *2* for the operation to occur.
4. The colon is the separator and is a part of all PILOT program lines. It separates the instructions to the computer from the rest of the program line. Do not type a character space after the colon.

V. PILOT Commands
   A. Type = *T:*
      1. Used to display text on the screen
      2. The text following the colon must be less that 40 characters per line
      3. Multiple contiguous text lines do not require additional *T:* Commands
         Format: T:This is the first line
                  :and this is the second
                  :and this is the last line.
   B. Remark = *R:*
      1. Used for programmer/author comments embedded in the lesson—program notes, memos, etc.
      2. Remarks are not visible on-screen when the lesson is "run"; they only appear in program line listings
   C. Wait = *W:*
      1. Used to time material or keep it displayed on the screen for a predetermined amount of time
      2. Causes lesson to pause for the number of seconds specified after the W:
         Format: T:You have 30 seconds to solve the following problem.
                  :2 + 6 - 4 - 2 + 7 =
                  W:30
   D. End of program/lesson = *E:*
   E. Practice these commands, beginning in Immediate Mode (*RUN/STOP–I*), using workshop-supplied handouts

VI. Write a sample lesson
    A. Enter Edit Mode (*RUN/STOP–E*)

Example: R:This is a test lesson
               T:Hello
               T: These spaces will
               T:do interesting
               T: things.
               W:10
               T:Was that wait too long?
               E:

    B. Clear memory using *SHIFT– CLR/HOME*)
    C. Enter Run Mode (*RUN/STOP– R*)
    D. Clear memory (*SHIFT– CLR/HOME*)

VII.   Editing
    A. Discuss the concept of editing and the importance of being able to change, delete, and add text in an existing lesson
    B. Introduce the editing commands available in PILOT
    C. Distribute a printed copy of a sample lesson/program which is missing both entire program lines as well as material from included program lines. Have workshop participants keyboard the incomplete lesson/program as it appears on the handout.
    D. Distribute a printed copy of the corrected sample lesson/program. Walk the workshop participants through the process of making the necessary changes using the editing commands.

VIII.   More PILOT Commands
    A. Accept = *A:*
       1. Used to accept student input when lesson is run
       2. Does not check student response for accuracy
          Format: T:What is the opposite of up?
                   A:
                   T:Good thinking!
    B. Match = *M:*
       1. Used to check answers by allowing the teacher/programmer to identify matches
       2. Match is one of the most powerful and unique instructions in PILOT
       3. Creates a "window" and looks for an answer. Unlike BASIC, PILOT easily allows a variety of response types—sentence, phrases, one word.

Format: T:What is the opposite of up?

A:

M:down

4. To determine if the student answer matches the correct answer, use *TY:* (*Type if Yes*) and *TN:* (*Type if No*)

Format: T:What is the opposite of up?

A:

M:down

TY:Great job!

TN:The opposite of up is down.

E:

5. To indicate multiple correct responses, use & for *and* and *!* for *or*

Format: T:Which days are called the "weekend"?

A:

M:Saturday&Sunday!Sat&Sun!Sat.&Sun.

TY:Many people think Saturday and Sunday

TY:are the best days of the week.

TN:They are Saturday and Sunday.

6. To accommodate "wild card" answers, use the asterisk to stand for any letters. In this way, answers can be modified to accept variations in spelling.

Format: T:What is the capital of Connecticut?

A:

M:Hartford!H*rtf*d

C. Upper/Lower-case character answers = *PR:L* or *PR:U*

1. Used to indicate if all answers should be converted to upper or lower-case characters. Computer converts answer to all upper case (*PR:U*) or all lower case (*PR:L*) regardless of what case the student keyboards, so that matches can be determined without regard to case.

2. Be sure that the *PR:* designation and case in the Match Command are the same

3. Use the *PR:* Command as a separate instruction at the beginning of the lesson/program

D. Jump (Branching) = *JY:* and *JN:*

1. Used to branch to other lesson segments based on the student's responses. *JY:* indicates *Jump if Yes* and *JN:* indicates *Jump if No.*

2. Facilitates the development of tutorial lessons using PILOT

Format: JN:@A (to jump to last Accept on an incorrect
answer)
JY:@M (to jump to the next Match on a correct
response)
JY:@P (to jump to the next problem statement on
a correct response)
J:Label (to jump to a section with a specific label)
3. Use a sample lesson to demonstrate the Jump Command
E. Variables = *N*
1. Review the Accept Command (It accepts the student's input
but does not store that input.)
2. Variables are used to store information for later re-use,
i.e. the student's name, specific responses, etc. Can use
any letter designation: N, S, D, etc.
Format: T:What is your name?
A:N
T:Well, N, it's great to meet you.
3. Dimensions are assigned to variables to identify the
maximum number of characters the variable can store

IX. Hands-on practice
A. Distribute sample lessons in either written or disk form. Review
program lines. Note structure and use of PILOT commands.
B. Suggest lesson modifications for participants
C. Practice using the sample lessons. Practice making modifications
to the sample lessons.

Day Two of PILOT Workshop

I. Review previous day's material, particularly commands,
and answer questions

II. Mechanics
A. *Format* blank disks to be used to store authored lessons
B. Practice "loading" PILOT language
C. Practice "saving" and "loading" lessons

III. Additional commands
A. *%B* represents a special answer buffer variable, which has a
preassigned dimension of 89 character spaces
B. *C:variable = expression* represents a computation variable

1. This variable can represent a constant, a variable, or a mathematical expression
2. Acceptable math functions include: +, -, *, /,()
   Format: C:N=2 (constant)
   C:N=A (variable)
   C:N=2 + A (expression)

IV. Graphics and Color = *G:field*
   A. The Commodore screen has 320 x 200 pixels. PILOT uses 192 rows of 319 dots. Use X and Y coordinates to specify location. Point X = 0, Y = 0 is located in lower left corner.
   Formats: *G:E* = erases the full screen
   G:PX,Y = point, draws a point at X,Y location
   G:Q = unpoint, erases a point
   G:R = remove, erases a line
   Semicolon = allows multiple graphics commands to occupy one line. (*G:E;P1,1*)
   B. Using graph paper to "map" screen graphics simplifies the pre-computer design of complex graphics
   C. Color
   Formats: *G:X3* = sets exterior border
   G:B2 = sets background color
   G:C4 = sets foreground color

V. Subroutines = *U:Name* (where Name is name of subroutine)
   A. Subroutines are sub-programs within the larger program used for organization and clarity
   B. Useful to repeat sections of lessons—record-keeping, feedback routines, etc.
   C. All subroutines must end with the End Command (*E:*)
   D. Demonstrate jumps to subroutines (and automatic return to larger program at point of original departure)

VI. Special PILOT Features
   A. Programmable characters
   B. Sprites
   C. Sound
   D. Record keeping

VII. Demonstrate newly-introduced commands
   A. Distribute sample lessons, written and disk, and discuss program lines.

  B. Discuss lesson modifications
  C. Hands-on: Have participants make lesson modifications
      (workshop leader circulates to assist in programming process)
  D. Discuss other lessons participants might work on. Provide
      feedback on appropriateness of lesson ideas re: features
      of PILOT, programming skills of participants, etc.

VIII.   Conclusion
  A. General question-and-answer period
  B. Discuss options for follow-up training
  C. Distribute additional "take home" materials, if any
  D. Discuss other resources: coaches, software libraries,
      user's groups, etc.

As the sample outlines of these two workshops indicate, a guided, hands-on approach is a useful method for introducing new skills. However, since the purpose of a workshop is to meet the needs of the participants, the workshop leader and training coordinator should survey the participants to determine their priorities.

Follow-Up Training

"Training" should not refer simply to a session or two of instruction and practice. This is particularly true when dealing with the more complex authoring products (authoring systems and authoring languages). In these cases, training should extend beyond initial sessions. At the least, some workshops might be expanded to a third day which concentrates on programming activities. If teachers/authors are to use authoring products successfully, they must function in a supportive environment. The major forms of this support are discussed below.

Administrative Support

After the initial training sessions, teachers need some time to digest the new material and experiment on their own. Administrators can help by making available the copies of authoring products, computer equipment, and practice time. Practice time is probably the most crucial issue since developing a new technical skill requires uninterrupted time periods. Ideally, teachers/authors should have 2–3 periods (45–60 minutes long) per week during the first 2–3 weeks, post introduction, in which to practice applying the new skills being learned. It may be necessary to arrange for schedule changes, teacher aides, or substitutes to ensure that trainees have sufficient practice time. Some schools allow faculty to use professional leave time to develop their skills. Clearly, school administrators must recognize the long-term benefits which follow these short-term schedule changes.

Coaching

Another aspect of continued training is access to a "coach." The coach can be the original workshop leader or another individual who is knowledgeable about the authoring product and has experience in the classroom. The coach is a resource, working with the teacher/author during release time to develop lessons using the authoring product.

A coach can also be a demonstrator, linking the workshops with practical applications. In this role, a coach actually comes to the classroom while classes are in progress and demonstrates the use of the authoring product with the students. The authored lesson can be demonstrated to the class as a whole, to small groups, or to individual students. In this situation, teachers/authors have the opportunity to observe and ask questions. Concerns regarding the use of the authoring product and other issues such as student management are more specifically and easily handled in this environment.

Some schools have expanded the coaching model to include later visits by a coach during lessons conducted by the teacher/author using the authoring product. A coach can then supply suggestions and answer any questions the teacher/author might have after using the authoring lesson in the classroom. This type of model can be extremely effective in assisting educators to gain new skills, develop confidence in using those skills, and, finally, in implementing the use of those new skills in the classroom.

The coaching model underlines the need for teachers/authors to have access to a support person or structure which encourages continued use of the authoring product and also helps teachers/authors solve problems before those problems cause them to abandon the use of authoring products as useless or too demanding upon time and energy. In conjunction with, or instead of, classroom visits, it is valuable to have a coach on-call.

Communication

An additional step should be included in the follow-up training model to increase the effectiveness of the use of authoring products. Learning from others in a similar situation is an effective teaching device. After training and some follow-up sessions with a coach or individual practice, it is helpful for the teachers/authors to be able to share their lessons with each other. In sharing sessions and experiences, teachers learn new ideas, exchange authored lessons, and evaluate authored lessons and authoring products. (See Chapter 9.) These sharing sessions are often structured as users' groups, formal or informal.

Duration of Training

The length of time needed to implement the various aspects of a training plan differs based on the commitment of the school administrators, the experience of the staff, and the complexity of the authoring product being learned. The more training and practice time made available, the faster educators will become comfortable using the authoring product. The less complex software, such as mini-authoring programs, requires shorter training periods and less follow-up time. Many educators are comfortable and knowledgeable enough after a demonstration and two hours of hands-on practice to begin constructing their own computer-based lessons using this type of authoring product.

Authoring systems are more complex and require more training. Follow-up needs also tend to be more extensive. Additional release time to develop lessons is advised. However, as with other authoring products, the time required to construct lessons using authoring systems decreases as experience increases.

Of course, using an authoring language, such as PILOT, requires the most training and follow-up time. Programming, even using an authoring language developed for instruction, is more difficult than using preprogrammed software. The trade-off is one of greater control and flexibility for a commitment of more learning time and effort.

Summary

Training, then, does not end with a workshop. Rather, it is important that follow-up be provided in terms of time, equipment, and support personnel. Information sharing also serves an important purpose.

For the use of authoring products to be successful and effective in education and to expand on the role of the computer as an instructional tool, it is critical that school systems provide support for educators. This support should include training workshops, available software and computers, accessible information resources, flexible time allowances, and encouragement. If more than the individually motivated educator is going to explore this alternative to commercially available software, school administrators must communicate their philosophical support and remove the practical roadblocks from teachers' paths.

8

Enhancements and Special Features

The preceding Chapters describe the general attributes of the three stages of authoring: mini-authoring, authoring systems, and authoring languages. Each stage or category is characterized by features and capabilities particular to that type of package. In addition, there are special characteristics contained in many authoring products which provide the educator with more presentation and response flexibility. One of the major advantages to the use of authoring products with students, particularly special needs students, centers around these special characteristics.

Included among these enhancements are such things as special graphics capabilities, variable print sizes and types, modified input and output devices, and even the integration of advanced video-disk technology. This Chapter discusses many of these special features and enhancements, and illustrates their application to lesson development. The Chapter closes with a scenario which demonstrates the type of educational situation which could soon exist, given the combination of authoring products and continuing technological advances.

Graphics and Character Sets

One of the most useful features now available with many authoring systems and authoring language packages is the capability to vary the size of the printed text. Apple SuperPILOT (from Apple Computer, Inc.), for example, uses simple commands to set parameters for the height, width, thickness, color, and spacing of characters. This means that the teacher/author can tailor the written portions of the lesson to meet both the physical and educational needs of particular students. A few examples demonstrate the wide range of potential uses of these features of graphics and character sets.

Large type is useful with young children and visually impaired students. Text in some authoring products can be enlarged several times so that each letter or character is as tall as an inch or more. For the visually impaired, larger type can make the difference between being able to read independently or requiring that information be read aloud by the teacher or another student. The ability to alter text size enables the teacher/author to produce customized software to meet the needs of a wide range of potential users.

Other text variations (color, spacing, width, or thickness) allow the teacher/author to change the degree of emphasis on a word or phrase within the text. Color, width, etc. can be used to highlight words of particular importance as well as words that the student needs to recall. For example, students with reading disabilities often become bewildered by pages of text and have difficulty finding the appropriate information. Teachers can use these character set options to help these students locate material. When learning to read paragraphs, many special needs students have difficulty identifying "the main idea." If the topic sentence in each paragraph is visually differentiated by print of a different size or color, the student's attention can be more easily directed to these important sections.

These text variations can also be used to highlight parts of speech or sounds. Hearing-impaired individuals often have difficulty understanding poetry or the cadence in prose because they cannot physically experience the sounds. Authoring products make it possible to visually communicate the rhythm or rhyme in speeches or poetry so that hearing-impaired students can "see" the flow of language. For example, though the words *whey* and *way* rhyme, they are not spelled the same. It is difficult, if not impossible, for a hearing-impaired child to appreciate the music in many nursery rhymes by just seeing the printed text. Using an authoring product, a teacher can color code the words or parts of words which rhyme. In the above example, the *ey* and *ay* could be printed in the same color, but in a different color than that used for the other letters. This type of highlighting can assist students in developing some language skills.

The use of highlighting also provides a type of cuing which can help learning disabled students. Many computer-based color-coded reading lessons use color cues to focus a student's attention on such things as letter-sound correspondences. Highlighting can also be used to assist students who approach reading tasks from left to right. In a similar fashion, math problems can be presented so that correct positioning and sequencing are evident. For example, addition problems requiring regrouping can use green numbers for the right-most column and red for the left-most column, cuing students to "start" on green and "stop" on red. When these special features are coupled with the ability to construct computer-based lessons which are tailored for individual needs, the results are dynamic.

Another example of the use of enhanced visual displays exists in the authoring system *BLOCKS '82* (from California School for the Deaf). A large library of prerecorded graphics is available with this package. Subjects include such diverse areas as maps, time, buildings, and transportation. *BLOCKS '82* was designed for use with deaf populations, and the emphasis on visuals is particularly appropriate for these students. The ease with which pictures can be incorporated into the text allows teachers and language pathologists to create many useful lessons designed to meet specific student needs. Other features include the ability to "draw" pictures on the screen using a graphics tablet, game paddles, and joysticks. A graphics tablet allows the teacher/author to draw in a more natural fashion, while the game adapters turn the screen into an Etch-a-Sketch pad. Again, these extra capabilities make it possible for the teacher/author to construct customized lessons for individual students using the interactive capabilities of the computer within the tutorial framework of an authoring product.

One other graphics feature that is useful with special needs students is the use of the LOGO-like commands which some versions of PILOT contain. This feature is valuable for both teachers and students who are using authoring products to construct lessons. For student authors, this added feature of drawing is particularly motivating. In addition, the special characteristics of learning to draw with LOGO-like commands are beneficial for many students who have difficulty working from left to right and, correspondingly, are not comfortable reading English texts.

Modified Input Devices

Another enhancement built into many authoring languages, including most versions of PILOT, as well as many authoring systems is the ability to use a variety of input devices. By adapting to the student's needs, the computer becomes an instructional tool which literally opens new worlds for many, including the physically impaired. To be able to couple customized lessons with individualized input is especially exciting for teachers working with non-verbal students who have limited motor skills. More and more adaptation devices are becoming available. Some of the more common devices which can be attached to the computer include light pens, game paddles, joysticks, voice devices, or simple on/off switches. These devices can actually replace the keyboard.

Other authoring products include a simplified response framework. *Special Needs Volume I - Spelling* (from Minnesota Educational Computing Consortium) is an example of one such product. Designed to teach beginning spelling to students who are motor impaired or have poor coordination, this product contains 20 preprogrammed multiple-choice exercises which can be used as is, with no authoring activity on the part of the teacher. In addition, the teacher/author has the option of modifying lesson content to meet student needs. The lesson's answers (preprogrammed or authored) are displayed in a multiple-choice format. A box "scans" across the answers at a rate determined by the teacher/author. When the desired answer is within the box, the student responds by using game paddles or pressing any key on the keyboard.

Another type of input modification with much potential is the speech recognition device. The *Voice Based Learning System* or *VBLS* (from Scott Instruments Corporation) is an example of this type of input adaptation. A physically disabled person is able to use lessons constructed with this authoring product by simply speaking the lesson's answers into a microphone. Simplified, the sound waves (analog signals) are converted into digital signals and recorded within the program. These recorded student responses are then compared with earlier recorded teacher/author responses. In this manner, *VBLS* can interpret specific words spoken by the students.

During the authoring of a *VBLS* lesson, the teacher/author completes a verbal script with the computer to provide a basis upon which the computer can interpret the sound of student voices. The teacher can author lessons with his or her own voice or with other voices. If the students and teacher/author are in the same voice category (children, females, males, mixture of females and males, or special needs), the teacher can complete the verbal script with only his or her own voice. If the teacher and students are in different voice categories, the teacher/author must include other voices in the verbal script. Although the scheduling of multiple voices can be difficult, the preparation of the verbal script itself is straightforward. *VBLS* guides the teacher/author and accompanying voices through the authoring process with clear on-screen instructions.

Speech recognition devices like *VBLS* allow individuals with no movement capabilities to learn and practice skills on a computer, thereby greatly increasing the user's autonomy and independence. Currently, these products require significant periods of time to "train" the computer to understand and accept certain words. As the technology develops further, the potential of speech recognition in computer-based lessons will be realized and the performance of verbal input systems will become more reliable.

Voice and Speech Synthesis

The use of speech and sound with computer-assisted instruction has incredible implications for the education of special needs students. Students for whom English is a second (and unreliable) language, those students who do not have a useful voice, and those students needing individualized instruction in spelling skills and the language arts can greatly benefit from lessons which speak clearly and accurately. Several speech synthesizers are currently on the market, and many can be accessed from specific authoring systems or versions of the authoring language PILOT.

Although quality is improving and prices have decreased, the use of speech synthesis with authoring products is limited mostly to products designed for the blind/visually impaired and individuals without speech. Voice output is often the most useful, and sometimes only, means of computer interaction for these students. When both speech production and speech recognition are fine-tuned, the results of using these devices with authoring products to meet the needs of disabled individuals will be enormous. These output devices allow the physically disabled student without a usable voice to participate in regular classes when equipped with a computerized voice. The computer can become a prosthesis as common as the hearing aid has become for the hearing impaired.

Using Taped Speech for Authoring

Although speech synthesis has great potential, there are still major drawbacks. Fine tuning the sounds to be as "natural" as possible is a time-consuming task and requires some programming skill. Even the commitment of time and skill is not enough to overcome the drawbacks: The quality of speech is often difficult to understand and is not currently accurate enough for many speech and language uses. What is needed is speech as clear as that in taped recordings.

At present, an affordable hardware device does exist which allows educators to incorporate tape - recorded speech into customized lessons. Developed and marketed by Hartley Courseware, Inc., and named the Cassette Control Device (CCD), this adapter allows sound to be synchronized with material presented on the computer screen.

The CCD, a small 5 x 2" box, plugs into the game-paddle port on an Apple computer and the remote jack on any standard tape recorder/player. (A specially adapted CCD can be ordered for Apple IIc computers.) An experienced programmer can use the CCD in original programs. For the inexperienced programmer, using the Hartley Courseware authoring software is probably the most practical approach. Hartley Courseware has developed several programs which use the CCD: *Create - Vocabulary, Create CCD Lessons,* and *Create - Spell It.* Another of these programs, *Create Fill-in-the-Blanks,* illustrates the use of the CCD.

Before *Create Fill-in-the-Blanks* can be used by students, the teacher/author must add the lesson content. There are two steps to authoring lessons using the CCD:

1. The teacher/author must create a word list. This word list is where the textual on-screen information is placed.
2. The teacher/author must then create a tape to be used with the word list.

The process for both of these steps is clearly explained in the on-screen directions and accompanying written documentation.

Create Fill-in-the-Blanks

After accessing the Teacher's Main Menu, the following screen appears:

> *** MENU ***
>
> 1 - RUN LESSONS
> 2 - CREATE WORD LIST
> 3 - CORRECT/CHANGE WORD LIST
> 4 - MAKE TAPE
> 5 - STUDENT PLANNING
> 6 - DELETE A LESSON
> 7 - SEE A CATALOG
>
> ENTER SELECTION
> AND PRESS RETURN

To begin creating a lesson, select Option # 2 (Create Word List). After typing in a name for the list, the next screen appears. The name of the word list just assigned by the teacher/author appears on the first line.

> CREATE WORD LIST (NAME OF LIST APPEARS HERE)
>
> TYPE '#' TO QUIT AND SAVE LIST
> TYPE '@' FOR ''
>
> STIM:
> RESP:
>
> FRAME # 1

At this point, the teacher/author enters the information as it should appear to the student on the screen. For example, a teacher/author types *BOB IS A* after the word *STIM* (*stimulus*). The prompt then moves to the next line, where the teacher/author types the correct answer or *RESP* (*response*), in this case *BOY.* After ' Return' is pressed, the space after the stimulus and response prompts are cleared; and Frame # 2 appears. Approximately 20-30 different stimulus and response pairs can be entered for each word list. Larger sets should be avoided because they can disrupt

the synchrony between the tape recording and computer screen. When #is
typed, the screen prompts the user with

SAVE THIS LIST (Y/N)

After saving the list on a disk by typing *Y*, the next task is to prepare
the corresponding tape recording. Short ten-minute cassette tapes are most
useful for this type of authoring so that only one lesson is recorded on each
side. This arrangement avoids confusion when students use the lesson as
well as helps to ensure the proper synchrony between the tape recording
and the computer screen.

The computer guides the teacher/author through the steps of preparing
the tape by providing on-screen prompts. After selecting Option # 4 for
making a tape from the Teacher's Main Menu, the teacher/author is asked
to enter the list name which to be used with the tape. The following screen
then appears:

LIST NAME: (NAME OF LIST APPEARS HERE)
NUMBER OF WORDS: (NUMBER OF WORDS APPEARS HERE)

INSERT THE CASSETTE
PRESS THE REWIND BUTTON
AND PRESS 'RETURN' WHEN IT HAS FINISHED REWINDING.

The computer screen continues to provide prompts for setting up the
tape recorder. When the teacher/author is ready to make the tape recording, the computer screen informs the teacher/author that there will be
approximately eight seconds available for each recorded stimulus statement. To begin, the teacher/author presses 'Return'. The computer screen
displays a series of asterisks, marking the time. The time points to begin
and end speaking are clearly identified, and the teacher/author can use
part or all of the time allotted. In the example presented above, the
teacher could record the sentence: *Bob is a boy. Spell boy.* After making a
recording for each stimulus, the teacher/author is given the choice of working on another word list or returning to the Teacher's Main Menu.

When a student works on a lesson which employs the CCD, the computer displays precise on-screen instructions for using the tape recorder.
[For some students, it is necessary for the teacher to perform the preliminary set-up.] When using the lesson, the student looks at the screen and

listens to the synchronized tape recording. The student responds using the computer keyboard.

As this brief example demonstrates, using the CCD is a relatively simple way to include clear speech in a customized drill-and-practice lesson. The added dimension of speech expands the student population which can benefit from the lesson and more fully employs the computer as an instructional tool.

Interactive Video Disks

The possibilities of using various enhancements with authoring products are unlimited. One of the most exciting recent innovations in educational technology is interactive video-disks. Some authoring systems and versions of PILOT allow the author to access video-disks for lesson development. Imagine the possibilities only hinted at in the following brief scene.

A moderately mentally retarded class of adolescents is working on a restaurant skills unit. Several of the students would be able to work in the rehabilitation center restaurant if they were able to demonstrate the ability to correctly set tables. Their teacher has designed a practice-and-test lesson using an authoring language on a computer system hooked to a camera and a video-disk. On a table in full view of the camera are several sets of utensils and plates. The practice lesson begins.

"Hello, John," says the computer, "I'm glad to see you back. What will you do today?"

John responds verbally, "I want to practice setting the table."

The computer's voice-recognition system cues on the words *practice, set,* and *table,* and retrieves the necessary lesson. Now the computer's voice directs John to set the table for two.

When John is done, he presses the Start Button on the camera. The camera takes a photo of the table setting, sending the information for analysis to the computer. John has made just one error.

"Good work, John." John smiles at the computer-spoken praise. "There's just one little thing we should probably go over. Look at the screen while I tell you about it. On the screen are two place settings. The one on the left with the green background is correct. The one on the right with the orange background is the one you did. Do you see the difference?"

John looks closely. After a few minutes he responds, "Oh, I put the spoon on the wrong side of the knife. I'll go fix it." John returns to the table, rearranges the place settings and presses the Start Button on the camera again. This time, the computer praises John for setting the table correctly, and the lesson continues.

Summary

This Chapter's examples of enhancements and special features for use with computerized authoring products only hint at the potential for the future. Technological advances should provide creative and interactive capabilities beyond our imagination. One thing is clear: The direction for the future will continue to make the computer more accessible and better suited to the needs of users with a range of educational needs, regardless of their physical limitations.

9

Lesson Development and Evaluation

This Chapter provides the reader with both guidelines for developing computer-based lessons and various criteria for judging the relative merits of computer software. For some teachers, it is more appropriate to use the services of an experienced programmer to do the actual authoring of lessons. This is particularly true for authoring languages. A final section of this Chapter makes recommendations about communicating with programmers.

Teachers should always evaluate the educational validity and effectiveness of material for the intended student population. The need to carefully evaluate computer software is compounded by the relative scarcity of microcomputers within the classroom. To ensure that the computer is used to maximum effectiveness, the teacher must critically examine the software being used on the computer.

When that software is an authoring product, the teacher/author has the added responsibility of making sure that teacher-designed software adheres to good teaching and learning practices. The teacher who is planning on creating educational material using authoring products needs to follow guidelines for good lesson development.

The way to approach development and evaluation is determined by the type of authoring product. As discussed in Chapter 4, mini-authoring programs provide little leeway for instructor-initiated changes and modifications. Mini-authoring programs should be evaluated using general software evaluation standards (see Chapter 9 and Appendix 2 of Budoff, Thormann, & Gras, 1985). Authoring systems, though more flexible than mini-authoring programs, still have a level of predetermined structure and require another format for evaluating effectiveness. Authoring languages require the most specialized design and evaluation procedures to ensure the appropriate use of the computer as an instructional tool.

Evaluating Mini-Authoring Programs

Just as commercially available drill-and-practice or tutorial software packages differ in quality, so does software designed for mini-authoring. As more mini-authoring programs become available, special educators need to be aware of general software evaluation and selection guidelines. Poorly designed mini-authoring programs are no more helpful than poorly designed preprogrammed software, except that the teacher/author determines the lesson content.

Unlike authoring systems and authoring languages, mini-authoring programs allow the educator little flexibility in lesson format. By definition, the teacher/author plugs his or her lesson content into the mini-authoring program's framework. For this reason, it is usually most effective to evaluate a mini-authoring program using standard software evaluation criteria. It is wise to evaluate the software before using it for authoring, and, ideally, before purchasing it. Several commercially available software evaluation forms exist, and many school systems are developing their own. In general, these forms rate general information, documentation, educational content and quality, and technical and presentation characteristics. Each rated category contains several important evaluation criteria.

General Information

Briefly, within the general information category, educators should consider the following eight points:

1. Learning theory and educational procedures.
2. Required hardware and peripherals.
3. Stated goals and objectives.

4. Publisher statements regarding applicability to special populations.
5. Policies regarding preview, backup disks, and guarantees.
6. Recommended type of use: drill and practice, drill and practice after traditional classroom lesson, integral part of lesson, focus of lesson, motivation/reward.
7. Teacher prerequisite skills for authoring.
8. Student prerequisite skills for use.

Documentation

Within the area of documentation (written or on-screen), educators should look for the following points:

1. Type of documentation—for teacher, for student; written or on-screen.
2. A clear explanation of operation.
3. Directions for using any special authoring characteristics and any management and record-keeping features.
4. Suggestions for curriculum inclusion and classroom use.
5. An explanation of any preprogrammed data sets (those requiring no authoring).
6. An explanation of any student or teacher supplementary materials enclosed with the software.

Educational Content and Quality

In terms of educational content and quality, evaluation forms should include the following points:

1. Use of grammar and syntax.
2. Spelling.
3. Reinforcement and feedback.
4. Motivational aspects, including graphics.
5. Program sequence.
6. Average amount of time required to author a lesson.
7. Average amount of time required for a student to complete a lesson.

Technical and Presentation Characteristics

Technical and presentation aspects should be evaluated in the following areas:

1. Ease of use. Completeness of management and record-keeping features.
2. Program reliability during normal use.
3. Clarity of screen display.
4. Appropriate use of graphics, color, animation, and sound.
5. Learner control of pace and sequence.
6. On-screen assistance and/or easy menu access.

Additional Considerations

Each of these points should be included when evaluating a mini-authoring program. They comprise the bare framework of an evaluating system. Each evaluator should add additional points and make other modifications, thereby continually improving the form.

It is also helpful to approach software evaluation from the standpoint of the skill level required. By analyzing the minimum competencies required of anyone using the authored lesson, it should be possible to determine the appropriateness of the authoring software for developing lessons to be used by a given student or student population. Areas such as reading level, keyboarding skills, and visual and auditory acuity can all be analyzed while evaluating mini-authoring programs. If the target population is able to perform the minimum skills required, then the authoring product would be appropriate from that standpoint.

The wide variety of handicapping conditions makes it difficult for any one piece of software to be appropriate for all special needs students. Special educators will also want to include criteria particular to the area of special education. Among the additional topics which special educators should consider are modification possibilities and skill level requirements. The special educator needs to keep in mind the particular characteristics of his or her students and ask a range of other questions, including the following:

1. Is the reading level appropriate, or can it be changed?
2. Can the mini-authoring program be modified to use speech synthesis?

3. Can the teacher/author or student adjust the rate of presentation, rate of response, and other aspects of timing?
4. Can the teacher/author or student modify the graphics, use of sound, and the print size?
5. Can modified input devices (light pens, graphics pads, game paddles) be used instead of the keyboard?

Evaluating Authoring Systems

Authoring systems allow the teacher/author more flexibility and control of lesson format. Whereas it is sufficient to evaluate mini-authoring programs, without lesson content, authoring systems place more demands upon the evaluator. It is not sufficient to evaluate just the authoring system: The lessons constructed using that system must be evaluated because so much of the lesson development depends upon the teacher/author.

It is best to begin by evaluating the lessons produced with an authoring system by using criteria similar to those listed for evaluating mini-authoring programs. However, because much of the lesson development depends upon the teacher/author, it is important that additional aspects be considered.

When selecting an authoring system, the educator should first delineate the needs of the students. The individual educational plans of special needs students often indicate characteristics which the teacher/author should require in an authoring system. For example, if students have visual acuity deficits, the authoring system should have alternate character sets or other provisions which allow the teacher/author to use large-size print or color cues. Branching capabilities are also extremely important with special needs students. Knowing that the authoring system includes these special features is insufficient: The teacher/author should also determine how easy it is to use these special features.

The educator should research several different authoring systems, list the types of features available on each system, determine which features are most important for the target student population, and make a selection based on these factors. Comparing the features among authoring systems will help make the educator aware of their differing capabilities and limitations. In addition, evaluating the software will assist the teacher/author in determining the educational quality of a given authoring system.

Due to his or her increased involvement using authoring systems, the teacher/author becomes more responsible for establishing and maintaining the quality of the lessons. It is important for the teacher/author to use all available features appropriately, including reinforcement, screen displays, and branching techniques. The educator should take into account the learning styles and learning needs of the intended students, and make sure that the lesson meets those needs as closely as possible within the framework of the authoring system. For example, learning theory regarding reinforcement schedules and feedback should be considered when developing the lesson. Response modes should be geared for individual student needs. The rate of presentation and the amount of information presented on a screen should be in keeping with the student's learning capabilites. If the student learns best through a multi-sensory approach, and the authoring system contains these capabilities, the teacher/author needs to use this approach in the lessons.

As authoring systems share some evaluation criteria with mini-authoring programs, so too they overlap authoring language considerations. Points of good lesson design, usually associated with evaluating authoring languages, should be considered. The teacher/author has significant impact upon the structure of the lesson constructed using an authoring system, being responsible for a significant portion of the lesson design as well as the total lesson content. Points of good lesson design are the backbone of the evaluation criteria for authoring languages.

Developing and Evaluating Lessons Written Using Authoring Languages

Of all types of authoring products, authoring languages offer an educator the greatest flexibility. This flexibility demands more detailed development procedures on the part of the author. Before using an authoring language, an educator should become familiar with its features. These special characteristics must be kept in mind throughout the lesson-writing process to insure that the computer's capabilities are fully utilized.

Lesson development is a time-consuming and demanding process, even when the teacher/author is familiar with the authoring product. It is not unusual that 90% of lesson preparation takes place before the teacher/author moves to the computer keyboard. These pre-computer planning stages determine the quality of the resulting lesson. The following steps comprise the lesson writing process.

1. Identify the student population.
2. Identify the problem area, goals, and objectives.
3. Determine the instructional preparation.
4. Determine the content and prepare a general outline.
5. Fill in the outline details and assign labels.
6. Develop the lesson flowchart.
7. Design the lesson segments and screen displays.
8. Test and debug the lesson.
9. Prepare the documentation and support materials.
10. Consult with other teachers and programmers.

Identify the Student Population

The teacher/author using an authoring language, such as PILOT, needs first to identify and analyze the needs of the student population. The teacher/author needs to ask questions:

- For which students will the lesson be geared?
- What are the special learning needs and characteristics of those students?
- Do the students have any particular handicapping conditions which would interfere with computer use?
- What are the academic skills, such as the reading level, of the target population?

Identify the Problem Area, Goals, and Objectives

The formal process of developing the lesson begins with an analysis of the objectives of the lesson, usually a tutorial, and the identification of the specific area in which the student is having difficulty. The formal goals of the computer lesson should be determined since goals provide a reference point for the teacher/author when deciding what material and information to include. Specific objectives expressed in behavioral terms need to be identified to define the shape of the lesson. This process forms the outline of the scope and sequence of the lesson being developed. In developing the lesson's objectives, the teacher/author should keep in mind the capabilities of the computer and the special features of the authoring language as well as the student's instructional needs.

Determine the Instructional Preparation

Preparation here refers to the prior preparation of both the student and the teacher. For the teacher, it is necessary to determine what additional types of instructional materials should be used prior to the computer-based lesson. For example, some lessons might benefit from ditto worksheets prepared by the teacher. Others might require pictures which are referred to within the computer-based lesson. The entry level skills of the student, and the information required for the student to use the lessons, must be considered. The teacher/author needs to determine what prior preparation, both lessons and orientation, are necessary for the lessons to be beneficial to the students. The teacher's preparation consists of providing these materials to the students.

It is meaningful to view this preparation step in the context of the computer and authoring language as instructional tools used within an instructional scenario to achieve a curriculum goal. In order to integrate the computer-based lesson into the curriculum, a teacher should begin with an instructional scenario. The computer is just one instructional tool used within that scenario. At other stages within the scenario, other instructional tools are used to teach, drill and practice, test, etc. For instance, class discussion and reading might be used to teach material. The computer might be used to drill and practice the material. Teacher-prepared dittos might be used to test the material. In this way, the computer-based lesson becomes one stage in the instructional scenario. The teacher and student preparation refers to all steps in the instructional scenario which precede and even follow the computer-based lesson.

Determine the Content and Prepare the General Outline

The general outline of the lesson content should be defined. This initial outline is still broad in scope with only major areas noted. It is used to prompt any research necessary to verify content. At this stage the outline also serves as a set of signposts indicating the sequence of the lesson content.

Fill in the Outline Details and Assign Labels

Once a general outline has been established, the full outline of the lesson can be developed. During this stage, specific lesson content is identified.

Labeling parts of the outline is useful. Labeling consists of giving each section of the outline a short name which indicates the purpose or content of that section. These labels will be used later when writing the lesson to help the flow and branching. It is convenient to limit the labels to six letters, since most authoring languages limit labels to six characters. At this stage, many teachers/authors begin noting the types of presentation, activities, reinforcement schedules, and management aspects they intend to use. These notes often include specific ideas or approaches which the teacher/author wants to keep in mind while developing the lesson further. Keeping a memo pad handy and noting these ideas as they occur adds to the quality of the finished lesson.

Develop the Lesson Flowchart

A flowchart is a detailed pictorial and word description of how the lesson will "work." A flowchart serves as the actual structure of the lesson and contains the sections of the outline as well as any instructional or response-handling features. For instance, flowcharts illustrate branching by actually tracking the path the student will take in the lesson. The teacher/author uses the flowchart as a lesson "walk-through," watching for any errors in logic or "flow."

Design the Lesson Segments and Screen Displays

At this point, the teacher/author begins to design the screen displays: The outline is translated into the actual visual text. Because the screen is smaller than a typical worksheet page, the teacher/author should take care in determining the screen layout. Using graph paper usually facilitates this process. By following the outline and flowchart, reinforcement pages and branching sections can be developed in context with the rest of the material.

In general, there are four major lesson segments to consider:

- the initial material such as the instructions and lesson introduction,
- the main body of the lesson or teaching segment,
- the sections which will be re-used throughout the lesson, such as rewards and timing procedures, and
- record-keeping and student-response management.

The record-keeping and student-response management segment is of particular importance for teachers who wish to monitor the actual responses given by students. It is also closely related to the development of the teaching segment since it provides feedback as to whether the segment is too difficult or too easy.

The special effects are also designed and included at this stage. These effects include special character sets, graphics, animation, sound, and color. It is important to be aware of the impact these features have on the students who use the lesson. Some students find special effects distracting, while others are motivated and captivated by them. The use of various character sets can also enhance the ability of some students to use the lesson. For example, the use of large-size print for the visually impaired can make the difference between accessible and inaccessible lessons. Special highlighting can also draw attention to important information which students might otherwise overlook. Graphics can be used to represent a concept or idea which might be difficult to grasp through the written word alone.

Test and Debug the Lesson

After the lesson has been authored, the teacher should carefully *debug* it — inspect it for any design or programming flaws. The content should be factual and accurate, and the presentation clear. Continuity and "flow" should be analyzed. The teacher/author should "walk-through" the sequence several times, choosing alternative answers which lead to different branching procedures. Attempting to anticipate the students' potential responses and incorrect usage assists in pinpointing lesson weaknesses. Having another teacher or a student use the lesson during this testing and debugging stage is also useful. Revision can take place at this point and again after class use, until the final lesson accomplishes the desired task.

The teacher/author should finish his or her lesson development by using a software evaluation form to analyze the various features of the lesson. A form similar to that used for evaluating mini-authoring programs is a good place to begin. If the lesson passes that test, chances are it has been designed and written well.

Prepare the Documentation and Support Materials

Finally, the teacher/author should develop documentation and support materials to accompany the lesson. The level of documentation depends on how the lesson will be used. If the lesson will be used by other teachers or is designed for district use, the documentation should include the lesson's

- prerequisites,
- goals and objectives,
- features, and
- directions for use.

Management and modification procedures are of particular importance—they allow other educators to change the lesson to meet their students' needs. This is particularly important for teachers dealing with special needs students. The documentation should indicate the range of possible adaptations and the instructions for accomplishing them. The description of these features should be detailed enough for other teachers to use without having to contact the author. This type of documentation converts the finished lesson into a mini-authoring shell.

Even if the material is not intended for distribution to others, the teacher/author will find this documentation helpful for his or her own future reference. Time lapses often obscure original thoughts, procedures, and processes. In addition, clear documentation lets the teacher/author use segments of the one lesson in future lessons.

Other support materials might include non-computer worksheets, tests, reinforcement aids, etc.

Consult with Other Teachers and Programmers

At times, the teacher/author will find that consultation with other teachers or programmers helps refine and finalize the lesson. Field testing with populations other than the original classroom or group of students can provide more information regarding the lesson's effectiveness. The teacher/author also needs to determine whether the lesson will be available for distribution. If this is the case, methods of distribution need to be considered. User groups and computer clubs for education, as well as resource centers and libraries, are all possibilities for field testing a lesson as well as possible markets for its distribution. Although time-consuming, sharing lessons and lesson development processes can assist teachers/authors in producing quality software which achieves its intended purpose and meets individual student needs.

Developing Lessons with Programmers

Sometimes, educators do not have the resources of time, training, or expertise to develop original computer-based lessons. In some school systems, professional programmers are hired to work with classroom teachers to develop computer-based instructional lessons for specific student populations. In these cases, the programmer often has little or no educational background, and is not familiar with learning theory or various aspects of instructional design.

When this situation arises, the educator can be of great assistance to the programmer. Many of the steps discussed in the preceding section can help maximize the usefulness of the programmer's lessons. There are additional steps the educator can follow to assure that the final lesson is useful, usable, and appropriate for the student population.

Using the guidelines discussed above, the educator should develop a series of storyboards for the programmer. Storyboards are complete renditions of each sequence of computer screens. Based on objectives determined by the teacher, the precise physical layout of each screen should be specified. The teacher should note where such features as branching would take place and how those screens should appear. In essence, the teacher is authoring the lesson, but only from the standpoint of the *flowchart*. The programmer is responsible for writing the code to make the computer perform in the desired fashion. The teacher needs to be very clear and precise regarding how each screen should look as well as articulate the flow of the material. The programmer should also be told if management features are required and what types of record keeping the educator would like. If the teacher can provide the programmer with written documentation for the layout of each screen (including graphics), and the sequence of material, the programmer will be better able to provide a lesson that fits the needs of the classroom and meets the expectations of the teacher.

Summary

As noted, evaluating computer-based lessons is critical, particularly lessons constructed using authoring products. This Chapter outlines evaluation criteria for all three types of authoring products. More importantly, it also discusses guidelines for the development of good lessons. The great majority of lesson development occurs before the teacher/author begins work at the computer keyboard. Underlying the entire issue of lesson development is the importance of integrating the computer-based lesson into the instructional scenario, thereby utilizing the computer as the powerful instructional tool that it can be.

10

Issues
and Concerns

Educators and educational administrators need to consider a number of issues when making and executing plans to introduce microcomputers to teachers and students. This Chapter examines general issues related to using computers and more specific issues concerning authoring products and their future. They include:

- defining the instructional roles of the computer,
- thinking in instructional scenarios,
- determining where computers should be located,
- determining how students should use computers,
- defining computer literacy,
- determining when to use authoring products,
- recognizing limitations to be considered in selecting authoring products,
- providing teacher training and support,
- new directions for authoring, and
- a prospectus for the immediate future of development.

Defining the
Instructional Roles of the Computer

When first introduced in schools, microcomputers were too often heralded as all-purpose solutions to every educational problem. School administrators and parents uncritically accepted claims that computers would revolutionize learning in the schools. In spite of their inadequate understanding of the roles the computer should play in the learning process, administrators, parents, and policy makers pressed to make computers available.

However, there were two initial roadblocks to the successful integration of computers into the curriculum:

- excessive expectations for what the computer could accomplish; and
- the general recognition that much of the available software was of poor quality, and presented activities and content in a manner which did not enhance instruction.

In the years since the introduction of microcomputers, administrators, parents, teachers, and policy makers have learned that the successful utilization of microcomputers in education requires thoughtful and careful planning. Many educators recognize the potential of the technology and are eagerly exploring a variety of classroom adaptations. At the other extreme are individuals who want nothing to do with computers. Perhaps they have seen inappropriate applications or are disenchanted with unfulfilled commercial promises. Still other teachers are simply uncomfortable with or even fearful of the new technology. These educators are understandably disturbed by administrative directives that require they use computers with their students.

However, the vast majority of teachers are neither overly enthusiastic about or completely disinterested in computers. Today, more and more educators are aware of the educational contributions that computers can make. These include:

- stimulating more and higher quality writing output through word processing programs;
- teaching classification and organization of materials by using database software;
- practicing sequencing, problem solving, communicating, and following directions by learning to program;

- accessing specialized information—for example, from an electronic encyclopedia; and
- enhancing other classroom learning through computer-based drill-and-practice or tutorial lessons.

A key step in ascertaining the instructional role of the computer is to begin viewing the computer as an instructional tool, powerful but limited. Computers do not replace teachers—computers are teaching tools to be used by teachers.

Thinking in Instructional Scenarios

Budoff et al. (1985) have argued for thinking about learning activities as sequences arranged in an *instructional scenario.* The concept often helps teachers identify the instructional roles of the computer for their students. An instructional scenario describes the variety and sequence of instructional procedures planned for the student and reflects the tasks' prerequisite skills, the conditions under which the student learns best, and those instructional procedures that will help him or her attain an objective. Scenarios detail the different activities in the learning sequence, how they are ordered, and what instructional operations and media are to be used. The concept of the instructional scenario is intended to help the teacher identify the unique roles the computer can play in teaching students.

The computer is an instructional tool, albeit a powerful one. Successful integration of computers into the classroom depends on a recognition that the computer is an addition to the teacher's arsenal of instructional tools. Computer-based lessons should be viewed as enhancing the teacher's instruction. The computer should not be viewed as replacing elements of the curriculum. Computer software and hardware do not provide a complete instructional system.

Even the most successful computer-based learning system does not provide a total instructional environment. Yet a common stance among computer users and software developers has been that the computer is destined to become the teacher. Software is evaluated as to whether, considered independently, it can provide an alternate means to teach elements of the curriculum. The computer as sole teacher is not a solution. The teacher must be in the position to design the instructional scenario so that it includes a wide range of instructional tools. Non-computer activities are critical to the student's progress since they reinforce the work on the computer within an orderly context in an instructional setting. Computer-based lessons reinforce learning from other classroom activities and, in tutorials, expand upon that learning under the teacher's supervision.

Thus, the computer makes a unique contribution as just another medium of instruction. The challenge for teachers, then, is to define the unique roles the computer can play as an instructional tool—whether these are to motivate, to provide direct instruction, or to review the student's prowess with the materials. Used in the context of an instructional scenario, the computer can make significant contributions to the student's learning experiences. However, the teacher remains the designer and manager of the student's learning experiences: He or she determines what part the computer will play in that experience.

Often new technologies are not integrated in the schools for instructional purposes because they have not been presented as extensions of the current activities of the school. Instead they are made to seem to be dramatic new teaching processes; and therefore frightening. New approaches must be heralded as revolutionary to attract attention, but unless their claims are realistic and well packaged, they will discourage potential users. Any new technology needs time for applications to be developed and a body of practice to evolve. New technologies have never totally replaced existing learning materials, and it is misleading and irresponsible to promote computers as replacements for teachers.

Recognizing the role of the computer as an instructional tool, and locating appropriate software, will equip educators to design instructional scenarios which include the computer.

Determining Where
Computers Should Be Located

A major issue teachers, administrators, and policy makers face is determining the instructional setting in which computers should be utilized. Should computers be clustered in laboratories, or distributed in classrooms? Initially, the group-teaching orientation of regular education prevailed in the majority of schools. Computers were grouped in clusters of 5-20 in a room (computer lab) and used for class-size activities. Access to computers was usually scheduled and supervised by a specialist rather than the classroom teacher. This arrangement made the limited number of computers in the school available to all students, assuring that the students in each class had the opportunity to work with the computer under the supervision of an experienced instructor.

Placing computers in labs has advantages and disadvantages. Computer-lab activities are usually scheduled in class-size groups during the school week. Student involvement with the computer becomes a scheduled activity—such as a course in computer literacy, LOGO, or programming. This arrangement prevents students from moving to the computer when their progress in an activity suggests a useful computer application—maybe a drill-and-practice exercise to review long-division problems, word processing a report, or playing a game as a reward.

Another result of clustering computers in a laboratory is that classroom teachers are not necessarily part of the computer activity. Regular class teachers often view the computer lab as a free period for themselves— much as music, art, or shop periods. The result is that teachers do not learn about the computer, do not see what their students are working on in the computer laboratory, and are not encouraged to build relationships between their students' computer activity and the instructional activities in the classroom. In addition, because teachers are trained in the artificial settings of computer-literacy workshops and in-service meetings, often without follow-up support, they are unequipped to answer computer-related questions which crop up when their students return to the classroom.

In contrast, placing computers in labs with experienced teachers does have some advantages. Being able to introduce an entire class to computers at the same time, with one or two students working at each computer, saves both time and teacher effort. Experienced teachers are more likely to have a working knowledge of a wider range of software. Schools may be better able to afford 5-20 computers for a lab than several in each classroom. In addition, placing computers in labs rather than classrooms allows schools to maintain tighter security over equipment—an important consideration in some schools.

Computers in labs also circumvent the problems created in some classrooms when students working on computers distract other students. Most often, this is a by-product of computer software which is rich in special effects—sound, graphics, etc.

Ultimately, placing computers exclusively in laboratories makes it unlikely that they will become an intrinsic part of the instructional scenario because they are not physically convenient and readily accessible.

Placing computers in classroom with students has its own advantages and disadvantages. A primary advantage is the increased accessibility of the computer. This location enhances the role the computer can play as an instructional tool in a variety of activities including writing; drill and practice as part of an instructional sequence; and simulations in social studies, science, and mathematics. Placing the computer in the classroom provides the teacher with the incentive to find ways to integrate the computer into the student's instructional scenario. The teacher alone controls access to the computer.

If the computer is going to be used as an instructional tool, not just a game machine, placing it in the classroom seems the most sensible policy. This location allows it to be utilized for a greater range of applications. Some schools group computers in labs as a temporary measure. After a transition stage—when teachers are trained and sufficient resources are available—computers are moved into classrooms. If it is not possible to ultimately locate computers in the classroom, a combination of the two placements should be considered.

Determining How Students Should Use Computers

What activities are important for students to engage in during their computer time? The response to this questions differs depending on where the computers are located: laboratory clusters or individual classrooms. In computer laboratories, LOGO clearly interests and absorbs many students and can be used to teach sequencing, following directions, geometry, etc. LOGO doesn't teach programming but can introduce students to the computer and interest them in pursuing programming. In labs, all students can acquire an understanding of what computers can and can't do, and learn to recognize them as another tool in an instructional or work setting. Whether they can become effective users depends on access.

The placement of computers in classrooms in addition to or instead of labs allows students to have access to the computer as their learning needs dictate, whether they are mastering a skill, writing a report, or creating a program for work or play. When each classroom has several computers, they can be used in the same way as tape recorders and books. Students can use the computer, either individually or in small groups, as they progress through the learning unit. In short, the computer becomes an interactive instructional tool as the students work through problems that involve independent learning and discovery. It is more likely that standard applications become familiar, and that students acquire more than a sense of what computers can and can't do.

The computer is particularly valuable for those students experiencing difficulties in learning in school. However, an excessive reliance on the computer should be avoided. Excessive use of the computer, particularly by special needs students, can result in these students limiting their learning to the computer, thereby escaping from other instructional settings where they have experienced failures. Even though the computer can be highly motivating and teachers may be tempted to utilize the computer extensively, the special needs student must be routinely exposed to other instructional learning media (workbooks, books, and direct small-group instruction). It is also critical for these students to demonstrate to themselves that they can apply what they have learned on the computer in other instructional settings. The special needs student's attachment to the computer can be used as an inducement for him or her to work in other instructional formats, e.g., a reward for other class work.

Defining Computer Literacy

Within the concept of instructional scenarios, it is assumed the computer will make a number of contributions to a student's learning. These include drill-and-practice and tutorial instruction, stimulating higher quality writing, and teaching classification and organizational skills.

In addition, two underlying goals for including computers in the schools are often identified: to make students computer literate and to have them develop some proficiency in programming. In the early days of microcomputers, computer literacy was often defined as the ability to program. It was generally assumed that using the computer and being able to program were one in the same. However, in view of further technological developments, questions should be raised about the necessity of being a proficient programmer and the working definition of computer literacy. Is it necessary to be able to program a computer? Does computer literacy require the ability to program?

One of the most significant features of the microcomputer marketplace is the speed with which it has developed. Our economy has shifted from agricultural to industrial and is now shifting from industrial to service. The computer is the tool of the service economy much as the tractor was the tool of the agricultural economy and the assembly line was the tool of the industrial economy. Microcomputers are notable for their convenient size and low cost—both assure a growing popularity.

As the marketplace grows and computer applications multiply, computer hardware will become more specialized and software will become more "user friendly." Novice users will be able to use sophisticated and complex software and hardware that perform new and useful functions.

Today, it can now be argued that most persons don't need to become computer programmers because technology has made programming a skill most individuals will never need. Rather, it is suggested that computer users should become familiar with the various applications (word processing, spreadsheets, etc.) they find useful in their everyday lives. Computers should be viewed as tools which can be used to manipulate information. In the classroom, computers help students learn in a structured, interactive way. In the workplace, computers are another tool.

The question is how much does the student need to know to be able to use a computer-based cash register, do word processing, or successfully utilize the applications software likely to be found in an office. It is these jobs that will proliferate in the next decade, not programming jobs. All of us successfully utilize the biggest computer systems in the world—the American telephone systems—and know nothing of how they work.

Today's working definition of computer literacy seems to be the ability to use the computer to meet your everyday needs. School policy makers must grapple with what students need to know about computers in order to use them today and in the near future: What computers can do and what they can't do. Determining the answers to the questions of what the computer can do is a byproduct of including the computer in the instructional scenario. Using the computer as an instructional tool acquaints the student with its limitations and capabilities. Studying "the computer" is not the most efficient way to become computer literate.

This working definition of computer literacy does not mean that students should not learn programming. Some educators view learning computer programming as an excellent way to work on an assortment of skills: organizing, sequencing, problem solving, communicating, following directions, etc. However, it is not clear that computers, at present, are the best or only medium through which students can practice these skills. Clearly, learning to program can be a valuable experience. The question is the importance of this experience for all students.

The more distant future of computer development is harder to predict. However, the trend is clearly toward more user-friendly software and sophisticated hardware. The speed with which new hardware is being developed and new applications are becoming available demands that the working definition of computer literacy be reexamined on a regular basis.

Determining When
to Use Authoring Products

As indicated in earlier Chapters, the use of authoring products opens new avenues for teacher and student development of individualized educational material. Educators can use authoring products to construct customized computer-based lessons to meet the needs of students, regardless of the availability of appropriate preprogrammed lessons.

The three levels of authoring products allow educators to choose from a variety of special features and time/energy commitments. Well-designed authoring products facilitate lesson development through easy-to-follow directions on-screen or in written documentation, making it possible for teachers at all levels of experience to determine the authoring products most suited to their needs.

Early users of authoring products relied on the authoring language PILOT. Remembering that authoring languages are the most complicated of the authoring products, these early users of PILOT despaired that ordinary teachers with a minimum of computer knowledge could custom design lessons using an authoring product. Unfortunately, they equated all authoring products with PILOT.

Since those days, the range of authoring products has expanded. Today, educators can choose from a variety of special features and time/energy commitments. These products, with their predetermined formats, make lesson writing options available to all teachers. Well-designed authoring products facilitate lesson development through easy-to-follow directions on-screen or in written documentation, making it possible for teachers at all levels of experience to determine the authoring products most suited to their needs.

Several factors determine the appropriateness of particular authoring products within a given education setting. The educator must decide whether student goals can be best achieved through the use of computer-based lessons or computer-independent learning. It is important to keep in mind both the benefits and limitations of computer-assisted instruction and to carefully match student learning styles, interests, and needs with a variety of instructional materials and presentations.

The computer should never be the only instructional tool. It is important that knowledge acquired through computer-based lessons be generalized to other settings. In the same way, computer-based lessons can help cement learning acquired through other more traditional instructional tools.

The educator must also understand the limitations of authoring products so that realistic decisions can be made about instructional materials and presentations. Drill-and-practice or tutorial approaches to instruction are the most accessible ways to use computers for two reasons. First, these two formats are familiar and clearly understood. Second, the capabilities of microcomputers accommodate these types of exercises best. As other types of instruction are explored and the capabilities of computers increase, more varied instructional programs and authoring products will appear.

In determining when to use authoring products, teachers must consider their own needs and interests, as well as the resources available to them and the needs of their students. Authoring products differ in flexibility, style, and variety as well as ease of use (the time needed to learn to author lessons using the software). Mini-authoring programs require the least commitment to learn, often only an hour or two, and can meet the needs of many students. On the other hand, authoring languages make the construction of more complex customized lessons possible because they include more sophisticated branching and record-keeping capabilities. A teacher proficient in using authoring languages should be viewed as a resource for his or her colleagues, and should receive the support of school administrators.

Of equal importance is the software design (see Chapter 9). When using mini-authoring programs and authoring systems, educators should evaluate the lessons in much the same way as they would any piece of commercial software they might consider purchasing. The lessons, containing teacher-supplied content, need to be of high quality to maintain student interest and motivation. When using authoring languages, the teacher/author must be careful to follow good lesson development procedures so that the finished lesson is of sufficiently high quality.

Although increasing numbers of educators are making use of a variety of authoring products, little research has been done on the effectiveness of these products. Educators need this information. A major reason for encouraging teachers to meet together in user groups is to facilitate the sharing of lessons and evaluate their effectiveness. Evaluation of authoring products and lessons written with them should improve and strengthen the range of available software. While the concerns and practices of regular, remedial, and special educators differ significantly, these users can still benefit from sharing experiences with each other. User groups, consortiums, workshops, and conferences offer the opportunity for teachers to meet and discuss relevant issues.

For special educators, a national electronic bulletin board such as Special Net (see Resources) can provide an accessible source for sharing information.

Recognizing Limitations to be Considered in Selecting Authoring Products

There are limitations inherent in all authoring products. Any design with a predetermined structure restricts the options available to the lesson writer. In essence, authoring products use a template for lesson development. Mini-authoring programs employ a rigid template while authoring languages have a much more flexible command structure. The command options available in an authoring product dictate particular teaching approaches or strategies and prohibit others. Some applications are limited because different products omit different commands. Each product, being designed for instructional purposes, simplifies authoring but requires lessons be produced within the rule system.

Some authoring products address their own limitations by accommodating programs developed with other software. For example, Apple SuperPILOT (from Apple Computers, Inc.) contains commands for including lesson segments or modules written in BASIC; and *Author I* (from Tandy Co./Radio Shack) allows the inclusion of lesson segments written in BASIC or machine language. Teachers/authors who wish to include lesson segments already written in other programming languages should consider using authoring languages which facilitate this.

Authoring products are evolving, in particular authoring systems and authoring languages. Whether their capabilities will continue to expand depends on interest, and more directly, purchases. The more complex authoring systems appeal to both the school and business markets. Apple SuperPILOT was developed for the business, not the school, market. Industry, which spends billions of dollars training and upgrading its personnel, will continue to use authoring products. These business users stimulate the market, which in turn benefits the schools.

Providing Teacher Training and Support

Teacher training and support is an extremely important issue. Teachers require initial training and continuing support. Training should cover not only the use of computers but also the use of prepackaged software.

Perhaps most important is having the time to learn to use authoring products and having support while learning to apply them. If teachers are given adequate time to experiment, they can develop enough skills to author lessons independently. The time and support needed are not unreasonable. Teachers can become conversant with the mini-authoring programs in an hour or two. Authoring systems and authoring languages require more of a commitment. All authoring products require a continuing atmosphere of support.

Typically, teachers have been trained in short-term workshops designed to introduce them to the computer. Limited attention and resources are offered to support teachers who are using computers in classrooms. In regular education, this issue was sidestepped by grouping computers in laboratories where computer activities were taught by specialists. The classroom teacher was not included; computers were not available for the classroom and neither was support for the teacher interested in bringing the computer into his or her classroom. Only now are some school districts focusing attention on methods to support teacher efforts to adopt computers. These districts are placing computers in classrooms and integrating them into the curriculum.

It is important to recognize that these types of support are not routinely available. Yet, integrating computers into the school curriculum places more demands on teachers than the open schools and classrooms of the past. Many schools are still experimenting, trying to determine which computer applications are most appropriate and what the working definition of computer literacy is.

Locating Resources

If policy makers, administrators, and teachers are serious about the introduction and incorporation of microcomputers into the learning lives of all students, some type of support system has to become commonplace in school districts of any size (more than 3000 student enrollment) and most high schools. This is the minimum requirement. Given the current tide of fiscal austerity, these resources are unlikely to be made available. Clearly, schools wishing to implement computer-based instruction will have to take specific measures to accomplish these ends. It is realistic to expect that the burden will fall on interested teachers, who will spearhead and spread the integration of computers in the classroom. It is not realistic to expect this integration to be successful without the support of school administrators.

User Groups

There are several ways to provide this support. The user group is an interesting phenomenon of the microcomputer age. There has been a spontaneous growth of self-help and support groups of computer users, even for specific applications. These user/interest groups meet regularly to share their experiences with various types of applications. They serve as an important and low-cost source of continuing support and consultation among teachers. These groups are most evident in large cities. The phenomenon, however, also extends to smaller towns and sparsely populated areas since computer users seem eager to exchange experiences and information by mail or by telephone to electronic bulletin boards, many of which are free and offered as a public service.

Although the easiest method of support is user groups of teachers and administrators, teachers do not readily participate in them. Reasons for this are unclear. It would seem that teachers who have opted to use authoring products, as well as word processing or database programs in their classrooms, should be sufficiently interested in computer use that they would be willing to participate regularly in user groups. Clearly, the responsibility for organizing these groups must be assumed by someone. Attendance at these meetings can be facilitated if the school district shares time with the teachers; scheduling a time near the end of the school day allows sessions to run over into after-school hours. It is predicted that this shared-time arrangement will encourage teachers to participate. Such an arrangement indicates to teachers that the district recognizes the positive value of time spent in these in-service training activities. Recruiting administrators for these groups is valuable because they will understand better what teachers using the computer are attempting to do and will then support them more effectively.

District or Intermediate District Computer Centers

The goal of increasing knowledgeable computer use in the classroom can be served by curriculum training and support mechanisms at the district or intermediate educational district levels. A center can respond to specific software needs as they are defined by teachers. It can collect teacher-constructed, computer-based lessons, teachers' experiences with and evaluations of different types of software, and samples of software. Many centers also collect catalogs to help teachers locate software.

This multi-school base allows a center to respond to requests for specific lessons required for a students's learning needs. Ideally, a curriculum center should respond to the training needs of teachers in the affiliated districts and support these teachers' use of software with students. Centers can also introduce new applications. For example, the possibilities of telecommunications in public school applications is now under study.

In-School Computer Specialists

In some schools, teams of individuals (computer-experienced teachers, the head of the computer science department, computer-lab teachers, etc.) are on-call to teachers with problems in classroom applications. In addition, they can organize training sessions which are led by knowledgeable teachers. Almost every school has at least one educator who enthusiastically uses computers and spreads news of his or her use, encouraging others to join in the activity. Identifying these specialists or "zealots" allows schools to make the most of their own resources. Obviously, administrators must support these teams of specialists, recognizing the time and effort that goes into their activities.

Coaching

In addition to the activities already identified, teams, centers, in-school specialists, etc. can serve as coaches for teachers who are integrating computers into their classrooms. The coaching model (see Chapter 7) is a particularly valuable training mechanism.

New Directions for Authoring

Four developments can be anticipated which will affect the future of authoring products.

- Computer hardware technology will continue to evolve.
- Authoring products will utilize more alternative input and output devices.
- The range and types of computer-based instructional lessons will expand.
- The process by which computers are integrated into the classroom will be reexamined.

The relentless continuing evolution and expansion of hardware technology—videodisks, talking computers, and computers that recognize speech—will help to define the future of authoring. These new devices will benefit particular subsets of students. For instance, a computer that speaks can provide a language-disabled student with opportunities to communicate and allow him or her the chance to participate in the traditional classroom.

A major development, already available for corporate training systems, is combining other new technologies with the mass market computer. For example, videodisk technology, especially the laser disk, offers increases in readily available memory and high-quality visual illustrations. The costs of interfacing the computer-videodisk technology are currently too high for the school market. When these costs are reduced, computer-controlled videodisks, as exemplified by Thorkildsen's (1982) work, will enormously increase the quality of the visuals which can be integrated into instructional software.

There are other technologies already available for more expensive computer models which will change the status of the mass market computer. Given the rate of technological change, these technologies will be available long before teachers are trained and equipped to utilize them.

Second, authoring products will become more flexible. Some of this flexibility will be the result of hardware developments. Some will be the result of new conceptualizations of computer assisted instruction. All will be stimulated by market activity. For these reasons, it will continue to be important for the school market to present itself as a powerful factor, either independently or in partnership with the business market.

Currently, computer-based lessons are usually drill and practice or tutorial. To date, most lesson formats have been dictated by workbooks rather than by the interaction that goes on between teacher and students in classrooms. A computer can interact with students, unlike a workbook, but new formats are needed to harness this capability. Simulation programs are beginning to make their presence felt in the school market. Clearly, other new formats for instructional lessons will be developed. Realizing the goal of fulfilling the computer's potential as an instructional tool will require research which involves observing the teaching-learning process in the classroom. More knowledge is needed about how creative teachers elicit positive learning from their students. The challenge is to determine those interactive formats for which the computer is uniquely suited and to design lesson formats in which these interactions can occur. Educators must be able to determine the usefulness of these new formats. Hence, the need for training and readily available support will continue. The time dimension for the advent and introduction of new formats is probably a function of the interest in authoring products reflected in the marketplace.

The fourth direction is rethinking the process by which computers are integrated into the curriculum. This consists of a number of considerations, most of them identified as issues in this Chapter. It demands that the role of the computer be determined and implicitly includes the concept of instructional scenarios. The location of the computer—labs or classrooms—is another factor. The definition of computer literacy, and the ways we expect students to use the computer, are also included. The type of support given teachers is another factor. All of these issues, and others, must be examined and reexamined on a continuing basis. Today's answers may not be relevant for tomorrow, just as yesterday's are not relevant for today.

A Prospectus for the
Immediate Future of Software Development

To date the most popular computer applications, the ones for which manufacturers are creating software, have grown from the buying patterns of users. Manufacturers are responding to the demand for certain types of applications. A brief examination of computer applications in schools indicates that many were popularized in the more monied non-school markets. These applications include word processing, databases, and spreadsheets. The school market has benefitted because the demands of the business market have resulted in increasingly sophisticated applications in these areas.

Software development for the school market was initially stimulated by Federal funding when the microcomputer was just being developed for the mass market. Much of this development was premature. While the instructional possibilities of the microcomputer were recognized, there was insufficient attention to the realities of installing microcomputers in schools. Teachers and administrators were generally unfamiliar with the technology and unable to provide reasonable and experienced direction. Little time was allotted to training, hardware and software were not always easily accessible, and there was no clear understanding of how to introduce and integrate computers into the curriculum of the school.

The failure of these early efforts to install computers in education settings disillusioned the Federal educational leadership. Software development monies were withdrawn and Federal leadership in stimulating experimentation in developing instructional applications dissipated. This withdrawal has further retarded the efforts of teachers and administrators to incorporate the microcomputer into the curriculum. This money has been especially critical in the area of special education since these markets are recognized as unable to support the development, publishing, and marketing efforts of private sector companies. These markets are referred to as "thin" markets, and products for handicapped and disabled persons have often been subsidized. Software development for special needs students requires these leadership funds to develop appropriate software. The active withdrawal of Federal leadership bodes poorly for the introduction of microcomputer technology into the school curriculum.

Without this source of funding, schools must take a more aggressive stance in stimulating certain types of development. Realistically, schools must develop partnerships in the private sector which will result in a growing body of appropriate software and hardware for educational applications. In some cases, education can continue to ride the coattails of business, benefitting from the sophisticated applications originally developed for that market. Of particular note is the developing area of simulations. Simulations are a popular tool for business and hold enormous potential for education. The needs of the two settings are separated by differing requirements for sophistication. In spite of these differences, advances in simulation programs for business will certainly be of use to the school market.

Educational leaders can also stimulate software development by establishing partnerships with software developers in areas that appear promising. School purchases will increase the number of software developers: Software developers flow toward application's areas that command sales' markets which can support the costs of developing and supporting software. School purchases, in sufficient numbers, can therefore stimulate the interest of software developers and bring new developers into the market. To accomplish this, schools must combat their reputation for making illegal copies of disks and manuals—actions which naturally discourage developers.

A hope (or fantasy) has been that as more knowledgeable grassroots constituencies of teachers express needs for particular types of software, school districts, singly or in combination, can respond by initiating their own software development efforts. This is unlikely, since historically there has been little creative energy for such organized efforts at the district or multi-district level unless external funding can be found. There will be less money now that public schools are under attack. The curriculum centers of the sixties that trained and supported teachers in applying new curricula in mathematics, reading, or science no longer exist; and the retrenchment in spending for new services in education indicates they will not reappear soon.

Summary

The key, then, is to find ways to help the teachers and administrators become involved productively and comfortably with microcomputers, integrate them into the instructional process of the classroom, and provide increasingly sophisticated ways to engage students with them. The challenges and opportunities are there. Teachers can utilize word processing applications software to facilitate writing and language arts skills; database software to help students learn how to identify, classify and access the hierarchically-arranged elements within an array of facts; or authoring products to customize lessons in a range of areas for a variety of students. The school policy makers must encourage teachers to learn at least the rudiments of this technology and use it with their students. They must make computers available to teachers and students in the natural course of their learning, and support these teacher efforts with on-going training and other resources.

The pressure to introduce computers has been dramatically reduced. Schools now have a period in which to implement the technology at a more reasonable pace, with both positive and negative experiences behind them. Rather than abandoning the computer as a misplaced hope, the fading spotlight and pressure for its adoption can allow time and energy to be expended in planning how best to implement the technology in schools.

A major benefit of this change of pace is that schools can slowly develop a capability to use computers. Schools should use this time to educate and support those teachers interested in using computers in their classrooms. This quiet period in the revolution will enable educators to feel their way gradually into the uses of the technology. At the same time, the school market must affect the future direction of software and hardware development by presenting the school market as a viable one as well as forging partnerships with other forces in the market. As these new developments result in new pressures to use the computer, there will be teachers in every school district who can develop a more constructive response.

References

Budoff, M., Thormann, J., & Gras, A. (1985) *Microcomputers in special education: An introduction to instructional applications, Rev. ed.* Cambridge, MA: Brookline Books, Inc.

Chiang, A., Stauffer, C., & Cannara, A. (Feb. 27–March 1, 1979) *A teacher-controlled, computer-assisted instructional system for special education.* Paper presented at the annual convention of the Association for the Development of Computer-Based Instructional Systems, San Diego, CA. (ERIC Document Reproduction Service No. E 175 448)

Conlon, T. (1984) *PILOT: The language and how to use it.* Englewood Cliffs, NJ: Prentice-Hall International, Inc.

Dence, M. (1980) Toward defining a role for CAI: A review. *Educational Technology* 20(11), 50–54.

Gershman, J., & Sakamoto, E. (1981) Computer-assisted remediation and evaluation: A CAI project for Ontario secondary schools. *Educational Technology,* 21(3), 40–43.

Grimes, L. (1981) Computers are for kids: Designing software programs to avoid problems of learning. *Teaching Exceptional Children,* November, 49–53.

Hallworth, H.J., & Brebner, A. (1980) *Computer assisted instruction in schools: Achievements, present developments and projections for the future.* Calgary: Faculty of Education Computer Applications Unit.

Malone, T.W. (1980) *What makes things fun to learn? A study of intrinsically motivating computer games.* Palo Alto, CA: Xerox Palo Alto Research Center.

Mason, M. (March, 1983) Presentation at the Council for Exceptional Children Conference on Technology in Special Education.

McDermott, P.A., & Watkins, M.W. (1983) Computerized vs. conventional remedial instruction for learning-disabled pupils. *The Journal of Special Education,* 17(1), 81–88.

Ryba, K., & Chapman, J.W. (1983) Toward improving learning strategies and personal adjustment with computers. *The Computing Teacher,* 11(1), 48–53.

Thorkildsen, R. (1982) *Microcomputers/videodisc authoring system for instructional programming.* Paper presented at the annual meeting of the American Educational Research Association, New York.

Trifilette, J.J., Frith, G.H., & Armstrong, S. (1984) Microcomputers and resource rooms for L.D. students: A preliminary investigation of the effects on math skills. *Learning Disability Quarterly,* 7(1), 69–76.

Vitello, S.J., & Bruce, P. (1977) Computer-assisted instructional programs to facilitate mathematical learning among the handicapped. *Journal of Computer-Based Instruction,* 4, 26–29.

Glossary

This Glossary details computer hardware components and some software considerations. Also included in this Glossary are working definitions of some disabling conditions.

It is important to remember that the tide of technology is rushing in at a rapid rate. Some of this information will be out of date very soon. On the other hand, many of the exciting developments described here are still emerging. It usually takes some time for the latest breakthroughs to trickle down to affordable, reliable applications and mass-produced components.

Authoring languages: Commercially available high-level computer programming languages designed to facilitate the development of computer assisted instruction, particularly tutorial and drill-and-practice lessons. This type of authoring product is more complex than either mini-authoring programs or authoring systems.

Authoring products: Commercially available software packages designed for ease of use in constructing customized computer-based lessons, usually for computer assisted instruction. Authoring products are usually divided into three major types: mini-authoring programs, authoring systems, and authoring languages.

Authoring systems: Commercially available software packages which use a menu-driven approach to assist the user in developing customized instructional lessons. This type of authoring product is more complex and more flexible than mini-authoring programs but less complex than authoring languages.

Blindness: A term which refers to severe visual impairments, though not necessarily the complete loss of sight. Some professionals define legal blindness as visual acuity of 20/200 or less after correction. Therefore, it is possible for some individuals who have been designated as blind to read large-size print at close range.

Bug: Refers to an error in a computer program/lesson which prevents it from running correctly.

Bus: A hardware unit for carrying data. All computers have buses within the CPU (central processing unit). Some provide external buses as well for adding on multiple peripherals or system enhancements.

Cassette Control Device (CCD): Developed and marketed by Hartley Courseware, Inc., this electronic device serves as an interface between a microcomputer and a cassette tape recorder, and allows vocal input and output to be coordinated with computer software.

Central Processing Unit (CPU): The *brains* of the computer. The CPU acts as a traffic controller, interpreting and executing instructions.

Cerebral palsy: Often referred to as *C.P.* A permanent non-progressive neuromuscular disorder which usually results from prenatal or birth injury to the motor-control centers of the brain. The severity of motor impairment varies widely. Seizures, sensory disorders, and mental retardation are common with this disorder.

Command language: Each Operating System has its own sets of commands that users can call on without the support of other software. For example, *DIR* to display a disk directory, *ERA* followed by file name to erase a file, *PIP* to copy files from disk to disk, and *STAT* to see how much free space is left on a disk. Some command languages are easier to use than others. Unfortunately, there is no standard terminology.

Computer: A programmable machine capable of processing information when correctly instructed to do so by a programmer.

Computer assisted instruction (CAI): A category of educational software that refers to lessons written for educational purposes using computer technology. Computer-based drill-and-practice, tutorial, and simulation lessons can all be referred to as computer assisted instruction.

Computer-managed instruction: Computer software packages which both instruct and maintain a record of individual student progress.

Concurrency: Also called *multi-tasking.* Allows the computer user to to use the central processing unit for more than one task at a time. One program can run in the "background" and another in the "foreground." Also, the user can interrupt one program, call up another, and return to the first where it was interrupted.

Courseware: A term referring to software packages which have been designed specifically for educational instruction. These packages often consist of more than one program, and can cover a range of skills.

CRT (Cathode Ray Tube): Technically, refers to the monitor or screen that is attached to a microcomputer and is used for viewing software. However, the term has been generalized and is often used to refer to the video terminal unit, including both the screen, or CRT, and the keyboard.

Cursor: The small square or other special symbol on the monitor or screen that indicates position. The cursor can be moved around the screen, and is often used to indicate the location for entering text.

Deafness: A term referring to hearing impairment of a degree to prevent accurate and consistent sound or speech perception.

Debug: To remove program/lesson errors or *bugs* so that the software runs correctly to conclusion.

Digitizer tablet: Requires software that knows how to interpret the input signals. Using a digitizer tablet is rather like drawing or writing or tracing on a sheet of fine graph paper. Each square is given a pair of coordinates, x and y. A square 5 inches from the left margin and 4 inches from the bottom might have an x coordinate of 500 and a y coordinate of 400. If a writing instrument entered that square, the values 500, 400 would be sent to the computer (in binary).

An obvious use of the digitizer tablet is for entering graphics— anything drawn on the tablet can be stored in code form. These graphics can then be reproduced on the screen or sent to a graphics printer. The tablet can also be used to enter responses to multiple-choice tests and questionnaires by associating certain blocks of squares with certain questions. With the right software, digitizer tablets can even be used for handwritten entry of letters and numbers. Their standards of legibility are somewhat higher than ours—they might be used in the future to teach penmanship.

Disability: Refers to a wide variety of handicapping conditions which interfere with functional skills in daily living.

Disk file: The Operating System, working with the disk controller, allocates space for files as they are created. It records on a *disk directory* the name, type, starting track, and sector of each file. Most users never know exactly where a file resides on its disk, but most users never need to know—the Operating System keeps a perpetual up-to-date inventory of all files.

ASCII file: American Standard Code for Information Interchange (pronounced "asky"). ASCII is a widely accepted code in which numbers are assigned to all the standard letters, digits, and punctuation marks as well as special non-characters such as line feed and backspace. ASCII files store everything in this code, using one byte per character.

ASCII files can be easily read by the computer without any special software and can be copied directly from the disk to the screen or the printer, or transmitted by modem, without losing any characters.

Programs and numeric data, by contrast, are often stored in *binary coded decimal* or some other space-saving code. Only computer experts and the software that created the file can make sense of these codes. If such a file is copied directly to a screen or printer, it will be illegible.

Data file: A file containing data, usually in a well-defined format of records and fields within records. As with office files, one should be able to access any record at any time—the progress record of one student, the schedule of one teacher, the students enrolled in one class. For handling data, *random access* and *ISAM* files are the most convenient.

ISAM data file: Indexed Sequential Access Method. The ISAM method creates and maintains a sorted index for each data file. The index stores a *key* for each record in the data file. The key might be a name on some systems; on others the key must be numeric. Stored with each key is the location of the associated record in the data file. This allows instant random access to any given record. Because the index is always sorted, it can be used to access the data file sequentially but in sorted order.

Program file: A file containing a unit of software. Unlike data files, these are usually read from beginning to end, so no random access or index is needed. If the program has already been translated, by a compiler or assembler, the central processing unit can read the file but most users cannot. If the program is still in source code form, it can be read by the same interpreter used in writing it. If it is in ASCII code, it can also be read by users.

Random access file: Permits instant access to any given record by its record number. Usually the records are stored in the same order they are entered. They must be sorted every time a report in sorted order is required.

Sequential file: A method of file organization that does not permit random access. Sequential files are not really suited for data: To find *Wagner,* one has to look at *Anderson, Bach, Beethoven, Chopin, Debussy..* . . Text and program files are usually sequential files.

Text file: A file containing text, which can include numbers as well as letters. Text files are usually created with the aid of a word processor. Text editors, which existed long before word processors, can also be used but are much less powerful. Word-processed files often include a great many special characters, and even unprintable characters, for controlling the printed format. If copied directly from disk to screen, text files are only partly legible.

Disk storage: Almost all microcomputers today offer disk storage. Disk storage can refer to either floppy disks or hard disks. Most computers now provide two disk drives in their standard configurations. Those that provide only one drive or only tape as a standard feature usually offer disk drives as optional add-ons. An important feature of disk storage is that the computer can access any part of an on-line disk almost simultaneously (random access).

Disk drives: The mechanisms for making the disks go around, and for rapidly positioning the *head* at any location to read or write magnetically coded bits on the disk surface. A disk drive can only handle one size of disk and only one type. However, for a given disk size and type, the drives of several manufacturers may be interchangeable.

Floppy disks: While indeed flexible, they do not flop. As of 1986, there are three standard sizes: the 3-inch microfloppy, the 5 ¼-inch minifloppy, and the 8-inch floppy. However, the actual capacity of any floppy disk is not standard: It is related less to its diameter than to the drive design (e.g., whether the disk drive can access both side of the disk or just one) and the *format* (see below).

Compared with *hard disks,* floppies are inexpensive and convenient. They can be easily removed from the disk drives and replaced. This convenience also means they are more subject to damage from careless handling.

Format: The organization and density of storage on a disk. The available surface of a disk is divided into *tracks*; each track is divided into *sectors*; each sector can store a specific number of bytes. Formats differ in number of tracks, sectors per track, and bytes per sector. Many computer manufacturers develop proprietary formats. In this case, the Operating System includes a format routine which ensures that the Operating System will be able to read its own disk, and other computers will not.

A *hard-sectored* disk has been given a format by the disk manufacturer, a format that cannot be changed. *Soft-sectored* disks are formatted by the user to match the proprietary format required by the computer. Storage capacity depends on the format: For example, the same 5 ¼-inch minifloppy can store 80,000 bytes with one format and 400,000 with another.

Hard disks: Allow considerably more storage than floppies, as well as faster reading and writing. Like floppies, hard disks come in many sizes, not necessarily related to their storage capacity. A hard disk the size of a minifloppy can store many megabytes. Most hard disks are fixed in place, and software and data must be transferred to other devices for back-up. Some are paired with removable disks, combining capacity and flexibility.

Laser disks: A disk that stores information by optics rather than magnetism. The laser writes a bit of data by changing the surface at a given point from amorphous to crystalline, or vice versa. The crystalline surface is highly reflective, the amorphous is not, and so the bits can be read optically. One manufacturer predicts the storage of 5,000 pages of text on a 2-inch disk.

A more important feature of laser disks is that they are already in use for audio and video recordings. When the problems of non-standardization and incompatibility are solved, a single disk will be able to store music, pictures, and movies side by side with computer text, data, and software.

Documentation: The materials which accompany computer software and explain its use and intended applications.

Flowchart: A graphic map or chart which indicates the sequence or "flow" of steps involved in a computer program/lesson. Flowcharts are often considered essential for clear software design.

Graphics pad: An input device consisting of a flat drawing surface that senses the location of a stylus, pencil, or finger and transmits this information to the computer.

Hardcopy: The tangible paper copy of computer information produced by a printer.

Input: Data or information which has been entered into the computer via a variety of devices.

Input/output device: Devices which are used for both input and output, such as video monitors or disks.

Interface: A hardware unit, a software unit, or a combination of both that allows communication between two units not specifically designed for each other.

Joystick: Widely used in video games. To use a joystick, tilt the stick on its base in any direction. The cursor, spaceship, or other indicator moves around the video display screen in response. A skillful user can guide the cursor through an intricate maze. Another use of joysticks is for moving the cursor to a desired location in a context provided by the software, as in selecting from a menu. The user can press a button on the joystick to indicate "This is my selection."

An educational game for beginning readers might display the word *CAT* on one side of the screen and pictures of a cat, bat, hat, and mat on the opposite side. A player could use a joystick to "point" to the picture that he or she thinks matches the word. (See also *Paddle* and *Mouse.*)

Keyboard: The most commonly used input device. Most people feel comfortable with a keyboard—perhaps because of its similarity to a typewriter keyboard or because the keys are labeled with familiar symbols. Students with low-level motor skills who have trouble with handwriting find it relatively easy to use a keyboard.

Keyboards are rarely purchased as stand-alone units: They usually come built into or ready to plug into the same cabinet as the computer or CRT. Plug-in models are equipped with cords for comfortable positioning. A recent innovation uses infrared signals instead of a physical connection: The keyboard can be moved freely up to several yards from the receiver as long as there is no wall or similar object in between to interfere with the signals.

The buyer of a computer system does not usually have a choice of keyboards. If a choice is available, the buyer should look for comfort and ease of use. Remember, the keyboard is one of two hardware elements with which the user will spend the most time.

The differences between one keyboard model and another are subtle. However, in the long run, they can make a big difference. Variations include the size of the key tops, spacing of keys, amount of pressure required to activate a key, sculpturing to keep the fingers from sliding off the keys, and location of seldom-used keys. On some models, the "home keys" (F and J) are identified by special sculpturing as an aid to correct hand positioning for touch typing.

Braille keys: Standard key whose tops are embossed in braille. These embossed keys are helpful to the blind, and sighted persons using them can become familiar with braille in the process.

Caps lock key: Essential if the keyboard and computer support upper- and lower-case characters. This key is different from the shift lock on a typewriter. It causes all alphabetic characters to be upper case, but has no effect on numbers and special characters. Thus, to get a % instead of a 5, the normal shift key is used.

Cursor control keys: Four keys usually labeled with arrows (up, down, left, right). Cursor control keys let the user position the cursor at any point on the screen for input. They are convenient for such applications as editing text. They do require appropriate software: The software must keep track of the cursor's location, but it must not treat the use of these keys as inputting data or text.

Dvorjak keyboard: Instead of standard QWERTYUIOP layout, the Dvorjak arranges keys according to frequency of use and ease of typing. For example, all vowels and the most frequently used consonants are on the middle row of alphabetic character keys. The Dvorjak keyboard on a word processor is claimed to increase productivity by 50% or more once the user has learned it. (The

QWERTYUIOP layout, by the way, was actually designed to slow the typing pace so that mechanical typewriters could keep up.)

Function keys: Special keys used to enter commands. These keys are labeled with their functions. A word processing system might provide *Append, Edit, Save, Print*, and so on. Once again, the function must be recognized by the software or the Operating System.

> **Programmable function keys:** Usually labeled F1, F2, F3, etc. A great convenience for people who learn how to use them. The user can define and redefine key functions at will. The function can be a command and/or a string of characters. When a key's function has been defined by the user or predefined by the software, that function can be called up with one keystroke.

Membrane keyboard: Found in some of the more inexpensive computers. Membrane keyboards use a flat surface with printed keys instead of raised, separate keys. One problem is the lack of tactile feedback. To compensate, some manufacturers provide a click or other mechanical sound.

Numeric key pad: A separate bank of keys like that on an adding machine. Handy for entering numeric data.

One-hand keyboard: Advertised as a revolutionary device that permits rapid text and data entry with only one hand. (It's not clear whether there are models for left-handed users.) The device is small, not much larger than a pack of cards, and provides a small number of keys, all of which can be reached moving only one hand. The keys can be used singly and in combinations to provide at least as many characters as a regular keyboard.

Learning disability: This term refers to a large class of disorders characterized by one or more significant deficits in essential learning processes which require special education remediation techniques. The precise definition of learning disabilities has undergone much change and revision. Learning-disabled students usually evidence a discrepancy between expected and actual achievement in one or more areas. These areas can include spatial orientation; mathematics skills; and written, read, or spoken language. A learning disability is not primarily the result of intellectual, motor, sensory, or emotional handicaps, nor it is due to lack of opportunity to learn.

Light pen: By-passes both keyboard and cursor. The user holds a pen-like object connected to the computer by a cord and touches the screen directly. Special hardware is required to detect and identify the point of contact and special software is needed to interpret the input. Software permitting, light pens can be used to draw and edit graphic images on the screen with great precision. (See also *Touch screen.*)

Listing: A printed image, on the monitor or on printer paper, of the statements or program lines within a given computer program.

Load: The process of entering a computer program into computer memory from a peripheral device. Sometimes called "booting" the program.

Memory: The information storage area of the computer which is readily accessible to the computer, and does not require the use of peripheral devices.

Mental retardation: This term refers to a condition marked by deficits in adaptive, intellectual, emotional, or social development.

Menu: A list of options available to the user of a given software package.

Microcomputer: A small computer that uses a microprocessor as the central processing unit.

Microprocessor: A very small processor or integrated circuit stored on a single chip. In a microcomputer, the central processing unit is a microprocessor.

Mini-authoring programs: Preprogrammed commercially available software packages which serve as program "shells" and allow the teacher/author to insert lesson content into a predesigned lesson format in order to construct an individualized computer-based lesson. This type of authoring product is less complex than both authoring systems and authoring languages.

Modifiable program: A type of mini-authoring program, generally drill and practice, preprogrammed with subject matter which can be used as is or easily modified by the teacher/author.

Modem: The name is derived from a contraction of *modulator-demodulator*. A modem allows two computers or a computer and a terminal to communicate through standard telephone lines. At the input end, it converts digital signals from the computer into audio signals for transmission. At the output end, it converts sound into digital signals. A modem is needed at both the input and output end. Some computers, especially portable models, have built-in modems. Some units can be set up to dial a given telephone number or to answer incoming calls. Direct-connect modems plug directly into modern telephone jacks, bypassing the telephone itself. More primitive models use an acoustic *coupler* that provides a special cradle for the telephone handset. These are not as reliable for transmitting data as the direct-connect.

Monitor: The screen which serves as an input and output device for most microcomputers. Also called a VDT (video display terminal).

Mouse: A device held in one hand and rolled around the tabletop. Its motion is echoed on the video display. One or more buttons are provided to enter predefined commands. The most common use of a mouse is for selecting from an array of options, but some claim the mouse is good for drawing graphics. For that purpose, however, a digitizer tablet might allow greater precision.

> **Mechanical mouse:** Uses rotating balls in contact with the table top or other surface to detect the motion. It functions better on slightly rough surfaces than on formica or glass.

> **Optical mouse:** Must be used on a board marked with horizontal lines in one color and vertical lines in another color. The mouse uses a light beam and reflectors to sense and count the lines being crossed. It is said to be more durable than the mechanical mouse. However, the user must play close attention to alignment.

Multi-user system: Usually, a system in which several users at several terminals share the same central processing unit and disk storage. Multiple users can even access the same data files. The CPU is assigned to one user for a fraction of a microsecond, to another for the next fraction, and so on. (The fractions of time are sometimes called "time slices.") The Operating

System has responsibility for time-slice scheduling and data integrity, in addition to its usual duties.

Multi-user capability is provided by most if not all mainframe and minicomputer systems. As microprocessors and disk storage approach the power and economy of mainframes, more multi-user operating systems will become available. At least one multi-user system on the market provides a separate microprocessor and RAM for each user, while all users share the same hard disk.

Network: A wiring and interface arrangement by which many computers, terminals, and peripherals can share resources, such as storage, data, and printers. This technology is making rapid progress, even to the point of allowing communication between otherwise incompatible hardware units. Networks require special Operating System capabilities.

Operating system: The first program to run when the computer is initially turned on. The Operating System contains the main control programs for the computer.

Paddle: Works rather like a joystick or mouse but has less freedom of motion. The user turns a knob on its base, and an associated bar, like a long cursor, moves up and down or back and forth along a straight line. Paddles are used for a great many action games; in these the true cursor often represents something like a hockey puck or soccer ball. Under the control of the software, the cursor whizzes about the screen and bounces off paddle bars, obstacles, and screen edges. The angles of reflection follow at least some of the laws of physics. Parents of youthful addicts say that joystick and paddle games develop excellent hand-eye coordination. (See also *Joystick* and *Mouse.*)

Peripheral devices: Devices connected to the computer, but not part of the main unit. Peripheral devices include disks, disk drives, printers, and other input/output devices.

Port: An electrical connection through which a computer communicates. The central processing unit has one or more ports of its own, and the computer provides one or more ports for the user to connect peripheral devices. A device and the port it is connected to must be of the same type, unless a special interface is used.

Parallel port: Allows data to be sent more than one bit at a time; for example, 8 bits can be sent simultaneously over 8 parallel wires.

Serial port: Allows data to be transmitted one bit at a time over a single wire. (Other wires are required for grounding and for sending messages such as "Are you ready for more?" and "Yes, go ahead.")

Printer: Used primarily for text, but some models have graphics capabilities. Printers have come a long way in the last decade. More and more features are available at ever lower prices. It is important to remember that printing is controlled primarily by software. Special features usually require special software support.

Impact printer: Works somewhat like a typewriter, using a ribbon between the paper and the print head. All impact printers are noisier than non-impact printers.

Band printer: Big workhorse used mostly in busy data processing departments. Now being offered in smaller sizes at lower prices.

Dot matrix printer: Works with a moving print head that contains a matrix (rectangle) of tiny movable pins. According to the character code received, the necessary pins are projected against the ribbon and each pin prints a small dot. The more dots, the clearer the character.

New models are extremely flexible. They can print draft copy at very high speed, correspondence-quality copy at lower speeds, and graphics as well. The user can specify compressed print, expanded print, double-size print, etc. Some use multicolored ribbon and variable dot density to produce shaded color graphics.

At least one manufacturer controls the typeface by codes stored in ROM cartridges. The typeface can be changed by changing the cartridge. Three or four cartridges can be inserted at once, allowing you to mix typefaces in the text. With some units, you can also create special characters and small graphics, store them on disk, and insert them in the text as you would other characters.

Formed character printer: Produces *letter quality* print like that produced with a good electric typewriter. This category includes *daisywheel* and *thimble* printers, the names referring to the shape of the changeable printing element. The print head moves along the line, and each character code received makes the element spin to place the right character in front of the hammer that makes it print. Changing the typeface requires changing the print element—a rather clumsy procedure to carry out in the middle of printing.

Line printer: Prints an entire line at once. Like band printers, their speed, reliability, and cost make them most suitable for large data processing centers where massive reports are being printed 24 hours a day.

Non-impact printer: Make less noise than impact printers. Cannot make carbon copies. Most require special paper, special ink, special chemicals, or other supplies that add to the operating cost.

Electrostatic and electrographic printers: Quieter and faster than impact printers. Some require special paper. Can produce graphics, but not in color. Similar in many ways to *thermal printers.*

Ink-jet printer: Relatively expensive but becoming less so. Can print anything in black and white or color.

Laser printer: Relative newcomer. Can print anything in black and white. Incredibly fast, and correspondingly expensive. Popular for the speed and quality of their output. In appearance, they resemble a copying machine and work on a similar principle.

Plotter: Don't print at all, but actually draw with pens. Can draw almost anything and are excellent for color graphics. Plotters require special software, but some are reasonably priced.

Thermal printer: Similar to the *electrostatic/graphic printer* but use a different chemical process to produce the image.

Printing features: The importance of each of the following features depends on the primary use, frequency of use, and location of the printer.

Buffer memory: Text and data are often sent to a printer faster than the printer can print. The buffer takes up the slack. When the buffer fills up at the input end, the computer is told to wait until there's room. The bigger the buffer, the better.

Clarity of print: In general, formed character printers are better than dot matrix printers at producing clean crisp characters. With dot matrix printers, the clarity is a function of the dot density.

Color: Produced with colored ribbon on formed character printers, multicolored ribbon on dot matrix printers, colored ink on plotters and ink-jet printers. Generally, the last two provide the brightest colors and sharpest images.

Descenders: A descender is the part of certain lower-case characters, such as *g* and *y*, that is printed below the baseline. Some dot matrix printers with small matrices do not print below the baseline, and letters that should have true descenders appear deformed. Printed text looks better, and is easier to read, with true descenders than without.

Graphics: An increasingly popular feature, available with some quite inexpensive dot matrix printers. Plotters are designed primarily for graphics. Laser printers handle graphics as easily as text. Very limited graphics can even be produced with a formed character printer. In all cases, special software is required.

Interface to computer: A printer has a serial interface, a parallel interface, or both. The type of interface used must match the computer's port. There are differences among interfaces. Even the common RS-232 connector is not completely standardized. If computer and printer do not match, a special interface is required.

Justification: Many users like to see pages of text neatly lined up, or *justified,* on the right as well as the left. One means to this end is to insert extra spaces between words where necessary. A more sophisticated method is *microjustification.* With this method, any extra space is evenly distributed between characters and spaces throughout the text line. Either method can be used with proportional spacing.

Noise level: Noisy printers seem to become more noisy with use, though this is purely imaginary. Acoustic cabinets can be purchased for most printers. Thermal, electrosensitive, ink-jet, and laser printers are virtually silent.

Paper feed: If you plan to purchase only one printer, it is preferable to have one that can handle all types of paper stock in a variety of sizes: Single sheets, envelopes, and pin-feed.

> **Pressure or friction feed:** The paper is gripped by rubber rollers as with a typewriter. Pin-feed (fan-fold) paper feeds continuously; single sheets must be inserted one at a time.

> **Sheet feeder:** An attachment that stores a few hundred single sheets of paper and feeds them to the printer. Expensive but much easier than feeding single sheets by hand.

> **Tractor feed:** Also called *pin-feed.* Eliminates hand feeding at very little cost. The paper is continuous, fan-folded, with perforations along the folds and holes along the sides. The tractors have pins that fit the holes and pull the paper along. This permits perfect alignment and registration. The paper can be pre-printed with user-specified forms or letterheads. If you do not like the holes, you can buy paper, even fine quality bond, with perforated hole strips that tear off to leave a neat edge.

Paper width: Common maximum widths that printers can accommodate range from 8–14 or more inches. The number of columns for printing text depends on the pitch (characters per inch) at which the text is printed.

Pitch or spacing: Most printers can be set to either of the two standard pitches available with electric typewriters: 10 characters to the inch or 12. A few offer 17 pitch. Some can be controlled by software to print at almost any pitch.

Proportional spacing: Results in very handsome copy, similar to that in a printed book. With true proportional spacing, the *m* is wider than the *n* and the *n* wider than the *i*.

Speed: Formed character printers are limited in speed because the printing element has to spin to the correct position for each character. Their speeds range from 12–55 cps (characters per second). Dot matrix printers are usually faster; quite inexpensive models print at 130 cps or better. Line and band printers print at speeds of 2,000 lpm (lines per minute), while electrostatic printers manage 18,000 lpm and electrographic, 30,000 lpm. Some ink-jet printers offer speeds of up to 45,000 lpm, others use lower speeds to achieve higher print quality. Laser printers combine very high speed with versatility and clarity of print.

Variable type: Formed character printers allow changes of typeface but this must be done manually by changing the print element. Some dot matrix printers provide many typefaces and varying sizes through programmed codes or ROM cartridges. Ink-jet and laser printers can print anything the software can define.

Program: A set of instructions which tells the computer what to do.

Programmer: A person who designs and writes the lines or instructions which make up software.

Programming language: A language that is used by a programmer to develop the set of instructions which the computer will follow. Authoring languages are a category of programming languages. Examples of programming languages include PILOT, BASIC, and Fortran.

RAM: Random Access Memory works with microscopic switches that can be turned on or off, by means of electric current, to represent bits of data or instructions. RAM is actually not accessed randomly but under the very precise control of the Operating System and other software. Any byte in RAM can be read or written to at any time.

RAM is used for temporary storage of programs and data copied into it from a disk. It also stores input from the keyboard or other devices and whatever data is generated from the central processing unit. Depending on the system, RAM may also have to accommodate the Operating System and an interpreter. Obviously, the more memory the better. Fortunately, memory chips are becoming less and less costly.

Battery-backed RAM: Ensures the survival of the RAM contents in the event of a power failure.

NOVRAM: Non-Volatile RAM, also called EEPROM (Electronically Erasable Programmable Read Only Memory). The bit switches in these chips can be reset, as in RAM, but will then remain fixed, even without electricity, as in ROM. So far, this form of memory has the disadvantages of slower access and greater power consumption.

User memory: Usually refers to the amount of RAM that is not reserved for the Operating System and other software required by the central processing unit. If the operating system is in ROM, user memory and RAM may be the same.

Robot: Listed here because it often combines both input and output, involving two-way communication with the outside world. Robots can see, hear, measure, sort, count, lift objects, walk, talk. They can be programmed to perform specific tasks such as putting wheels on automobiles. Some things they do as well as humans. Robots can also be very entertaining to build and a number of make-it-yourself kits are on the market at surprisingly low prices.

ROM: Read Only Memory is memory in which software has been made permanent—software in this form is called *firmware*. ROM chips cannot be changed as the software is in the form of fixed switches. The contents of ROM chips are secure even without electricity. The central processing unit can read faster from ROM than from RAM.

Some systems use hard-wired ROM chips to store always-needed software such as Operating Systems and interpreters. Some of these, however, do offer other options: The normal CPU/Operating System team can by bypassed by inserting a board with a different CPU accompanied by its own Operating System in a ROM chip. In a sense, the user then has two computers even though they cannot read each other's disks.

Some systems provide for the insertion, removal, and replacement of various ROM cartridges. Game cartridges for home computers are one example. Another is the removable ROM cartridge that controls the variable typefaces of certain printers.

Run: After a program/lesson has been written or loaded into the computer, it is executed or "run." Run is the command used to execute the program/lesson.

Save: The process whereby a computer program/lesson is stored on a peripheral device, such as on a disk or tape. Save is also a command used to cause a program/lesson to be *saved* onto a given storage device.

Screen: The monitor or display portion of the computer. Also called a VDT (video display terminal).

Shell programs: Mini-authoring programs which consist of an outline or format, but no specific information. The user is able to insert individualized material into the basic outline or *shell,* thereby creating a customized lesson which will follow the logic of the original outline.

Software: Most simply, software is another name for computer programs. Generally, software is divided into two major categories. Systems software refers to those programs necessary for the computer to carry out common functions. Applications software refers to programs which are designed for specific uses. Authoring products are included in the applications software category.

Tape files: On tape, all files are treated sequentially, regardless of the type of file. When a disk is backed up on tape this does not matter: If the disk must be restored, all files will automatically be read back in sequence. (Disk back-up and restore operations generally use large tapes.)

The sequential nature of tape becomes a problem when working with disk files and newly created software. In reading from and writing to tape cassettes, the Operating System cannot keep track of what is where. Instead, the user must note the location counter on the tape drive/reader. It is very easy to save one program or data file on top of another, whether by choice or accident.

Tape storage: The tape media used for storage in computer systems range from standard audiotape cassettes and special data tape cartridges to giant reels. For general purposes, the main advantage of tape storage over disk is its low cost. It is very useful for backing up disk files: Data and software from an entire hard disk can be copied onto tape for safekeeping; then, if the disk files are destroyed, they can be restored from the tape.

Tape storage also has some definite advantages for classroom use. If a system can use both disk *and* tape, software stored on tape frees up disk space for data files. Tape cassette cartridges are less vulnerable to careless handling than disks. At least one popular and inexpensive home computer uses two-track tape; one track can be used to record and play back voice or music or sound effects, the other for software. Both tracks are read simultaneously.

Tape cassettes have two major drawbacks. (1) Loading software from cassettes can take two or three minutes, as opposed to a few seconds from disk. (2) Tape *must* be read sequentially. It cannot provide, as disk storage can, instant access (random access) to given data. The first of these drawbacks is merely a nuisance, a matter of time and convenience. The second is more important in that it severely limits the usefulness of tape for data files.

Terminal: Another input-output device. Many terminals look just like desktop computers—they have keyboards and video screens even though they have no central processing units. Most computers can pretend to be dumb terminals. Mainframe computers and microcomputers with multi-user Operating Systems serve several terminals at one time. A printer can be called a terminal, especially if it has a keyboard for sending data and instructions to the computer.

Touch screen: Requires special hardware, which can sometimes be added to a standard CRT. As the name implies, the user merely touches the screen, usually with a finger. One means of detecting the touch and its location is by optical sensors ranged around the screen's edges. Because of the size of human fingers, control is less precise than with a light pen. The primary use of touch screens is for selecting from an array of choices (such as a menu) presented by the software.

Utility programs: This term refers to two basic types of software. The most common reference is to software which allows the computer to carry out generalized functions, such as copying disks or tapes. Another type of utility package is related to mini-authoring programs and is used to create dittos, worksheets, tests, etc. in a predesigned format with teacher/author determined subject matter.

Videodisk: The disk on which moving pictures can be stored. Similar in appearance to phonograph records, the pictures on a video disk can be directly accessed by other devices such as microcomputers.

Video display: The most commonly used output device for interactive computer systems. As of this writing, nearly all video displays are cathode ray tubes (CRTs), similar to those used for television. Many home computers are even designed to use television sets as their displays. *Plasma* *displays,* the latest wrinkle in display terminology, have one big advantage over CRTs—they are thin and flat. Because of their high cost per square inch, plasma displays are usually limited to a display size of 10 or fewer lines of text. The price is falling, and their use and usefulness will expand.

Most desktop computers and terminals come with built-in video displays. Other computers may not include any display: The user is expected to hook up a separate *monitor,* which must of course be compatible with the computer.

Video displays vary greatly, not always according to price. The following features should be considered in their evaluation.

Character size: Controlled by software, but the lower limit is determined by the *resolution* (see below) of the screen. As in a printed book, large characters make reading easier for small children and visually handicapped persons. On the other hand, more text can be displayed on the screen at one time if the characters are small. Some systems allow the user to select from a range of character sizes or height-width ratios. This feature is most likely to be found in systems offering graphics.

Color: Multicolor, actually, as meaning combinations of 8, 16, or more colors, both foreground and background. Color has great appeal, especially for children, and can clarify distinctions and associations among separate elements of a display. A color CRT and special software are required.

Even among monochrome CRTs, there is some choice: Green on black, white on black, amber on grey. Studies in Europe determined that amber was the easiest on the eyes for long-term use, but other studies disagree: There is no clear consensus. For continuous reading of text, the clarity of the characters may be the most important factor in reducing eyestrain.

Descenders for lower case: Each character displayed on the screen has a rectangle of space reserved for it. Within that rectangle is a smaller one from which dots are selected to form the character. (This block of dots has to be smaller so that the characters do not all run together.) On some displays this smaller *print block* rests on the baseline rather than extending below it. In this case, the tails of the lower-case characters (*g, j, p, q,* and *y*) cannot be shown below the baseline. These characters end up looking rather odd, with their tails tucked up under them. The difference is small but sometimes annoying and might add to the difficulties of dyslectics and others with reading problems.

Graphics: Recently introduced in the business systems but, for years, included in small home computers as a matter of course. Graphics have proven to be a valuable communications tool. Image quality depends primarily on screen resolution (see below). The determining factor is the size of the smallest area that can be controlled.

On some systems, the smallest block of dots that can be controlled is the *character block*. In text mode, a given block can display one of the standard text characters; in graphics mode, it can display a graphics character (such as a bar, diamond, or triangle); in either mode, it can be an empty block set to dark or light or color. In true graphics systems, the software can control *pixels*, which are much smaller. A typical character block is 10 x 10 pixels; thus the pixel is 100 times smaller than the character block.

With low-resolution screens or *character graphics*, the effect is grainy or blocky. Curves and diagonals look stepped. High-resolution screens with *pixel addressing* can produce smooth curves and realistic images, but at a very high price. Fortunately, there are many alternatives between the two extremes.

Resolution: Indicates the number of pixels on the screen. A pixel is the smallest area that can be individually lighted or colored. Dedicated graphics equipment can provide resolutions of 1,280 x 1,024 pixels, while inexpensive monitors and television sets typically offer around 256 rows by 192 columns on the same size screen.

Screen size, in inches: Measured on the diagonal. The 13-inch screen is the most common size in current use, presumably because it is comfortable for the user. Large screens are difficult to view in their entirety, and small screens often feel confining. However, portable computers with screens as small as 5 inches on the diagonal have been popular, and some displays used for word processing have screens measuring more than 20 inches. The optimum screen size for any purpose depends on the desired character size and the number of lines and columns.

Screen size, in lines and columns: A great deal of packaged software has been written for the common screen layout of 24 or 25 lines top to bottom and 80 columns (characters) across. At present, many of the home computers used in schools allow for a maximum of 40 columns.

Voice digitizer: Breaks down the wave forms of human speech into "slices." Each slice is converted to a group of binary codes. Code groups are compared to standards, each of which represents a word in a vocabulary file. Voice digitizers are used by workers whose hands are occupied with manual tasks, as well as by persons who do not have full use of their hands.

Most voice digitizers have very limited vocabularies and must learn to recognize the individual speaker's voice. They become confused if the regular speaker has a cold. High-pitched voices also cause confusion. However, this technology is advancing rapidly.

Voice synthesizer: The potential applications of this technology are so many and varied that a great deal is being invested in its development. The voice synthesizer calls on groups of binary codes representing discrete sounds, syllables, or words and produces recognizable speech through a speaker. The quality of the sound varies in rather the same way as the quality of graphic images—by the size and number of individual particles that can be defined.

However, to store all the codes representing all the nuances in 5 seconds of true human speech would fill an entire floppy disk. One solution is to store code groups representing phonemes. If there are enough phonemes on file, they can be assembled in various combinations to form a large number of words and even sentences. A dictionary of words and their associated phonemes is still required—one researcher predicts that written language will evolve (or devolve) into phonetic spelling so as to be easily recognized by computers.

Those working in this area are finding ways to reduce or even eliminate the mechanical, robotic sound of synthetic speech. While researchers are perfecting voice synthesis, future users are planning for its most effective applications.

Word processing: A process whereby text can be edited and revised using the capabilities of computer technology.

Authoring Resources

Regional Resource Centers

Great Lakes Area Regional
   Resource Center
Ohio State University
101 Student Service Building
154 West 12th Avenue
Columbus, OH 43210-1390

Mid South Regional
   Resource Center
University of Kentucky
128 Porter Building
Lexington, KY 40506-0205

Mountain Plains Regional
   Resource Center
Utah State University
Exceptional Child Center - UMC 68
Logan, UT 84322

Northeast Regional
   Resource Center
Trinity College
Colchester Avenue
Burlington, VT 05041

South Atlantic Regional
   Resource Center
Florida Atlantic University
1236 North University Drive
Plantation, FL 33322

Western Regional
   Resource Center
College of Education
University of Oregon
Eugene, OR 97403

Resources for Locating
Software or Interesting Applications

Association for Computing
  Machinery (ACM)
1133 Avenue of the Americas
New York, NY 10036

Association for Development
  of Computer-Based
  Instructional Systems (ACDIS)
ACDIS Headquarters
Computer Center
Western Washington University
Bellingham, WA 98225

Association for Educational
Data Systems
1201 Sixteenth Street, N.W.
Washington, DC 20036

Council for Exceptional Children
1920 Association Drive
Reston, VA 22091

International Council for
  Computers in Education
Department of Computer
  and Information Science
University of Oregon
Eugene, OR 97403

Microcomputer Education
  Applications Network
256 N. Washington Street
Falls Church, VA 22046

National Association of
  State Directors of
  Special Education (NASDSE)
1201 Sixteenth Street, N.W.
Suite 610
Washington, DC 20036

National Council of
  Teachers of Mathematics
1906 Association Drive
Reston, VA 20091

National Science
  Teachers Association
1742 Connecticut Avenue, N.W.
Washington, DC 20009

Technology and Marketing
  Branch
United States Department
  of Education
Office of Special Education
Washington, DC 20202

Bulletin Boards

Handicapped Educational
Exchange (HEX)
11523 Charlton Drive
Silver Spring, MD 20902
(301)593-7033

Special Net
National Association of
   State Directors of
   Special Education (NASDSE)
1201 Sixteenth Street, N.W.
Suite 610
Washington, DC 20036
(202)822-7933

Software Review Sources

The Apple Journal
   of Courseware Review
Apple Computer, Inc.
10260 Bandley Drive
Cupertino, CA 95014

Classroom Computer Learning
19 Davis Drive
Belmont, CA 94002

Applesauce
PO Box 598
Venice, CA 90291

Compute!
515 Abbot Drive
Broomall, PA 19008

BYTE
70 Main Street
Peterborough, NH 03458

Computing Teacher
Department of Computer
   and Information Science
University of Oregon
Eugene, OR 97403

Call - A.P.P.L.E.
Apple Puget Sound Program
Library Exchange
304 Main Avenue South
Suite 300
Renton, WA 98055

ConnSense
Special Education
   Resource Center
Hartford Graduate Center
Windsor Street
Hartford, CT 06120

Courseware Report Card
Educational Insights, Inc.
150 West Carob
Compton, CA 90220

Electronic Learning
Scholastic, Inc.
902 Sylvan Avenue
Englewood Cliffs, NJ 07632

C.U.E. Newsletter
PO Box 18457
San Jose, CA 95158

Hardcore Computing
14404 E.D. Street
Tacoma, WA 98445

*The Digest of
    Software Reviews*
School & Home Courseware, Inc.
1341 Bulldog Lane
Suite C
Fresno, CA 93710

Interface Age
16704 Margueret Avenue
Cerritos, CA 90701

The Disc Project
Oakland Schools
2100 Pontiac Lake Road
Pontiac, MI 48054

*Journal of Computers
    in Mathematics and
    Science Technology*
1331 E. Thunderhead Drive
Tucson, AZ 85718

Educational Computer
PO Box 535
Cupertino, CA 95015

Kilobaud Microcomputing
80 Pine Street
Peterborough, NH 03458

80 Microcomputing
80 Pine Street
Peterborough, NH 03458

Microcomputer Digest
103 Bridge Avenue
Bay Head, NJ 08742

Electronic Classroom
Educational Insights, Inc.
150 West Carob Street
Compton, CA 90220

MicroSIFT News
MicroSIFT
Northwest Regional
    Educational Laboratory
300 S.W. Sixth Avenue
Portland, OR 97204

Electronic Education
Electronic Communications, Inc.
1311 Executive Center Drive
Suite 200
Tallahassee, FL 32301

Nibble
PO Box 325
Lincoln, MA 01773

Personal Computing
PO Box 1408
Riverton, NJ 08077

School Microware Reviews
Dresden Associates
PO Box 246
Dresden, ME 04342

Pipeline
Conduit
PO Box 388
Iowa City, IA 52244

Sector
Utah State University
Logan, UT 84322

Popular Computing
70 Main Street
Peterborough, NH 03458

T.H.E. Journal
PO Box 992
Acton, MA 01720

Educational Software Directories

*Apple Computer Clearinghouse
for the Handicapped*
Prentke Romich Co.
769 Turnpike Road
Shreve, OH 44676

K-12 Micromedia
6 Arrow Road
Ramsey, NJ 07446

*The Educational
Software Selector*
T.E.S.S.
EPIE Institute and
Teachers College Press
EPIE Institute
Water Mill, N.Y. 11976

*Opportunities for
Learning, Inc.*
8950 Lurline Avenue
Chatsworth, CA 91311

*Educator's Handbook and
Software Directory*
Vital Information, Inc.
350 Union Station
Kansas City, MO 64108

Queue
5 Chapel Hill Drive
Fairfield, CT 06432

Reference Manual for
  Instructional Users
  of Microcomputers
JEM Research
Discovery Park
University of Victoria
PO Box 1700
Victoria, BC V8W 2Y2
CANADA

Scholastic Microcomputer
  Instructional Materials
904 Sylvan Avenue
Englewood Cliffs, NJ 07632

School Microware Directory
Dresden Associates
PO Box 246
Dresden, ME 04342

Sources for Courses
TALMIS
115 North Oak Park Avenue
Oak Park, IL 60301

Special Ware Directory
LINC
1875 Morse Road
Columbus, OH 43229

Swift's Educational
  Software Directory
Sterling Swift
  Publishing Company
7901 South IH-35
Austin, TX 78744

Manuals for Creating Software/Courseware

Author's Guide
H.J. Peters and
  J.W. Johnson
CONDUIT
PO Box 388
Iowa City, IA 52244

Designing Instructional
  Computing Materials
Minnesota Educational
  Computing Consortium
  (MECC)
3490 Lexington Avenue North
St. Paul, MN 55126-8097

Mini-Authoring Programs

The following listing of mini-authoring programs is arranged alphabetically. This list is suggestive, not exhaustive, and is intended to serve as a reference rather than a recommendation.

BRAINZ-GAMEZ

Designed primarily for drill-and-practice exercises, this mini-authoring program supports English, French, Spanish, and German. Lessons can include up to 30 screens of text or questions displayed in regular or oversized type. Other special features include graphics, customized response possibilities, two presentation formats, and extensive on-screen instruction for teachers/authors.

Bainum Dunbar, 6427 Hillcroft, Suite 133, Houston, TX 77081
Available for Apple IIe, Apple IIc, and IBM

C-BITS III

A simple mini-authoring program using teacher-supplied questions. Correct responses allow two players to take a turn on a *Tic-Tac-Toe* screenboard.

Educational Software Midwest, 414 Rosemere Lane, Maquoketa, IA 52060
Available for Apple

CONCENTRATION

A fifteen-item gameboard is available for the creation of matching games. Teachers/authors select items to be included in lessons.

School & Home Courseware, 1341 Bulldog Lane, Suite C, Fresno, CA 93710
Available for Apple, Atari, Commodore 64, PET, and TRS-80

CREATE FILL-IN-THE-BLANKS

A menu-driven mini-authoring program allowing the use of speech from a cassette tape recorder. A special device, called the Cassette Control Device (CCD), is used to synchronize the lesson on the screen with the tape recording. Lessons consist of visual displays on the screen coupled with tape recorded instructions and information. Stores student responses for record-keeping purposes. (Note: Cassette Control Device available from Hartley Courseware, Inc.)

Hartley Courseware, Inc., 133 Bridge Street, Dimondale, MI 48821
Available for Apple and Franklin (CCD required)

CREATE LESSONS

An easy-to-follow, menu-driven system that "walks" the teacher/author through the process of creating lessons using a multiple-choice format. Provides for hint screens and feedback frames. Teachers/authors can determine the number of tries and use of early lesson termination. Large-character set and record-keeping capabilities included.

Hartley Courseware, Inc., 133 Bridge Street, Dimondale, MI 48821
Available for Apple and IBM

CREATE LESSONS - ADVANCED

Similar to *Create Lessons*. Does not include the large-character set but does include additional features. Allows students to flip back-and-forth within information sections, print lessons, and make-up personal reinforcers. Uses 40 character keyboard.

Hartley Courseware, Inc., 133 Bridge Street, Dimondale, MI 48821
Available for Apple IIe and IIc

CREATE CCD LESSONS

Designed for use with the Cassette Control Device (CCD). Lessons are presented using synchronized screen displays and tape recorded information. Combined auditory and visual presentation enhance student learning capabilities. Can be used for a variety of formats.

Hartley Courseware, Inc., 133 Bridge Street, Dimondale, MI 48821
Available for Apple (CCD required)

CREATE - MEDALISTS

Has special format which can utilize 50 categories with 40 clues. Can be used for any content area.

Hartley Courseware, Inc., 133 Bridge Street, Dimondale, MI 48821
Available for Apple and IBM

CREATE - SPELL IT

Used to create up to 40 individualized spelling lists. Provides instant feedback to student response. Has record-keeping capabilities. Designed for use with the Cassette Control Device (CCD).

Hartley Courseware, Inc., 133 Bridge Street, Dimondale, MI 48821
Available for Apple (CCD required)

CREATE - VOCABULARY

Uses a drill-and-practice format and the Cassette Control Device (CCD) to present student with auditory feedback when learning how to say new words.

Hartley Courseware, Inc., 133 Bridge Street, Dimondale, MI 48821
Available for Apple (CCD required)

CRYPTO-GEN

Allows the teacher/author to create a cipher puzzle using teacher-determined content. Clues can be provided, and there are three different levels of difficulty for the puzzles.

XPS, 323 York Road, Carlyle, PA 17013
Available for Apple

DT MENTOR MASTER WITH GAME SHOW

A teaching aid which allows the teacher/author to insert information into a drill-and-practice format with animated rewards. Correct responses allow students to shoot at space missiles.

Datatech Software Systems, 19312 East Eldorado Drive, Aurora, CO 80013
Available for Apple

EARLY SKILLS

A simple matching lesson format for basic reading skills. Consists of two disks. One disk is preprogrammed with sample lessons which can be modified. The other disk is for creating lessons. Both disks include record-keeping capabilities.

Hartley Courseware, Inc., 133 Bridge Street, Dimondale, MI 48821
Available for Apple

GAME SHOW

An animated drill-and-practice game based on *Password*. Up to ten definitions or "clues" are allowed per word. Additional disks can be used to create as many files as desired. Sound effects can be turned off.

Advanced Ideas, Inc., 2902 San Pablo Avenue, Berkeley, CA 94702
Available for Apple II series, IBM, and Commodore 64

THE GREAT COMPUTER GAMEWORKS

Teachers/authors create their own quizzes within an open-ended database format. Students select one of three racetracks and playing pieces and move around the racetrack as they answer questions. Includes prerecorded quizzes.

Creative Publications, PO Box 10328, Palo Alto, CA 94303
Available for Apple

HANGMAN

Traditional "hangman" game which allows the teacher/author to supply word lists. Also contains several prerecorded lists.

Comaldor, PO Box 356, Postal Station O, Toronto, Ontario M4A 2N9, CANADA
Available for PET

INDIVIDUAL STUDY CENTER

Matching and completion tests, drills, crossword games, and timed exercises. More than 50 prepared Subject Data Files are available, or the teacher/author can create original files for use in the various formats. Includes record-keeping capabilities.

Teach Yourself by Computer, 2128 West Jefferson Road, Pittsford, NY 14534
Available for Apple and TRS-80

KID BITS WORD FAIR

This mini-authoring program consists of a predesigned lesson format containing ten questions each. The teacher/author can tailor the material to meet individual student needs. The student selects parts to be added to a clown face for each correct response. Includes record-keeping capabilities.

Potomac Micro Resources, PO Box 277, Pittsford, NY 14534
Available for Apple

THE LEARNING BOX

A mini-authoring program using a *Tic-Tac-Toe* format. Teachers/authors create drills. Contains color and sound. Does not include record-keeping capabilities, but questions and answers can be printed.

M.D. Fullmer Associates, 1132 Via Jose, San Jose, CA 95120
Available for Apple

MAGIC SPELLS

Consists of a scrambled word spelling game set in a fantasy adventureland. Fourteen word lists are included. Authoring capabilities allow insertion of individualized word lists within the game format.

> *The Learning Co., 545 Middlefield Road, Suite 170, Menlo Park, CA 94025*
> Available for Apple and TRS-80

MASTER MATCH

Teachers/authors supply lesson content to create matching games based on the tv quiz-game format. Special features include animated color graphics. Teachers/authors can also design their own graphics. Includes preprogrammed lessons in a variety of subject areas.

> *Advanced Ideas, Inc., 2902 San Pablo Avenue, Berkeley, CA 94702*
> Available for Apple II series, IBM, and Commodore 64

MULTIPLE CHOICE FILES

Allows teachers/authors to construct quizzes which use up to five multiple-choice answers for each question. Randomizes question presentation and provides immediate feedback. Students select answers using single-letter keystrokes. Tests can be printed. Does not include record-keeping capabilities.

> *Computations, PO Box 502, Troy, MI 48099*
> Available for Apple and Atari

PRINT YOUR OWN BINGO

This mini-authoring program enables teachers/authors to generate customized *bingo* cards for test, review, and many other purposes. Each bingo card is unique.

> *Hartley Courseware, Inc., 133 Bridge Street, Dimondale, MI 48821*
> Available for Apple

PRINT YOUR OWN CALENDAR

A multi-faceted program which generates calenders from various databases or allows the teacher/author to create individualized calenders with special events or other listings.

> *Hartley Courseware, Inc., 133 Bridge Street, Dimondale, MI 48821*
> Available for Apple

PUZZLES & POSTERS

Includes a number of game formats such as word searches, cross-word puzzles, and mazes as well as posters and banners. Teacher-generated word lists can be stored for use in a variety of formats.

Minnesota Educational Computing Consortium, 3490 Lexington Avenue North, St. Paul, MN 55116-8097
Available for Apple, Atari, Commodore 64, IBM, and TRS-9200

THE SHELL GAMES

Four quiz-game formats into which teacher-supplied content can be inserted. Formats include true/false, matching, and multiple-choice. Uses data alteration for program changes. Also includes prerecorded topics.

Apple Computer, Inc., 20525 Mariani Avenue, Cupertino, CA 95014
Available for Apple

SIMULATION CONSTRUCTION KIT

A multi-level mini-authoring program which stimulates computer literacy. Students design their own simulations using research, flowcharts, and programming to learn about the sequencing and consequences of making decisions.

Hartley Courseware, Inc., 133 Bridge Street, Dimondale, MI 48821
Available for Apple

SPIDE ATTACK

This mini-authoring program includes hi-resolution graphics. Contains multiple-choice, true-false, and fill-in-the-blank formats. Maintains a quick pace.

Ahead Designs, 699 North Vulcan #88, Encinitas, CA 92024
Available for Apple

SQUARE PAIRS

A matching game using teacher-supplied matched pairs in boxes on the screen. Variations include shape match, problem and answer, and word pairs in addition to exact answer.

Scholastic Wizware, 902 Sylvan Avenue, Englewood Cliffs, NJ 07632
Available for Apple and Atari 400, 800

STUDY QUIZ FILE

A mini-authoring program which allows teachers/authors to create lessons within a quiz framework of questions and answers with a word-match format. Questions are presented randomly and can be revised.

Computations, PO Box 502, Troy, MI 48099
Available for Apple and Atari 400, 800

SUPER WORDFIND

Similar but more advanced than *Wordsearch* (see below), this mini-authoring program enables teachers to create larger puzzles. Words are embedded in the puzzles. Students are given either the word or clues with which to determine the word. Word lists can be stored for later use in new puzzles.

Hartley Courseware, Inc., 133 Bridge Street, Dimondale, MI 48821
Available for Apple

TEACHER'S QUIZ DESIGNER

Allows teachers/authors to create and edit quizzes. Also scores and keeps track of student averages.

International Business Machines Corporation, PO Box 152750, Irving, TX 75015-2750
Available for IBM

TIC TAC SHOW

Based on *Tic-Tac-Toe*, this is an animated quiz game for one or two players, or small teams. Teachers/authors can generate 18 questions per subject, and more than one correct answer per question.

Advanced Ideas, Inc., 2902 San Pablo Avenue, Berkeley, CA 94702
Available for Apple II series, IBM, and Commodore 64

WORDSEARCH

Teachers/authors can create fun wordsearch puzzles of varying degrees of difficulty with the options of diagonal or backward spelling. Word lists can be printed at the bottom of puzzles. Answer sheets can also be printed.

Hartley Courseware, Inc., 133 Bridge Street, Dimondale, MI 48821
Available for Apple and IBM

Authoring Systems

The following listing of authoring systems is arranged alphabetically. This list is suggestive, not exhaustive, and is intended to serve as a reference rather than a recommendation.

ADVICE
>This authoring system gives students advice on and remedial help with a concept or objective. Teachers/authors do not need programming knowledge to construct lessons. (All grades)
>
>*Diversified Educational Enterprises, Inc., 725 Main Street, Lafayette, IN 47901*
>
>Available for Apple II series and TRS-80 I, II

ADVOCATE AUTHORING SYSTEM
>Uses simple English and numeric responses for lesson creation. Editing capabilities allow deletion, insertion, and revision of entered information.
>
>*Edu-CAItor, Inc., 38 Main Street, Hudson, MA 01749*
>
>Available for Apple

THE AUTHOR
>Enables teachers/authors with very little experience to create their own computer courseware. Includes a student record-keeping routine and telephone support. (All grades)
>
>*Phoenix Performance Systems, Inc., 64 Lake Zurich Drive, Lake Zurich, IL 60047*
>
>Available for IBM, Apple II series, and Wang-PC

AUTHOR I
>A menu-driven screen-oriented authoring system that simplifies the creation of CAI materials. Features include full-screen editing, graphics, branching, student management, and score-keeping. Allows access to routines written in BASIC and machine language for experienced programmers.
>
>*Tandy Co./Radio Shack, One Tandy Center, Fort Worth, TX 76102*
>
>Available for TRS-80

THE AUTHOR PLUS

Combines the features of *The Author* with more extensive graphics, full screen entry/editing, and answer judging. Includes a record-keeping routine and telephone support. (All grades)

Phoenix Performance Systems, Inc., 64 Lake Zurich Drive, Lake Zurich, IL 60047

Available for IBM

AUTHORING SYSTEM

An authoring system designed for both education and business training. Includes student management. Capabilities include graphics, color, animation, special character sets, fonts, and text and graphics overlays.

McGraw-Hill/Courseware, 1221 Avenue of the Americas, New York, NY 10020

Available for Apple

BLOCKS '82

Provides teachers/authors with a very easy-to-follow format for creating drill-and-practice lessons and tests. Special features include hi-resolution color graphics and the use of external devices for graphics creation. A very large graphics library can be used to illustrate lessons.

California School for the Deaf, 39350 Galludet Drive, Fremont, CA 94538

Available for Apple

CAI*PLUS AUTHORING SYSTEM

An authoring system designed to be especially easy to use. Editing features provide teachers/authors with simple commands for text and data correction. Includes record-keeping capabilities.

Edu-CAItor, 38 Main Street, Hudson, MA 01749

Available for IBM and TRS-80

CAIWARE-2D

A structured approach to authoring, providing formats for true/false, multiple-choice and fill-in-the-blank questions. Includes editing and graphics capabilities. Text is automatically formatted.

Records lesson time for student, and contains score-keeping and classroom management features.

Fireside Computing, Inc., 5843 Montgomery Road, Elkridge, MD 21227

Available for TRS-80

CAIWARE-3D

Develops up to an hour of classroom material in eight to ten hours of authoring, without programming. Schedules presentation of lessons, tracks students day to day, and offers word processing and branching. (Grades 4 and above)

Fireside Computing, Inc., 5843 Montgomery Road, Elkridge, MD 21227

Available for TRS-80 I, III, 4

C.A.S.E.

A screen-oriented method for test construction, administration, correction, analysis, and storage. Employs item banking principles. (Grades 3-12)

Pogo Ware Educational Software, PO Box 55298, Madison, WI 53705

Available for Apple II series

CATGEN/CAT

A two-part computer-aided teaching system that consists of two parts. The teacher/author uses *Catgen* to create lessons, tests, and files. The student uses *Cat* to run the lessons. Contains an optional practice mode and editing capability. (All grades)

Dynacomp, Inc., 1427 Monroe Avenue, Rochester, NY 14618

Available for TRS-80 I, III, 4

CAVRI V INTERACTIVE VIDEO SYSTEM

Designed for educators who wish to write interactive video instructional lessons in BASIC. Includes five discrete modules on disk, interfacing hardware, and a user manual. (Grades 6 and above)

Cavri Systems, Inc., 26 Trumball Street, New Haven, CT 06511

Available for Apple II series

CLAS (COMPUTERIZED LESSON AUTHORING SYSTEM)

Computerized lesson-authoring system designed to help teachers/authors create their own courses. Lessons can consist of reading material followed by problem sets. Reading material can contain fill-in-the-blank questions. Students can also use the system to prepare for tests, learn new material, or write their own lessons. Includes user guide. (All grades)

> *Touch Technologies, Inc., 609 South Escondido Blvd., Suite 101, Escondido, CA 92025*
> Available for Apple II series, IBM, and Commodore 64

COMPUTER-GENERATED MATHEMATICS MATERIALS:
Volume 1-Problem Solving

Allows many tests or worksheets to be created quickly and easily. Selections can be made from 316 different objectives covering *Interpreting Tables, Selecting an Operation* (for use in solving word problems), *Reading Graphs* and *Working Backwards* (which is a collection of mazes, patterns, magic triangles, and squares). (Grades 3-8)

> *Minnesota Educational Computing Consortium, 3490 Lexington Avenue North, St. Paul, MN 55126-8097*
> Available for Apple II series

CREATE-a-TEST

Prints selected questions from question disks. Teachers/authors can prepare their own question disks using the built-in text editor. Prerecorded question disks are also supplied. Tests can be produced in ten minutes. (All grades)

> *Cross Educational Software, PO Box 1530, Ruston, LA 71270*
> Available for Apple II series

CUSTOMIZED TESTING

A courseware package that can generate aptitude tests. Teachers/authors can create customized questionnaires which meet their specifications.

> *Classroom Consortia Media, Inc., 57 Bay Street, Staten Island, NY 10301*
> Available for IBM

ELECTRIC ENGLISH AUTHORING

An authoring system that allows teachers/authors to modify the lessons supplied with the software or create their own computerized lessons without any knowledge of programming. In addition, teachers/authors can set up a management system for use with the lessons. The system can be used for a variety of subjects, not just English. (Grades 7-9)

Total Information Educational Systems, 1925 West Country Road, B2, St. Paul, MN 55113

Available for Apple II series

ELECTRIC POET

A text authoring system that allows the teacher/author to create demonstrations and lessons employing color, animation, graphics, music, and timing. Graphics and text can be moved around the screen, and color can be used to create emphasis.

International Business Machines Corporation, PO Box 152750, Irving, TX 75015-2750

Available for IBM

ELECTRONIC MASTER I

Quickly generates worksheets and mini-worksheets (horizontal setup) with answer keys for whole numbers, decimals, fractions, and integers. Allows teachers/authors to pick any single operation or mixture of operations and control the level of difficulty. Special options such as string addition, string multiplication, basic equations, one-number problems, and "even" division allow variety. A mini-word processor is also included for short messages, and an optional list of format changes allows worksheets to be customized further. An additional feature produces problems randomly from mathematical tables. (Grades 1-12)

Educational Software and Design, PO Box 2801, Flagstaff, AZ 86003

Available for TRS-80 I, III, Color Computer

ELECTRONIC MASTER I-S

Generates whole-number problems in large, workable print (vertical setup) and employs automatic line spacing and formatting. Different sets of problems can appear on the same sheet. Similar to *Electronic Master I* without the mixed operations feature. (Grades 1-8)

Educational Software and Design, PO Box 2801, Flagstaff, AZ 86003

Available for TRS-80 I, II, Color Computer

EnBASIC AUTHORING SYSTEM

A kit of programming tools for educators who wish to write computer assisted lessons. Assumes knowledge of BASIC. Key features include state-of-the-art answer judging, spelling markup, alternate fonts, subscripts and superscripts, and diacritic marks. (All grades)

COMpress, PO Box 102, Wentworth, NH 03282
Available for Apple II series

EXAM OPTIONS

Designed for use in computer assisted testing. Allows the creation of exams in any subject area. Features include six exam types, exam storage, creation of up to 40 questions using text and/or graphics, editing and automatic exam checking. Automatically computes the percentage of correct responses and saves the scores. Scores can be reviewed by printout or on the screen. Exams can be administered at the computer or by printout. (All grades)

Computer Applications Tomorrow, 24151 Telegraph Road, Southfield, MI 48034
Available for TRS-80 I, III

FASTRACK QUIZZER

An action computer game using a racetrack format to quiz students on memorized material. Comes with a variety of quizzes at varying levels of difficulty. Teachers/authors can also create their own quizzes. One- or two-player option. (Grades 3-9)

Creative Publications, PO Box 10328, Palo Alto, CA 94303
Available for Apple II series

FLASHCARD MAKER/FLASHCARD QUIZ

Prepares flashcards and provides options for studying questions and answers, full testing, and easy learning. Stores scores and allows studying or retesting. Sample data file with 50 states and capitals provided. (Grades 3 and above)

Academy Software, PO Box 6277, San Rafael, CA 94903
Available for Commodore VIC 20

GENIS I

Genis I contains *Courseware Development System I* (an authoring system) and *Mark-PILOT* (a version of the PILOT authoring language). Both sections can be used together. Includes low-resolution graphics, automatic text formatting, and commands for text location on the screen. Also includes record-keeping capabilities.

Bell & Howell Micro Systems, 7100 North McCormick Road, Chicago, IL 60645
Available for Apple

GHOSTWRITER AUTHORING SYSTEM

An English-language prompted authoring system that enables non-programmers to create computer assisted instruction using branching, scoring, graphics, and computer-managed instruction. (Grades 6 and above)

Carvi Systems, Inc., 26 Trumball Street, New Haven, CT 06511
Available for Apple II series

GHOSTWRITER INTERACTIVE VIDEO AUTHORING SYSTEM

Has all the capabilities of the *Ghostwriter Authoring System* plus the necessary software and interfacing hardware to integrate video into the instructional lesson. (Grades 6 and above)

Cavri Systems, Inc., 26 Trumball Street, New Haven, CT 06511
Available for Apple II series

THE GREAT CREATOR

This menu-driven system allows the teacher/author to create multiple-choice and fill-in-the-blank questionnaires in as many as 16 languages. No programming skills are necessary. Features include a scoring system, upper- and lower-case display, accented characters, custom designed title pages, and screen instructions. (All grades)

The Professor, 959 N.W. 53rd Street, Ft. Lauderdale, FL 33309
Available for Apple II series

THE INSTRUCTOR'S SYSTEM - EXAMINER

Used in conjunction with *Exams* (see below) to administer tests by computer. Provides immediate feedback at the teacher's discretion, grades exams, stores detailed student performance profiles, and generates a class summary of responses to each question. (All grades)

Shenandoah Software, PO Box 776, Harrisonburg, VA 22801
Available for TRS-80 III

THE INSTRUCTOR'S SYSTEM - EXAMS

Creates, modifies, stores, and prints multiple-choice and true-false exams. Also prints exams, answer sheets, and answer keys. Includes a built-in word processor to edit questions. A "keyword" search option speeds reorganization by searching question files for items containing specified words or phrases. (All grades)

Shenandoah Software, PO Box 776, Harrisonburg, VA 22801
Available for TRS-80 III

LIGHT PEN QUIZ

A general-purpose authoring system for use with CMA's light pen. Designed to enable teachers/authors to create and edit computer-based quizzes. (All grades)

CMA Micro Computer, 55722 Santa Fe Trail, Yucca Valley, CA 92284

Available for Apple II series

THE LINGUIST

A translation/tutorial package to create lessons in any of 20 languages. Teachers/authors specifies one or two languages and enter pairs of equivalent words, phrases, or definitions. (All grades)

Gessler Publishing Company, Inc., 900 Broadway, New York, NY 10003

Available for Apple II series

MATHEMATICS: A Worksheet/Test Generator

Designed for the creation of arithmetic worksheets and tests. Worksheets include explanations and examples. Answer keys provided. (Grades K-6)

The Continental Press, Inc., 520 East Bainbridge Street, Elizabethtown, PA 17022

Available for TRS-80 III, 4

MICRO TUTOR II: EZ Author/Author Plus Systems

Two systems available. Each allows lessons to be created without programming. Features include visual prompting, interactive individualized instruction, automatic review of missed items, and multiple formats. *EZ Author Plus* includes highlighting, special characters, renewable tutor disk, easy editing, and choice of lesson/test formats. Includes user's manual. (All grades)

Scandura Training Systems, Inc., 1249 Greentree Lane, Narbeth, PA 19072

Available for Apple II series and Franklin

MULTISENSORY AUTHORING COMPUTER SYSTEM (MACS)

Designed for the development of individualized lessons for students based on their specific instructional needs. The multisensory format allows the teacher/author to select how instructions, lesson content, feedback, and reinforcement will be presented to the student—visual, auditory, or a combination. Students can also use an alternate input switch.

For information, contact Dr. Marion Panyan, 100 Whitehead Hall, Division of Education, The Johns Hopkins University, Baltimore, MD 21218 (301)338-8273

Available for Apple II+, IIe, IIc (Echo or Echo + Speech Synthesizer required)

PRIVATE TUTOR

Designed for the creation of lessons using text, true-false, match, and question formats. Allows integration of a video disk file, graphics, and BASIC programs.

International Business Machines Corporation, PO Box 152750, Irving, TX 75015-2750

Available for IBM

QUIZ

Used to create tests and quizzes using a variety of question formats. Tests and quizzes can be administered by the computer or printed. Does not require programming knowledge. (Grades 9 and above)

Diversified Educational Enterprises, Inc., 725 Main Street, Lafayette, IN 47901

Available for Apple II series and TRS-80 I, III

THE SAGE

Designed to create quizzes and tests with up to four responses per question. Can be used for either drill-and-practice or tutorial lessons. (Grades 8 and above)

Jagdstaffel Software, 645 Borden Road, San Juan, CA 95123

Available for Apple II series and Franklin Basis 108

SOFCRATES: The Courseware Creator

Designed as a complete authoring system with many special features. Includes several learning formats, and can be programmed to accept more than one correct answer. Contains student record-keeping functions, hi-resolution color text, graphics, and animation.

SIMPAC Educational Systems, 1105 North Main Street, Suite 11-C, Gainesville, FL 32601

Available for Apple

SPELL AND DEFINE

Can be used for drill-and-practice applications in many subjects. Teachers/authors supply ten terms or spelling words along with their definitions. Includes record-keeping capabilities. (All grades)

Electronic Courseware Systems, Inc., 1210 Lancaster Drive, Champaign, IL 61821

Available for Apple II series, Commodore 64, Victor 9000, and IBM

SUPER QUIZ II

Enables teachers/authors to create a test bank of up to 10,000 multiple-choice questions (of up to 500 characters each) using add-on and editing capabilities. Multiple copies of the same exam can be composed, using up to 100 questions per exam. Supports upper- and lower-case characters. (All grades)

Sterling Swift Publishing Co., 7901 South IH-35, Austin, TX 78744

Available for Apple II series

SUPER SOFCRATES

Containing all the features found in *Sofcrates: The Courseware Creator,* this augmented version has several improved lesson creation capabilities as well as additional editing commands. Includes interactive video capabilities.

SIMPAC Educational Systems, 1105 North Main Street, Suite 11-C, Gainesville, FL 32601

Available for Apple

TAS (TEACHER AUTHORING SYSTEM)

Provides formats for drill-and-practice exercises. Allows the teacher/author to store and print student records, worksheets, review lessons, assignments, and tests. Can maintain lesson file. Includes illustration capabilities. (All grades)

Teach Yourself by Computer, 2128 West Jefferson Road, Pittsford, NY 14534

Available for TRS-80 I, III, 4

THE TEST BANK. . .Computer Assisted Test Construction for Microcomputers

Teachers/authors create tests using a built-in word processor. Includes search capability. Can automatically renumber and merge items from several databases for composite tests and randomly change question order for different test versions. Prints tests and answer keys. (All grades)

>   *Advanced Technology Applications, 3019 Grovenor Drive, San Diego, CA 92122*
>   Available for TRS-80 II, 4

THE TEST FACTORY

An administrative package that allows teachers/authors to create up to 15 different tests, save them automatically and permanently, and print student-ready copies. Multiple forms of the same test can be prepared in minutes. (All grades)

>   *Classroom Consortia Media, Inc., 57 Bay Street, Staten Island, NY 10301*
>   Available for IBM

TEST WRITER

Prepares equivalent form tests with most question types, including essay. Questions are selected from a teacher-generated question pool. (All grades)

>   *Persimmon Software, 502C Savannah Street, Greensboro, NC 27406*
>   Available for Apple II series

TORRICELLI EDITOR

Designed for full-function courseware authoring. Allows teachers/authors to create courses, lessons, and tests. Does not require programming knowledge. (All grades)

>   *The Answer in Computers, 6035 University Avenue, Suite 7, San Diego, CA 92115*
>   Available for IBM, Wang PC, and Texas Instruments Pro

TORRICELLI SCHOOL

Designed for full-function course presentation. Requires no computer expertise other than knowledge of the system's keyboard. (All grades)

>   *The Answer in Computers, 6035 University Avenue, Suite 7, San Diego, CA 92115*
>   Available for IBM, Wang PC, and Texas Instruments Pro

TORRICELLI SCRIBE

Designed as a menu-driven system to make courseware authoring easier and error-free. (All grades)

The Answer in Computers, 6035 University Avenue, Suite 7, San Diego, CA 92115

Available for IBM, Wang PC, and Texas Instruments Pro

TUTORIAL LEARNING SYSTEM

Provides a vehicle for creating tutorial lessons. Does not require knowledge of computer programming. (All grades)

Diversified Educational Enterprises, Inc., 725 Main Street, Lafayette, IN 47901

Available for Apple II series, I, III

THE WIZ

Designed for quizzes on any subject. Up to three lines of words and phrases are flashed on the screen with a fourth line for the student's response. (All grades)

Alphanetics, PO Box 339, Forrestville, CA 95436

Available for IBM

WORD WISE AUTHORING

Designed as an authoring system for creating sight vocabulary exercises for primary-level students. Students either fill-in-the-blank or match words and phrases with pictures. (Grades 1-3)

Total Information Educational Systems, 1925 West Country Road, B2, St. Paul, MN 55113

Available for Apple II series

WORKSHEET GENERATOR

Used to generate worksheets with addition, subtraction, or multiplication problems. (All grades)

Micro Learningware, PO Box 307, Mankato, MN 56001

Available for Apple II series and TRS-80 III, 4

WORKSHEET WIZARD

Prints an individualized math worksheet for every student in the class. (Grades 1 and above)

Edusoft, PO Box 2560, Berkeley, CA 94702

Available for Apple II series

ZENITH EDUCATION SYSTEMS (ZES)
>Designed as a menu-driven authoring system. Includes hi-resolution graphics, animation, and branching capabilities. Graphs can be created using math functions. Record-keeping capabilities feature both detailed and summary reports of student performance.
>*Avant Garde Creations, 37B Commercial Boulevard, Novato, CA 94947*
>Available for Apple

Major Authoring Languages

The following listing of major authoring languages is arranged alphabetically by computer brand. This list is suggestive, not exhaustive, and is intended to serve as a reference rather than a recommendation.

APPLE

APILOT II Edu-Disk
>A complete PILOT authoring language package. Includes both hi- and low-resolution graphics, a clock, a "tone" command, a "touch" command which works in conjunction with a Symtec light pen, and a "talk" command which produces vocal sounds from the Apple speaker when used with the Muse *Voice* software.
>*MUSE Software, 347 North Charles Street, Baltimore, MD 21201*

E-Z PILOT II
>A simplified version of the PILOT authoring language with special help commands. Designed for ease of use. Includes color, sound, and large-print capabilities. Uses only eight basic commands. Can be used with graphics tablet or graphics utility. Record-keeping routines can be programmed in BASIC. Also available with student's manual as *E-Z PILOT Training Package.*
>*Hartley Courseware, Inc., 133 Bridge Street, Dimondale, MI 48821*

SuperPILOT
>A complete version of the PILOT authoring language. Includes additional features: color graphics, sound effects, special character sets, multiple fonts, and multiple character sizes. Also includes a modified version of "turtle graphics" for drawing, and the ability to control audio-visual devices such as video-recorders and video disk

systems. Expanded and improved editing and record-keeping facilities.

Apple Computer Co., 20525 Mariani Avenue, Cupertino, CA 95014

ATARI

Atari PILOT

An easy-to-learn version of the PILOT authoring language containing color and music capabilities. Includes "turtle graphics" and automatic text formatting.

Atari, Inc., PO Box 61657, Sunnyvale, CA 94088

COMMODORE

Commodore PILOT

This version of the PILOT authoring language utilizes many of the unique features of the Commodore 64 microcomputer, including programmable characters, moveable sprites, and the creation of music and sound effects.

Commodore International, 1200 Wilson Drive, Brandywine Industrial Park, West Chester, PA 19380

Vanilla PILOT

An easy-to-learn version of the PILOT authoring language. Contains "turtle graphics" and color capabilities, as well as sound and joystick commands. Powerful extensions include find, trace, change, and dump. Allows full control of the sound effects synthesizer. Includes an extensive programmer's aid package.

Tamarack Software, PO Box 247, Darby, MI 59829

CP/M

Nevada PILOT

A modified string-oriented version of the PILOT authoring language designed for developing programmed instruction, drills, and tests.

Ellis Computing, Inc., 3917 Noriega Street, San Francisco, CA 94122

IBM

Common PILOT
A powerful and complete version of the PILOT authoring language.
Micropi, PO Box 5524, Bellingham, WA 98227

IBM PILOT
A powerful and complete version of the PILOT authoring language.
International Business Machines Corporation, PO Box 152750, Irving, TX 75015-2750

TRS-80

Color PILOT
A version of the PILOT authoring language which includes hi-resolution graphics and large and small letters, as well as additional graphics commands. Sound is available through language control of a tape recorder.
Tandy Co./Radio Shack, One Tandy Center, Fort Worth, TX 76102

Micro-PILOT
An extended version of the PILOT authoring language with both graphics and file management capabilities. Also contains musical tone generation.
Tandy Co./Radio Shack, One Tandy Center, Fort Worth, TX 76102

Authoring Products

COMPANY	*PRODUCT*
Academy Software PO Box 6277 San Rafael, CA 94903	Flashcard Maker/Flashcard Quiz
Advanced Ideas, Inc. 2902 San Pablo Avenue Berkeley, CA 94702	Game Show Master Match Tic Tac Show

Advanced Technology Applications
3019 Grovenor Drive
San Diego, CA 92122

Computer Assisted Test
  Construction
The Test Bank

Ahead Designs
699 North Vulcan, # 88
Encinitas, CA 92024

Spide Attack

Alphanetics
PO Box 339
Forrestville, CA 95436

The Wiz

The Answer in Computers
6035 University Avenue
Suite 7
San Diego, CA 92115

Torricelli Editor
Torricelli School
Torricelli Scribe

Apple Computer, Inc.
20525 Mariani Avenue
Cupertino, CA 95014

Shell Games
SuperPILOT

Atari, Inc.
PO Box 61657
Sunnyvale, CA 94088

Atari PILOT

Automated Simulations
1988 Leghorn Street
Mountain View, CA 94043

Jabbertalky

Avant-Garde Creations
37B Commerical Boulevard
Novato, CA 94947

Zenith Education Systems
  (ZES)

Bainum Dunbar
6427 Hillcroft, Suite 133
Houston, TX 77081

Brainz-Gamez

BCD Associates, Inc.
5809 Southwest Fifth
Oklahoma City, OK 73128

The Instructor

Bell & Howell Co.   Courseware Development System
7100 North McCormick Road   Genis I
San Diego, CA 92131

California School for the Deaf   BLOCKS '82
Computer Lab
39350 Gallaudet Drive
Fremont, CA 94538

Carvi Systems, Inc.   Carvi V Interactive
26 Trumball Street   Video System
New Haven, CT 06511   Ghostwriter Authoring System
                                           Ghostwriter Interactive Video
                                               Authoring System

Classroom Consortia Media, Inc.   Customized Testing
57 Bay Street   The Test Factory
Staten Island, NY 10301

CMA Micro Computer   Light Pen Quiz
55722 Santa Fe Trail
Yucca Valley, CA 92284

Comaldor   Hangman
PO Box 356, Postal Station O
Toronto, Ontario M4A 2N9
Canada

Commodore Business Machines, Inc.   Commodore PILOT
1200 Wilson Drive
Brandywine Industrial Park
West Chester, PA 19380

COMpress   EnBASIC Authoring System
PO Box 102
Wentworth, NH 03282

Computations   Multiple Choice Files
PO Box 502   Study Quiz File
Troy, MI 48099

Computer Applications Tomorrow
24151 Telegraph Road
Southfield, MI 48034

Exam Options

The Continental Press, Inc.
520 East Bainbridge Street
Elizabethtown, PA 17022

Mathematics: A Worksheet/Test
    Generator

Courseware Inc.
10075 Carroll Canyon Road
San Diego, CA 92131

Courseware Master Designer
    Series

Creative Publications
PO Box 10328
Palo Alto, CA 94303

Fastrack Quizzer
Great Computer Gameworks

Cross Educational Software
PO Box 1536
Ruston, LA 71270

Create-a-Test

Datatech Software Systems
19312 East Eldorado Drive
Aurora, CO 80013

DT Mentor Master with
    Game Show

Digital Equipment Corporation
360 Interstate North Parkway
Suite 560
Atlanta, GA 30339

Courseware Authoring System

Diversified Educational Enterprises
725 Main Street
Lafayette, IN 47901

Advice
Tutorial Learning System
Quiz

Dynacomp, Inc.
1427 Monroe Avenue
Rochester, NY 14618

CATGEN/CAT (Computer
    Aided Teaching)

Edu-CAItor, Inc.   Advocate Authoring System
38 Main Street   CAI*PLUS Authoring System
Hudson, MA 01749

Educational Software and Design   Electronic Master I
PO Box 2801   Electronic Master I-S
Flagstaff, AZ 86003

Educational Software Midwest   C-Bits III
414 Rosemere Lane
Maquoketa, IA 52060

Educational Systems Software   Patient Professor
23720 El Toro Road
El Toro, CA 92630

Edusoft   Worksheet Wizard
PO Box 2560
Berkeley, CA 94702

Eiconics, Inc.   Eureka Learning Systems
211 Cruz Alta Road
PO Box 1207
Taos, NM 87571

Electronic Courseware Systems, Inc.   Spell and Define
1210 Lancaster Drive
Champaign, IL 61821

Ellis Computing, Inc.   Nevada PILOT
3917 Noriega Street
San Francisco, CA 94122

Entelik   Micro Tutor
Dept. 1, Ward-Whidden House
The Hill
Portsmouth, NH 03801

Fireside Computing Inc.   CAIWARE 2-D
5843 Montgomery Road   CAIWARE 3-D
Elkridge, MD 21227

Gessler Educational Software, Inc.
900 Broadway
New York, NY 10003

The Linguist

Hartley Courseware, Inc.
133 Bridge Street
Dimondale, MI 48821

Create CCD Lessons (uses CCD)
Create Fill-in-the-Blanks
    (uses CCD)
Create Lessons
Create Lessons - Advanced
Create - Medalists
Create Spell-It (uses CCD)
Create - Vocabulary (uses CCD)
Early Skills
E-Z PILOT II
E-Z PILOT II Training Pkg
    (w/student manuals)
Print Your Own Bingo
Print Your Own Calendar
Simulation Construction Kit
Super Wordfind
Wordsearch

International Business Machines Corp.
PO Box 152750
Irving, TX 75015-2750

Electric Poet
IBM PILOT
Private Tutor
Teacher's Quiz Designer

Jagdstaffel Software
645 Borden Road
San Juan, CA 95123

The Sage

The Johns Hopkins University
Division of Education
100 Whitehead Hall
Baltimore, MD 21218

Multisensory Authoring
    Computer System

The Learning Co.
545 Middlefield Road, Suite 170
Menlo Park, CA 94025

Magic Spells

McGraw-Hill/Courseware 1221 Avenue of the Americas New York, NY 10020	Authoring System
M.D. Fullmer Associates 1132 Via Jose San Jose, CA 95120	The Learning Box
Micro Lab 2699 Skokie Valley Road Highland Park, IL 60035	The Learning System
Micropi PO Box 5524 Bellingham, WA 98227	Common PILOT
Micro Learningware PO Box 307 Mankato, MN 56001	Worksheet Generator

Minnesota Educational
Computing Consortium
3490 Lexington Avenue North
St. Paul, MN 55126-8097
	Computer-Generated
	    Mathematics Materials:
	    Vol. I-Problem Solving
	Puzzles & Posters
	Special Needs Vol. I - Spelling
	Teacher Utilities Vol. I

Muse Software 347 North Charles Street Baltimore, MD 21201	APILOT II Edu-Disk
Persimmon Software 502C Savannah Street Greensboro, NC 27406	Test Writer
Phoenix Performance Systems 64 Lake Zurich Drive Lake Zurich, IL 60047	The Author The Author Plus

Pogo Ware Educational Software   C.A.S.E.
PO Box 55298
Madison, WI 53705

Potomac Micro Resources   Kid Bits Word Fair
PO Box 277
Pittsford, NY 14534

The Professor   The Great Creator
959 N.W. 53rd Street
Fort Lauderdale, FL 33309

Scandura Training Systems, Inc.   Author Plus Systems
1249 Greentree Lane   EZ Author
Narbeth, PA 19072   Micro Tutor II

Scholastic Wizware   Square Pairs
902 Sylvan Avenue
Englewood Cliffs, NJ 07632

School & Home Courseware   Concentration
1341 Bulldog Lane, Suite C
Fresno, CA 93710

Scott Instruments Corp.   VBLS
1111 Willow Springs Drive
Denton, TX 76205

Shenandoah Software   The Instructor's System
PO Box 776   Examiner
Harrisonburg, VA 22801   The Instructor's System Exams

SIMPAC Educational Systems   Sofcrates
1105 North Main Street, Suite 11-C   Super Sofcrates
Gainesville, FL 32601

Skillcorp Software Inc.   Skillcorp Authoring System
1711 McGraw Avenue
Irvine, CA 92714

Spectrum Training Corp.   The Educator
18 Brown Street
Salem, MA 01970

Sterling Swift Publishing Co.   Super Quiz II
7901 South IH-35
Austin, TX 78744

Tamarack Software   Vanilla PILOT
PO Box 247
Darby, MI 59829

Tandy Co./Radio Shack   Author I
One Tandy Center   Color PILOT
Fort Worth, TX 76102   Micro-PILOT

TARA, Ltd.   The Puzzler
PO Box 118
Selden, NY 11784

Teach Yourself by Computer   Individual Study Center
2128 West Jefferson Road   TAS (Teacher Authoring
Pittsford, NY 14534   System)

Total Information Educational Systems Electric English Authoring
1925 West Country Road, B2   Word Wise Authoring
St. Paul, MN 55113

Touch Technologies, Inc.   CLAS (Computerized Lesson
609 South Escondido Blvd.   Authoring System)
Suite 101
Escondido, CA 92025

XPS   Crypto-Gen
323 York Road
Carlyle, PA 17013

Index

DATE DUE		SUBJECT TO RECALL
RETURNED		
APR 1 8 1993		

Demco, Inc. 38-293